AFTER PROGRESS

AFTER PROGRESS

REASON *and* RELIGION *at the* END *of* THE INDUSTRIAL AGE

JOHN MICHAEL GREER

new society
PUBLISHERS

Cover design by Diane McIntosh.
Cover image: © iStock Lee Yiu Tung. Crane hook illustration © MJ Jessen
Printed in Canada. First printing February 2015.

New Society Publishers acknowledges the financial support of the Government of Canada through the Canada Book Fund (CBF) for our publishing activities.

Paperback ISBN: 978-0-86571-791-6
eISBN: 978-1-55092-586-9

Inquiries regarding requests to reprint all or part of *After Progress* should be addressed to New Society Publishers at the address below. To order directly from the publishers, please call toll-free (North America) 1-800-567-6772, or order online at www.newsociety.com

Any other inquiries can be directed by mail to:
New Society Publishers
P.O. Box 189, Gabriola Island, BC V0R 1X0, Canada
(250) 247-9737

New Society Publishers' mission is to publish books that contribute in fundamental ways to building an ecologically sustainable and just society, and to do so with the least possible impact on the environment, in a manner that models this vision. We are committed to doing this not just through education, but through action. The interior pages of our bound books are printed on Forest Stewardship Council®-registered acid-free paper that is 100% post-consumer recycled (100% old growth forest-free), processed chlorine-free, and printed with vegetable-based, low-VOC inks, with covers produced using FSC®-registered stock. New Society also works to reduce its carbon footprint, and purchases carbon offsets based on an annual audit to ensure a carbon neutral footprint. For further information, or to browse our full list of books and purchase securely, visit our website at: www.newsociety.com

Library and Archives Canada Cataloguing in Publication

Greer, John Michael, author

After progress : reason and religion at the end of the industrial age / John Michael Greer.

Includes bibliographical references and index.
Issued in print and electronic formats.
ISBN 978-0-86571-791-6 (pbk.).--ISBN 978-1-55092-586-9 (ebook)

1. Progress. 2. Reason. 3. Religion. I. Title.

HM891.G74 2015   303.44   C2015-900790-9
                                         C2015-900791-7

Contents

Introduction

THE RISING SPIRAL OF CRISIS that besets the industrial world today
is a complex matter — far more complex than the comfortable
clichés beloved by politicians and the media might suggest. Behind the
turbulent surface of politics and economics, the ongoing movement
of nation after nation toward failed-state conditions and the widening
gap between the general prosperity that the world's developed economies are supposed to yield and the far less evenly distributed results
that they actually manage to produce, deeper patterns are at work:
above all, the disastrous mismatch between political and economic
ideologies that demand endless economic growth and technological
expansion, on the one hand, and the hard limits of a finite planet on
the other.

Still, there's another dimension to the crisis of our time that goes
deeper still. The ideologies just mentioned, after all, didn't show up
out of nowhere one fine day, springing full-blown from the head of
Adam Smith like Athena from the head of Zeus. Nor, for that matter, are they hardwired into the human psyche; there have been any

1

number of human societies that didn't share our obsessions on that score. The ideas that have guided the modern world into its head-on collision with ecological reality have a history; they emerged at a particular point in the past, and their roots can be traced far back into the soil of human experience.

Nor are those ideologies anything like as secular, rational and pragmatic as their proponents so often insist. Remarkably often, those who believe in growth, progress and development — consider for a moment the emotional loading the modern world places on these words! — seem unable to think of these things as means to an end, as tactics or strategies that might conceivably be useful in some cases and not in others. Growth and progress, to believers in the conventional wisdom of our time, are ends in themselves: we progress because progress is as inevitable as it is good; we grow so that we can keep on growing.

The rhetoric of modernity cheerfully admits that growth and progress bring problems as well as benefits, but then goes on to insist that we have no choice but to live with the former and gratefully accept the latter. The notion that individuals, communities and nations might reasonably weigh the benefits against the problems, and decide on that basis whether or not to have more growth, more progress, or more development, is quite literally unthinkable to most people nowadays. Make the suggestion anyway, and the most common responses you'll get are blank incomprehension and incandescent rage.

There are several ways to talk about this curious phenomenon, but the one that makes the most sense of the data is to see growth, progress and development as religious concepts, freighted with all the passionate convictions and the claims of ultimate value that the Western world once attached to such concepts as saintliness and salvation. I'm aware that any such analysis is bound to be controversial, not least because many of those who speak most glowingly of growth, progress and development like to use the word "religion" as a derogatory catch-all term for those notions about the universe in which they themselves don't happen to believe. Still, a less simplistic look at religion and at the contemporary trust in progress as a religious faith will cast a useful light on some otherwise baffling habits of contemporary thought.

It so happens that I come to this exploration from a somewhat unusual standpoint. In eighteenth-century Britain, the Hobson's choice then on offer between dogmatic Christianity and the first stirrings of an equally dogmatic scientific materialism inspired a number of religious movements to go looking for a third option. One of these, among the smallest and strangest of the lot, turned for inspiration to what was then known about the ancient Druids — the priestly caste of the Celtic peoples of pre-Christian Europe — and to the cycles and phenomena of nature which the ancient Druids revered. Somehow or other, while many other products of that era of religious innovation fell by the wayside thereafter, the Druid Revival prospered in its own eccentric way, and the movement it launched has been a living tradition ever since.

That is to say, I am a Druid, a participant and teacher in a contemporary Druid order, a believer in the holiness of nature and the presence of divine powers in and through the systems and cycles of the biosphere, and thus a participant in the lively if rarely discussed subculture of minority religions in today's industrial world. I mention this here partly because the readers of a book that discusses the tangled relationship between religion and rationalism might reasonably want to know where its author stands with regard to the contending parties. Partly, though, it's because some of the points I try to make in the following pages cut straight across the claims of all sides in that ongoing quarrel, and some advance warning of that fact is probably worth giving.

Be that as it may, this is not a book about Druidry. It's a book about belief in progress as a surrogate religion, a pseudosecular faith that rose to prominence and power under the banner of industrialization and is now fading to irrelevance as the grandiose hopes once reposed in it give way to frustration and failure. More generally, it's a book about the religious underpinnings of the crisis of our age — about the way that certain ideas in conflict with ecological reality were taken on faith across the modern industrial world, became central to most modern conceptions of the meaning, purpose and value of human existence, and now bar the way to any useful response to the troubles that beset us. It's also a book about how we might get past those ideas and re-imagine our lives and our place in a world after progress.

One

The Noise of the Gravediggers

THERE ARE ANY NUMBER OF WAYS we could talk about the religious dimensions of the crisis of our time. The mainstream religions of today's industrial societies offer one set of starting points, while my own Druid faith, which is very nearly as far from the mainstream as you can get, offers another set. Then, of course, there's the religion that nobody talks about and most people in the industrial world believe in, the religion of progress, which will be central to the discussion ahead and which has its own noticeably dogmatic way of addressing such issues.

Still, a starting point a little less obvious than any of these may be better suited to the exploration I have in mind, so we will begin in the Italian city of Turin, on an otherwise ordinary January day in 1889. Over on one side of the Piazza Carlo Alberto, a teamster was beating one of his horses savagely with a stick, and his curses and the horse's terrified cries could be heard over the traffic noise. Finally, the horse collapsed; as it hit the pavement, a middle-aged man with a handlebar mustache came sprinting across the plaza, dropped to his knees beside the horse and flung his arms around its neck, weeping hysterically. His name was Friedrich Wilhelm Nietzsche, and he had just gone hopelessly insane.

At that time, Nietzsche was almost completely unknown in the worlds of European philosophy and culture. His career had a brilliant beginning — he was hired straight out of college in 1868 to teach classical philology at the University of Basel, and published his first significant work, *The Birth of Tragedy*, four years later — but he strayed thereafter into territory few academics in his time dared to touch. When he gave up his position in 1879 due to health problems, the university was glad to see him go. His major philosophical works saw print in small editions, mostly paid for by Nietzsche himself, and were roundly ignored by everybody. There were excellent reasons for this, as what Nietzsche was saying in these books was the last thing that anybody in Europe at that time wanted to hear.

Given Nietzsche's fate, there's a fierce irony in the fact that his most famous statement of the core of his teaching is put in the mouth of a madman. Here's the passage in question, from *The Gay Science* (1882):

"Have you not heard of the madman who lit a lantern in the bright morning hours, ran to the market place, and cried incessantly, 'I seek God! I seek God!' As many of those who did not believe in God were standing around just then, he provoked much laughter. Has he got lost? asked one. Did he lose his way like a child? asked another. Or is he hiding? Is he afraid of us? Has he gone on a voyage? emigrated? — Thus they shouted and laughed.

"The madman jumped into their midst and pierced them with his eyes. 'Whither is God?' he cried: 'I will tell you. *We have killed him —* you and I. All of us are his murderers. But how did we do this? How could we drink up the sea? Who gave us the sponge to wipe away the entire horizon? What were we doing when we unchained the earth from the sun? Whither is it moving now? Whither are we moving? Away from all suns? Are we not plunging continuously? Backward, sideward, forward, in all directions? Is there still any up or down? Are we not straying as through an infinite nothing? Do we not feel the breath of empty space? Has it not become colder? Is not night continually closing in on us? Do we not need to light lanterns in the morning? Do we hear nothing as yet of the noise of the gravediggers who are burying God? Do we smell nothing as yet of the divine decomposition? Gods, too, decompose. God is dead. God remains dead. And we have killed him.'"[1]

Beyond the wild imagery — which was not original to Nietzsche, by the way; several earlier German writers used the same metaphor before he got to it, and it has a long history in ancient religious traditions as well — lay a precise and trenchant insight. In Nietzsche's time, the Christian religion was central to European culture in a way that's almost unthinkable from today's perspective. By this I don't simply mean that a much greater percentage of Europeans attended church then than now, though this was true; nor that Christian narratives, metaphors and jargon pervaded popular culture to such an extent that you can hardly make sense of the literature of the time if you don't know your way around the Bible and the standard tropes of Christian theology, though this was also true.

The centrality of Christian thought to European culture went much deeper than that. The core concepts that undergirded every dimension of European thought and behavior came straight out of Christianity. This was true straight across the political spectrum of the time — conservatives drew on the Christian religion to legitimize existing institutions and social hierarchies, while their liberal opponents relied just as extensively on Christian teachings for the ideas and imagery that framed their challenges to those same institutions and hierarchies. All through the lively debates of the time, values and ethical concepts that could only be justified on the basis of Christian theology were treated as self-evident, and those few thinkers who strayed outside that comfortable consensus quickly found themselves, as Nietzsche did, talking to an empty room.

It's indicative of the tenor of the times that even those thinkers who tried to reject Christianity ended up copying it right down to the fine details. Thus the atheist philosopher Auguste Comte, a well-known figure in the generation before Nietzsche's though almost entirely forgotten now, launched a "Religion of Humanity" with a holy trinity of Humanity, the Earth and Destiny, a calendar of secular saints' days, and scores of other borrowings from Christian theory and practice. He was one of dozens of figures who attempted to create pseudo-Christianities of one kind or another, keeping most of the moral, conceptual and behavioral trappings of the faith they were convinced they had rejected. Meanwhile their less radical neighbors went about their lives in the serene conviction that the assumptions their culture had inherited from its Christian roots were eternally valid.

The only difficulty this posed is that a large and rapidly growing fraction of nineteenth-century Europeans no longer believed the central tenets of the faith that structured their lives and their thinking. It never occurred to most of them to question the value of Christian ethics, the social role of Christian institutions, or the sense of purpose and value they and their society had long derived from Christianity. Straight across the spectrum of polite society, everyone agreed that good people ought to go to church, that missionaries should be sent forth to eradicate competing religions in foreign lands and that the world would be a much better place if everybody would simply follow the teachings of Jesus, in whatever form those might have been reworked most recently for public consumption. It was simply that a great many of them could no longer find any reason to believe in such minor details as the existence of God.

Even those who did insist loudly on this latter point and on their own adherence to Christianity commonly redefined both in ways that stripped them of their remaining relevance to the nineteenth-century world. Immanuel Kant, the philosopher whose writings formed the high-water mark of modern philosophy and also launched it on its descent into decadence, is among other things the poster child for this effect. In his 1793 book *Religion Within The Limits of Reason Alone*, Kant argued that the essence of religion — in fact, the only part of it that had real value — was leading a virtuous life, and everything else was superstition and delusion.

The triumph of Kant's redefinition of religion was all but total in Protestant denominations up until the rise of fundamentalism at the beginning of the twentieth century, and left lasting traces on the left-ward end of Catholicism as well. To this day, if you pick an American church at random on a Sunday morning and go inside to listen to the sermon, your chances of hearing an exhortation to live a virtuous life, without reference to any other dimension of religion, are rather better than one in two.

The fact remains that Kant's reinterpretation has almost nothing in common with historic Christianity. To borrow a phrase from a later era of crisis, Kant apparently felt that he had to destroy Christianity in order to save it, but the destruction was considerably more effective than the salvation turned out to be. Intellects considerably less acute than Kant's had no difficulty at all in taking his arguments and using them to suggest that living a virtuous life was not the essence of religion but a modern, progressive, up-to-date replacement for it.

Even so, public professions of Christian faith remained a social necessity right up into the twentieth century. There were straightforward reasons for this; even so convinced an atheist as Voltaire, when guests at one of his dinner parties spoke too freely about the nonexistence of God, is said to have sent the servants away and then urged his friends not to speak so freely in front of them, asking, "Do you want your throats cut tonight?" Still, historians of ideas have followed the spread of atheism through the European intelligentsia from the end of the six-teenth century, when it was the concern of small and secretive circles, to the middle of the eighteenth, when it had become widespread. From there it moved out of intellectual circles, spreading through the middle classes during the eighteenth century and then, in the nineteenth — continental Europe's century of industrialization — reaching the urban working classes, who by and large abandoned their traditional faiths when they left the countryside to take factory jobs.

By the time Nietzsche wrote God's epitaph, in other words, the central claims of Christianity were taken seriously only by a minority of educated Europeans, and even among the masses, secular substitutes for religion such as Marxism and nationalism were spreading rapidly at the expense of the older faith. Despite this, however, habits of thought and behavior that could only be justified by the basic presuppositions of Christianity stayed welded in place throughout European society. It was as though, to coin a metaphor that Nietzsche himself might have used, one of the great royal courts of the time busied itself with all the details of the king's banquets and clothes and bedchamber, and servants and courtiers hovered about the throne waiting to obey the king's least command, even though everyone in the palace knew that the throne was empty and the last king had died decades before.

⁂

To Nietzsche, this clinging to the habits of Christian thought in a post-Christian society was incomprehensible. The son and grandson of Lutheran pastors, raised in an atmosphere of more than typical middle-class European piety, he inherited a keen sense of the internal logic of the Christian faith — the way that every aspect of Christian theology and morality unfolds step by step from core principles clearly defined in the historic creeds of the early church. It's not an accident that the creed most broadly accepted in Western churches, the Apostle's Creed, begins with the words "I believe in God the Father almighty, Creator of heaven and earth." Abandon that belief, and none of the ideas that depend on it make any sense at all.

This was what Nietzsche's madman, and Nietzsche himself, were trying to bring to the attention of their contemporaries. Unlike too many of today's atheists, Nietzsche had a profound understanding of just what it was that he was rejecting when he proclaimed the death of God and the absurdity of faith. "When one gives up Christian belief one thereby deprives oneself of the right to Christian morality," he wrote in *Twilight of the Idols*. "Christianity is a system, a consistently thought out and complete view of things. If one breaks out of it a fundamental idea, the belief in God, one thereby breaks the whole thing to pieces: one has nothing of any consequence left in one's hands."[2]

To abandon belief in a divinely ordained order to the cosmos, he argued, meant surrendering any claim to objectively valid moral standards, and thus stripping words like "right" and "wrong" of any meaning other than personal preference. It meant giving up the basis on which governments and institutions founded their claims to legitimacy, and thus leaving them no means to maintain social order or gain the obedience of the masses other than the raw threat of violence — a threat that would have to be made good ever more often, as time went on, to maintain its effectiveness. Ultimately, it meant abandoning any claim of meaning, purpose, or value to humanity or the world, other than those that individual human beings might choose to impose on the inkblot patterns of a chaotic universe.

I suspect that many, if not most, of my readers will object to these conclusions. There are, of course, many grounds on which such objections could be raised. It can be pointed out, and truly, that there have been plenty of atheists whose behavior, on ethical grounds, compares favorably to that of the average Christian, and some who can stand comparison with Christian saints. On a less superficial plane, it can be pointed out with equal truth that it's only in a distinctive minority of ethical systems — that of historic Christianity among them — that ethics start from the words "thou shalt" and proceed from there to the language of moral exhortation and denunciation that still structures most of Western moral discourse today. Political systems, it might be argued, can work out new bases for their claims to legitimacy, using such concepts as the consent of the governed, while claims of meaning, purpose and value can be rebuilt on a variety of bases that have nothing to do with an objective cosmic order imposed on it by a putative creator.

All this is true, and the history of ideas in the Western world over the last few centuries can in fact be neatly summed up as the struggle to build alternative foundations for social, ethical and intellectual existence in the void left behind by Europe's gradual but unrelenting abandonment of Christian faith. Yet this simply makes Nietzsche's point for him, for all these alternative foundations had to be built, slowly, with a great deal of trial and error and no small number of disastrous missteps. It has taken centuries of hard work by some of our species' best minds to get even this far in the project of replacing the Christian God, and it's by no means certain even now that their efforts have achieved any lasting success.

A strong case can therefore be made that Nietzsche got the right answer, but was asking the wrong question. He grasped that the collapse of Christian faith in European society meant the end of the entire structure of meanings and values that had God as its first postulate, but he thought that the only possible aftermath of that collapse was a collective plunge into the heart of chaos, in which humanity would be forced to come to terms with the nonexistence of objective values, and would finally take responsibility for their own role in projecting values on a fundamentally meaningless cosmos; the question that consumed him was how this could be done. A great many other people in his time saw the same possibility, but rejected it on the grounds that such a cosmos was unfit for human habitation. Their question, the question that has shaped the intellectual and cultural life of the Western world for several centuries now, was how to find some other first postulate as a basis for meaning and value in the absence of faith in the existence and providence of the Christian God.

They found one, too — though one could as well say that one was pressed upon them by the sheer force of circumstance. The surrogate God that Western civilization embraced, tentatively in the nineteenth century and with increasing conviction and passion in the twentieth, was progress. In the wake of that collective decision, the omnipotence and benevolence of progress have become the core doctrines of a secular religion as broadly and unthinkingly embraced, and as central to contemporary notions of meaning and value, as Christianity was before the Age of Reason.

That in itself defines one of the central themes of the predicament of our time. Progress makes a poor substitute for a deity, not least because its supposed omnipotence and benevolence are becoming increasingly hard to take on faith just now. There's every reason to think that in the years immediately before us, that difficulty is going to become impossible to ignore — and the same shattering crisis of meaning and value that religious faith in progress was meant to solve will be back, adding its burden to the other pressures of our time. Listen closely, Nietzsche might have said, and you can hear the noise of the gravediggers who are burying progress.

To describe faith in progress as a religion, though, courts a good many misunderstandings. The most basic of those comes out of the way that the word "religion" itself has been tossed around like a football in any number of modern society's rhetorical scrimmages. Thus it's going to be necessary to begin by taking a closer look at the usage of that much-vexed term.

The great obstacle that has to be overcome in order to make sense of religion is that so many people these days insist that religion is a specific thing with a specific definition. It's all too common for the definition in question to be crafted to privilege the definer's own beliefs and deliver a slap across the face of rivals. This is as true of religious people who want to define religion as something they have and other people don't as it is of atheists who want to insist that the ideology in which they put their trust doesn't constitute a religion no matter how closely it resembles one. Still, there's a deeper issue involved here as well.

The word "religion" is a label for a category. That may seem like an excessively obvious statement, but it has implications that get missed surprisingly often. Categories are not, by and large, things that exist out there in the world. They're abstractions — linguistically, culturally and contextually specific abstractions — that human minds create and use to sort out the confusion and diversity of experience into some kind of meaningful order. To define a category is simply to draw a mental line around certain things as a way of stressing their similarities with one another and their differences from other things. To make the same point in a slightly different way, categories are tools, and a tool, as a tool, can't be true or false. It can only be more or less useful for a given job, and slight variations in a given tool can be useful to help it do that job more effectively.

A lack of attention to this detail has caused any number of squabbles, with consequences ranging from the absurd to the profound. Thus, for example, when the International Astronomical Union announced a few years back that Pluto had been reclassified from a planet to a dwarf planet, some of the protests that were splashed across the Internet made it sound as though astronomers had aimed a death ray at the solar system's former ninth planet and blasted it out of the heavens.[3] Now of course they did nothing of the kind; they were simply following a precedent set back in the 1850s, when the asteroid Ceres, originally classified as a planet on its discovery in 1801, was stripped of that title after other objects like it were spotted.

Pluto, as it turned out, was simply the first object in the Kuiper Belt to be sighted and named, just as Ceres was the first object in the asteroid belt to be sighted and named. The later discoveries of Eris, Haumea, Sedna and other Pluto-like objects out in the snowball-rich suburbs of the solar system convinced the IAU that assigning Pluto to a different category made more sense than keeping it in its former place on the roster of planets. The change in category didn't affect Pluto at all; it simply provided a slightly more useful way of sorting out the diverse family of objects circling the Sun.

A similar shift, though in the other direction, took place in the sociology of religions in 1967 with the publication of Robert Bellah's essay "Civil Religion in America."[4] Before that time, most definitions of religion had presupposed that a belief system could be given the label "religion" only if it involved belief in at least one deity. Challenging this notion, Bellah pointed out the existence of a class of widely accepted

belief systems that had all the hallmarks of religion except such a belief. Borrowing a turn of phrase from Rousseau, he called these "civil
religions," and the example central to his paper was the system of beliefs that had grown up around the ideas and institutions of American
political life.

The civil religion of Americanism, Bellah showed, could be compared point for point with the popular theistic religions in American
life, and the comparison made sense of features no previous analysis
quite managed to interpret convincingly. Americanism had its own
sacred scriptures, such as the Declaration of Independence; its own
saints and martyrs, such as Abraham Lincoln; its own formal rites —
the Pledge of Allegiance, for example, fills exactly the same role in
Americanism that the Lord's Prayer does in most forms of Christianity
— and so on straight down the list of religious habits and institutions.
Furthermore, and crucially, the core beliefs of Americanism were seen
by most Americans as self-evidently good and true, and as standards
by which other claims of goodness and truth could and should be measured: in a word, as sacred.

Americanism was the focus of Bellah's essay, but it was and is far
from the only example of the species he anatomized. When the essay
first saw print, for example, a classic example of the type was in full
flower on the other side of the Cold War's heavily guarded frontiers. During the period between the publication of *The Communist
Manifesto* and the implosion of the Soviet Union, Communism was
one of the modern world's most successful civil religions, an aggressive
missionary faith preaching an apocalyptic creed of secular salvation. It
shared a galaxy of standard features with other contemporary Western
religions, from sacred scriptures and intricate doctrinal debates all the
way down to street-corner evangelists spreading the gospel among the
downtrodden.

Even its vaunted atheism, the one obvious barrier setting it apart
from its more conventionally religious rivals, was simply an extension of a principle central to the Abrahamic religions, though by no

means common outside that harsh desert-born tradition. The unyield-
ing words of the first commandment, "Thou shalt have no other gods
before me," were as central to Communism as they are to Judaism,
Christianity and Islam; the sole difference in practice was that, since
Communist civil religion directed its reverence toward a hypothetical
set of abstract historical processes rather than a personal deity, its version of the commandment required the faithful to have no gods at all.

Not all civil religions take so hard a line toward their theist rivals.
Americanism is an example of the other common strategy, which
can be described with fair accuracy as cooptation: the recruitment of
the deity or deities of the locally popular theist religion as part of the
publicity team for the civil religion in question. The rhetoric of the
Christian right in today's America offers a fine example of the type,
blurring the boundaries between patriotism and religious faith in a remarkable bricolage of secular and religious images and themes. Such
habits of thought are far from unique to American culture. In the heyday of nationalism, few Western nations failed to find some excuse to
claim God as an honorary citizen who, like any other member of the
national community, could be drafted into service in the event of war
or crisis.

⚜

Other examples of civil religion would be easy enough to cite, but
the two I've just named are good examples of the type and will be
wholly adequate to illustrate the points I want to make here. First, it
takes only the briefest glance at history to realize that civil religions
can call forth passions and loyalties every bit as powerful as those
evoked by theist religions. Plenty of American patriots and committed Communists alike have laid down their lives for the sake of the
civil religions in which they put their faith. Both civil religions have
inspired art, architecture, music and poetry along the whole spectrum
from greatness to utter kitsch; both provided the motive force that
drove immense social and cultural changes for good or ill; both are

comparable in their impact on the world in modern times with even the most popular theist religions.

Second, the relations between civil religions and theist religions tend to be just as problematic as the relations between one theist religion and another. The sort of bland tolerance with which most of today's democracies regard religion is the least intrusive option, and even so it often demands compromises that many theist religions find difficult to accept. From there, the spectrum extends through more or less blatant efforts to coopt theist religions into the service of the civil religion, all the way to accusations of disloyalty and the most violent forms of persecution.

The long history of troubled relations between theist religions and officially nonreligious political creeds is among other things a useful confirmation of Bellah's thesis. It's precisely because civil religions and theist religions appeal to so many of the same social and individual needs and call forth so many of the same passions and loyalties that they so often come into conflict with one another. Believers in theist religions often condemn the more intolerant civil religions as idolatrous, and believers in the more intolerant civil religions condemn theist religions as superstitious: in both cases, what's behind these condemnations is a tacit recognition of the common ground to which both kinds of religion lay claim.

Third, civil religions share with theist religions a curious and insufficiently studied phenomenon that might best be called the antireligion. An antireligion is a movement within a religious community that claims to oppose that community's faith, in a distinctive way: it embraces essentially all of its parent religion's beliefs, but inverts the values, embracing as good what the parent religion defines as evil, and rejecting as evil what the parent religion defines as good.

The classic example of the type is Satanism, the antireligion of Christianity. In its traditional forms — conservative Christians among my readers may be interested to know that Satanism also suffers from modernist heresies — Satanism accepts essentially all of the presuppositions of Christianity, but says with Milton's Satan, "Evil, be thou my good." Thus you'll have to look long and hard among even the most devout Catholics to find anyone more convinced of the spiritual power of the Catholic Mass than an old-fashioned Satanist. It's from that conviction that the Black Mass, the parody of the Catholic rite that provides traditional Satanism with its central ceremony, gains whatever power it has.

Antireligions are at least as common among civil religions as they are among theist faiths. The civil religion of Americanism, for example, has as its antireligion the devout and richly detailed claim, common among American radicals of all stripes, that the United States is uniquely evil among the world's nations. This creed, or anticreed, simply inverts the standard notions of American exceptionalism without changing them in any other way. In the same way, Communism has its antireligion, which was founded by the Russian expatriate Ayn Rand and has become the central faith of much of America's current pseudo-conservative movement.

Pseudoconservatism? Well, yes; the historic tradition of Anglo-American conservatism, with its deep-dyed suspicion of abstract intellectual schemes for a perfect society, has been abandoned by the utopian true believers in the free market who claim the conservative mantle in America today. In the same sense, there's nothing actually conservative about Rand's Objectivism; it's simply what you get when you accept the presuppositions of Marxism — atheism, materialism, class warfare and the rest of it — but say "Evil, be thou my good" to all its value judgments. If you've ever wondered why so many American pseudoconservatives sound as though they're trying to imitate the cackling capitalist villains of traditional Communist demonology, now you know.

Emotional power, difficult relations with other faiths and the presence of an antireligion: these are far from the only features civil religions have in common with the theist competition. Still, just as it makes sense to talk of civil religions and theist religions as two subcategories within the broader category of religion as a whole, it's worthwhile to point out at least one crucial difference between civil and theist religions, which is that civil religions tend to be brittle. They are far more vulnerable than theist faiths to sudden, catastrophic loss of faith on the grand scale.

The collapse of Communism in the late twentieth century is a classic example. By the 1980s, despite heroic efforts at deception and self-deception, nobody anywhere could pretend any longer that the Communist regimes spread across the globe had anything in common with the worker's paradise of Communist myth, or were likely to do so on anything less than geological time scales. The grand prophetic vision central to the Communist faith — the worldwide spread of proletarian revolution, driven by the unstoppable force of the historical dialectic; the dictatorship of the proletariat that would follow, in nation after nation, bringing the blessings of socialism to the wretched of the earth; sooner or later thereafter, the withering away of the state and the coming of true communism — all turned, in the space of a single generation, from the devout hope of countless millions to a subject for bitter jokes among the children of those same millions. The implosion of the Soviet empire and its inner circle of client states, and the rapid abandonment of Communism elsewhere, followed in short order.

The Communist civil religion was vulnerable to so dramatic a collapse because its kingdom was entirely of this world. Theist religions that teach the doctrines of divine providence and the immortality of the soul can always appeal to another world for the fulfillment of hopes disappointed in this one, but a civil religion such as Communism cannot. As the Soviet system stumbled toward its final collapse, faithful believers in the Communist gospel could not console themselves with the hope that they would be welcomed into the worker's paradise after they died, or even pray that the angels of dialectical materialism might smite the local commissar for his sins. There was no refuge from the realization that their hopes had been betrayed and the promises central to their faith would not be kept.

This sort of sudden collapse happens tolerably often to civil religions and explains some of the more dramatic shifts in religious history. The implosion of Roman paganism in the late Empire, for example, had a good many factors driving it, but one of the most important was the way that the worship of the old Roman gods had been coopted by the civil religion of the Roman state. By the time the Roman Empire reached its zenith, Jove and the other gods of the old Roman pantheon had been turned into political functionaries, filling much the same role as Jesus in the rhetoric of today's Tea Party activists. The old concept of the *pax deorum* — the maintenance of peace and good relations between the Roman people and their gods — had been drafted into the service of the Pax Romana, and generations of Roman panegyrists insisted that Rome's piety guaranteed her the perpetual rulership of the world.

When the empire started to come unglued, therefore, and those panegyrics stopped being polite exaggerations and turned into bad jokes, Roman civil religion came unglued with it and dragged down Roman paganism in its turn. The collapse of belief in the old gods was nothing like as sudden or as total as the collapse of faith in Communism — all along, there were those who found spiritual sustenance in the traditional faith, and many of them clung to it until violent Christian persecution intervened — but the failure of the promises Roman civil religion had loaded onto the old gods, at the very least, made things much easier for Christian evangelists.

It's entirely possible that some similar fate awaits the civil religion of Americanism. That faith has already shifted in ways that suggest the imminence of serious trouble. Not that many years ago, all things considered, the great majority of Americans were simply and unselfconsciously convinced that the American way was the best way, that America would inevitably overcome whatever troubles its enemies and the vagaries of nature threw at it, and that the world's best hope lay in the possibility that people in other lands would finally get around to noticing how much better things were over here and be inspired to imitate us. It's easy to make fun of such opinions, especially in the light of what happened in the decades that followed, but it's one of the peculiarities of religious belief — any religious belief, civil, theist, or otherwise — that it always looks at least faintly absurd to those who don't hold it.

Still, the point I want to make is more specific. You won't find many Americans holding such beliefs nowadays, and those who still make such claims in public generally do it in the sort of angry and defensive tones that suggest that they're repeating a creed in which neither they nor their listeners quite believe any longer. American patriotism, like Roman patriotism during the last years of the Empire, increasingly focuses on the past: it's not America as it is today that inspires religious devotion, but the hovering ghost of an earlier era, taking on more and more of the colors of utopia as it fades from sight. Meanwhile politicians mouth the old slogans and go their merry ways. I wonder how many of them have stopped to think about the consequences if the last of the faith that once gave those slogans their meaning finally goes away for good.

Such things happen to civil religions far more often than they happen to theist faiths. I encourage my readers to keep that in mind as we turn to another civil religion, which has played even a larger role in the making of modern history than the two just discussed. That faith is, of course, the religion of progress.

⚜

To suggest that faith in progress has become the most widely accepted civil religion of the modern industrial world is to say something at once subtler and more specific than a first glance might suggest. It's important to keep in mind, as noted above, that "religion" isn't a specific thing with a specific definition; rather, it's a label for a category constructed by human minds — an abstraction, in other words, meant to help sort out the blooming, buzzing confusion of the cosmos into patterns that make some kind of sense to us.

To say that Americanism, Communism and faith in progress are religions, after all, is simply a way of focusing attention on similarities that these three things share with the other things we put in the same category. It doesn't deny that there are also differences, just as there are differences between one theist religion and another, or one civil religion and another. Yet the similarities are worth discussing: like theist religions, for example, the civil religions I've named each embody a set of emotionally appealing narratives that claim to reveal enduring meaning in the chaos of everyday existence, assign believers a privileged status vis-a-vis the rest of humanity, and teach the faithful to see themselves as participants in the grand process by which transcendent values become manifest in the world.

Just as devout Christians are taught to see themselves as members of the mystical Body of Christ and participants in their faith's core narrative of fall and redemption, the civil religion of Americanism teaches its faithful believers to see their citizenship as a quasi-mystical participation in a richly mythologized national history that portrays America as the incarnation of freedom in a benighted world. It's of a piece with the religious nature of Americanism that the word "freedom" here doesn't refer in practice to any particular constellation of human rights; instead, it's a cluster of vague but luminous images that, to the believer, are charged with immense emotional power. When people say they believe in America, they don't usually mean they've intellectually accepted a set of propositions about the United States. They mean that they have embraced the sacred symbols and narratives of the national faith.

The case of Communism is at least as susceptible to such an analysis, and in some ways even more revealing. Most of the ideas that became central to the civil religion of Communism were the work of Friedrich Engels, Marx's friend and patron, who took over the task of completing the second and third volumes of *Das Kapital* on Marx's death. It's from Engels that we get the grand historical myth of the Communist movement, and every part of that myth has a precise equivalent in the Lutheran faith in which Engels was raised.

The parallels are almost embarrassingly straightforward. Primitive communism is Eden; the invention of private property is the Fall; the stages of society thereafter are the different dispensations of sacred history; Marx is Jesus, the First International his apostles and disciples, the international Communist movement the Church, proletarian revolution the Second Coming, socialism the Millennium, and communism the New Jerusalem which descends from heaven in the last two chapters of the Book of Revelation. The devout Communist, in turn, participates in that sweeping vision of past, present and future in exactly the same way that the devout Christian participates in the sacred history of Christianity.

To be a Communist of the old school is not simply to accept a certain set of economic theories or predictions about the future development of industrial society. It's to enlist on the winning side in the struggle that will bring about the fulfillment of human history, and to belong to a secular church with its own saints, martyrs, holy days and passionate theological disputes. It was thus well placed to appeal to European working classes which, during the heyday of Communism in the late nineteenth and early twentieth centuries, were rarely more than a generation removed from the richly structured religious life of rural Europe. In precisely the same way, Americanism appealed to people raised within the framework of traditional American Christianity, with its focus on personal commitment and renewal and its tendency to focus on the purportedly timeless rather than on a particular sequence of sacred history.

If this suggests a certain dependence of civil religions on some older theist religion, it should. So far, I've talked mostly about the category "religion" and the ways in which assigning civil religions to that category casts light on some of their otherwise perplexing aspects. Still, the modifier "civil" deserves as much attention as the noun "religion." If civil religions can be understood a little better if they're included in the broad category of religions in general, as I've suggested here, they also have certain distinctive features of their own, and one of them — the

most important for our present purposes — is that they're derivative;
it would not be going too far to call them parasitic.

The derivative nature of civil religions reaches out in two directions.
First, where theist religions in literate urban societies generally have an
institutional infrastructure set apart for their use — places of worship,
places of instruction, organizations of religious professionals and so on
— civil religions generally don't, and make use of existing infrastructure in a distinctly ad hoc fashion. In the civil religion of Americanism,
for instance, there are sacred shrines to which believers make pilgrim-
ages. Valley Forge, Pennsylvania, where the Continental army under
George Washington spent the decisive winter of the Revolutionary
War, is a good example.

Among believers in Americanism, the phrase "Valley Forge" is one
to conjure with. While pilgrimage sites of theist religions are normally
under the management of religious organizations, though, and are set
apart for specifically religious uses, Valley Forge is an ordinary national
park. Those who go there to steep themselves in the memory of the
Revolution can count on rubbing elbows with birdwatchers, cyclists,
families on camping vacations and plenty of other people for whom
Valley Forge is simply one of the largest public parks in southeastern
Pennsylvania. There's a local convention and visitors bureau with a
lavish website that was at one point headlined, "Life, Liberty, and the
Pursuit of Fun,"[5] which may suggest the degree of reverence surrounding the site these days.

In the same way, it's hard to speak of the priesthood of a civil religion in other than metaphorical terms, since those who take an active
role in promoting a civil religion are rarely able to make that a full-time
job. A great many civil religions, in fact, are folk religions, sustained by
the voluntary efforts of ordinary believers. The existing political system may encourage these efforts, or it may make every effort to stamp
the civil religion out of existence, but the fate of civil religions is rarely
dependent on the actions of governments. Communism again is a case
in point; as a civil religion, it came under heavy persecution in those

countries that did not have Communist governments and received ample state support in those countries that did. Just as the persecutions usually failed to lessen the appeal of Communism to those who had not seen it in action, the state support ultimately failed to maintain its appeal to those who had.

The dependence of civil religions on infrastructure borrowed from nonreligious sources, in turn, is paralleled by an equivalent dependence on ideas borrowed from older theist religions. I've already discussed the way that the civil religion of Americanism derives its basic outlook from what used to be the mainstream of American Protestant Christianity, and the point-for-point equivalences between the theory of the Communist civil religion and the older sacred history of European Christianity. The same thing can be traced in other examples of civil religion — to return to an example already cited, the way that the civil religion of the late Roman world derived its theory and practice across the board from older traditions of classical Paganism. There's a reason for this dependence, and it brings us back to Nietzsche, kneeling in the street with his arms around the neck of a half-dead horse.

Civil religions emerge when traditional theist religions implode. In nineteenth-century Europe and America, the collapse of traditional social patterns and the lasting impact of the Enlightenment cult of reason made uncritical acceptance of the teachings of the historic Christian creeds increasingly difficult, both for educated people and for the masses of newly urbanized factory workers and their families. Nietzsche, whose upbringing in rapidly industrializing Germany gave him a ringside seat for that process, saw the ongoing failure of the Western world's faith in Christian revelation as the dawn of an age of tremendous crisis: the death of God, to use his trenchant phrase, would inevitably be followed by cataclysmic struggles to determine who or what would take his place.

In these impending conflicts, Nietzsche himself was anything but a disinterested bystander. He had his own preferred candidate, the

Overman: a human being of a kind that had never before existed, and could never have existed except by very occasional accident as long as religious belief provided an unquestioned basis for human values. The Overman was not a successor species to today's humanity, as some of Nietzsche's less thoughtful interpreters have suggested, nor some biologically superior subset of human beings, as Nietzsche's tenth-rate plagiarists in the Nazi Party liked to pretend. As Nietzsche envisioned him, the Overman was an individual human being — always and irreducibly individual — who has become his own creator in a perpetual process of self-overcoming, remaking himself moment by moment in the image of values that he himself has created.

Nietzsche was perceptive enough, though, to take note of the other contenders for God's empty throne and sympathetic enough to recognize the importance and value of theist religion for those who could still find a way to believe in it. In the prologue to *Thus Spoke Zarathustra*, the first person that Nietzsche's alter ego Zarathustra meets as he descends from the mountains is an old hermit who spends his days praising God. Zarathustra goes his way, being careful to do nothing to challenge the hermit's faith, and only when he is alone again does he reflect: "Could it be possible? This old saint has not yet heard in his forest that God is dead!"[6]

For the Overman's rivals in the struggle to replace God, Nietzsche had less patience. One alternative that he discussed at great length and greater heat was German nationalism, the local variant of the same civil religion that became Americanism on this side of the ocean. The state was to him a "cold monster" that claimed the right to replace the Christian deity as the source of values and the object of public worship; he hated it partly because of its real flaws, and partly because it stood in the way of his preferred candidate. "There, where the state *ceases* — look there, my brothers. Do you not see it — the rainbow and the bridges to the Overman?"[7]

Socialism was another alternative Nietzsche noted; here again, his assault on it was partly a harsh but by no means inaccurate analysis of its failings, and partly a matter of brushing another contender aside to make way for the Overman. Still, another rival attracted more of his attention, and it was the ersatz deity with which this book is principally concerned. The core challenge that Nietzsche leveled against belief in progress will be discussed later on, as it needs to be understood in the context of the most difficult dimension of his philosophy. That in turn needs to be put into its own much broader context, which will require more than a little explanation of its own. Still, the point that's relevant here is that Nietzsche's identification of faith in progress as an attempted replacement for faith in God is at least as valid now as it was in his own day.

Compare the civil religion of progress to the others just discussed and the parallels are hard to miss. Like other civil religions, to begin with, the religion of progress has repeatedly proven its ability to call forth passions and motivate sacrifices as great as those mobilized by theist religions. From the researchers who have risked their lives, and not infrequently lost them, to further the progress of science and technology, to the moral crusaders who have done the same thing in the name of political or economic progress, straight on through to the ordinary people who have willingly given up things they valued because they felt, or had been encouraged to believe, that the cause of progress demanded that sacrifice from them, the religion of progress has no shortage of saints and martyrs. It has inspired its share of art, architecture, music and literature, covering the usual scale from the heights of creative genius to the depths of kitsch; it has driven immense social changes and made a mark on the modern world at least as substantial as contemporary theist religions have done.

The relationships between the civil religion of progress and theist religions have been as challenging as those involving the civil religions we've already examined. The religion of progress has its own sects and denominations, and it bears noting that these have responded differently to the various theist faiths of the modern world. On the one hand, there have been plenty of efforts, more or less successful, to coopt Jesus, the Jewish prophets and an assortment of other religious figures as crusaders for progress of one kind or another. On the other hand, there have been any number of holy wars declared against theist faiths by true believers in progress, who hold that belief in gods is "primitive," "backward" and "outdated" — in the jargon of the religion of progress, these and terms like them mean roughly what "sinful" means in the jargon of Christianity.

The civil religion of progress also has its antireligion, which is the faith in apocalypse: the belief that the modern industrial world and all its works will shortly be annihilated for its sins. Like the antireligions of other faiths, the apocalyptic antireligion embraces the core presuppositions of the faith it opposes — in this case, above all else, the vision of history as a straight line leading inexorably toward a goal that can only be defined in superlatives — but inverts all the value signs. Where the religion of progress likes to imagine the past as an abyss of squalor and misery, its antireligion paints some suitably ancient time in the colors of the Golden Age; where the religion of progress seeks to portray history as an uneven but unstoppable progress toward better things, its antireligion prefers to envision history as an equally uneven but equally unstoppable process of degeneration and decay; where the religion of progress loves to picture the future in the most utopian terms available, its antireligion uses the future as a screen on which to project lurid images of universal destruction.

The diverse sects and denominations of the religion of progress, furthermore, have their exact equivalent in the antireligion of apocalypse. There are forms of the apocalyptic antireligion that have coopted the language and imagery of older, theist faiths, and other forms that angrily reject those same faiths and everything related to them. Just as different versions of the religion of progress squabble over what counts as progress, different versions of the antireligion of apocalypse bicker over which kinds of degeneration matter most and what form the inevitable cataclysm is going to take.

In either case, as with other religions and their antireligions, the level of hostility between different subsets of the same religion or

antireligion quite often exceeds the level that any branch of the religion directs at its antireligion, or vice versa. The one great divergence
between most forms of the religion of progress and most forms of its
antireligion is that nowadays — matters have been different at other
points in history — very few believers in progress expect the utopian
future central to their faith to show up any time soon. Most contemporary believers in the antireligion of apocalypse, by contrast, place all
their hopes on the imminence of the end.

The civil religion of progress, finally, shares the pattern of twofold
dependence with the other civil religions we've examined. Like them,
it is largely a folk religion, supported by the voluntary efforts and
contributions of its faithful believers, by way of an ad hoc network of
institutions that were mostly created to serve other ends. Those who
function as its priests and preachers have day jobs — even so important
a figure as the late Carl Sagan, who came as close as anyone in recent
times to filling the role of pope of the religion of progress, spent most
of his career as a tenured professor of astronomy at Cornell University,
and his putative successor Neil DeGrasse Tyson has a comparable day
job as director of a planetarium. Like most folk religions, the religion
of progress receives support from a variety of institutions that find it
useful, but routinely behaves in ways that embarrass at least some of
its sponsors.

The other side of its dependence — its reliance on a set of ideas borrowed from theist religion — is a more complicated matter. In order to
make sense of it, it's going to be necessary to look into the way human
beings in modern industrial societies, and in other societies as well,
think about time. That's a far from simple matter. In today's industrial
world, in particular, the way there leads through highly controversial
territory, because a refusal to deal with the implications of time is all
but hardwired into contemporary popular culture.

Two

The Shape of Time

ONE OF THE ODDITIES OF CONTEMPORARY LIFE is the way that Americans in particular, and people throughout the industrial world more generally, like to pretend that history has nothing to teach them. It's a remarkably odd habit, not least because the lessons of history keep whacking them on the head with an assortment of well-aged and sturdy timbers without ever breaking through the trance.

My favorite example, not least because I've profited personally by it, is the historical blindness that sees to it that the lessons taught by speculative bubbles never seem to make it out of our collective equivalent of short-term memory. It so happens that in my adult life, I've had a ringside seat at four big speculative frenzies, and the first of them, the runup to the 1987 US stock market crash, got under way right about the time I first read John Kenneth Galbraith's mordantly funny history *The Great Crash 1929*. With Galbraith's account firmly in mind, I proceeded to watch a stock market bubble all but indistinguishable from the 1929 example unfold in front of my eyes, complete with the usual twaddle about new economic eras and limitless upside possibilities. It was quite a learning experience, though I didn't have any money of my own in the market.

A decade after the 1987 crash, the same twaddle got deployed a second time as computer-technology stocks began their ascent to ionospheric heights. At the time I was living in Seattle, one of the epicenters of the tech stock mania, and I was approached more times than I can easily remember by friends who worked in the computer industry, and who wanted to give me a chance to cash in on the new economic era and its limitless upside possibilities. I declined and, when pressed, explained my reasons with reference to Galbraith, 1929, and the 1987 crash. The standard response was condescending pity, a lecture about how I obviously didn't know the first thing about tech stocks and enthusiastic praise of books such as James Glassman and Kevin Hassett's infamous *Dow 36,000*. Shortly thereafter, the market crashed, and my friends' intimate knowledge of the computer field didn't keep them from losing their shirts.

Fast forward to 2004, and the same twaddle was deployed a third time. This time the investment du jour was real estate, and once again I was approached by any number of friends who wanted to help me cash in on the new economic era and its limitless upside possibilities. Once again I declined and, when pressed, explained my reasons with reference to Galbraith, 1929, the 1987 crash and the tech stock bubble and bust. The response? Condescending pity, a lecture about how I obviously didn't know the first thing about real estate, and enthusiastic praise of books such as David Lereah's epically mistimed *Why The Real Estate Boom Will Not Bust*. I was confident enough this time that my wife and I stayed out of the real estate bubble, waited for prices to plummet and bought the home where we now live for an absurdly small amount of money. Meanwhile the people I knew who planned on becoming real estate millionaires got clobbered when the bottom fell out of the market.

It's a matter of curiosity what the next asset class to go through the same cycle will be. That some asset class will go through that cycle, though, is as certain as anything can be. Try to tell the people who are about to get crushed by the next round of bubble-and-bust that that's what's happening, though, and you'll get the same condescending pity and the same lecture about how you obviously don't know the first thing about whatever asset is involved this time around. No matter how precise the parallels, they'll insist that the painful lessons taught by every previous speculative bubble in history are irrelevant to their investment strategy this time around, and they'll keep on saying that even when your predictions turn out to be correct and theirs end up costing them their shorts.

There are any number of factors feeding into this weird and self-defeating blindness to the most painful lessons of recent financial history. To begin with, of course, there's the widening mismatch between the American dream of endlessly improving economic opportunity and the American reality of steadily declining standards of living for everyone outside a narrowing circle of the well-to-do. Our national mythology makes it impossible for most Americans to conceive of a future of accelerating contraction and impoverishment, and so any excuse to believe that happy days are here again will attract an instant and uncritical audience.

Consider the extraordinary fog of misinformation surrounding the current fracking bubble — the increasingly loud and frantic claims that the modest temporary gains in oil production driven by the fracking phenomenon guarantee a future of abundant energy and prosperity for all.[1] It's the same twaddle about a new era with limitless upside potential, but it's even more popular than usual because the alternative is facing the future that's taking shape around us.

There are plenty of other forces helping to drive the same blindness to the obvious in contemporary culture, to be sure, and one of them is particularly relevant to the theme of this book. It's the general neglect of a style of thinking that is of central importance in modern science, but remains curiously unpopular in American culture. At the risk of scaring readers away by using a long word, I'll give it its proper name: morphological thinking.

Morphology is the study of form. Applied to biology, it was the driving force behind the intellectual revolution we nowadays associate with Charles Darwin, but was under way long before his time. Johann Wolfgang von Goethe showed in 1784 that the bones of the human skull are modified vertebrae that still retain their original relationship to one another; in 1790 he applied the same logic to plants, demonstrating that all the aboveground parts of flowering plants are modifications of a single primitive leaf structure.[2]

Two generations of scholars built on Goethe's work to show that every living creature has deep structural similarities with other life forms, living and extinct. The bones of your wrist, for example, have exact equivalents in a cat's foreleg, a dolphin's flipper and a bat's wing, and a close comparative study of all of these makes it impossible not to see the ancient mammalian forelimb that, over millions of years of deep time, became all four. Darwin's achievement, great as it was, was simply that of providing a convincing explanation for the changes that earlier biologists had already sketched out.

The lesson of morphology is that you can learn an extraordinary amount by looking for similarities of structure across a series of related things, even if you don't know a thing about the forces that cause the differences between them. That makes morphology particularly useful for fields of study where it's impossible to know the causes of change. Evolutionary biology is a great example. We don't have the opportunity to go back into the thinning forests of East Africa five or six million years ago, scatter instruments across the landscape and figure out exactly why it was that several kinds of primates came down from the trees and took up a life on the open savannah around that time. What we do have are the morphological traces of that descent, and of the different adaptations that enabled those early primates to survive — the long legs of the patas monkey, the hefty muscles and sharp teeth of the baboons, your upright posture and so on. From that, we can figure out quite a bit about what happened to each of those primate lineages, even in the absence of videotapes from the Pliocene.

Science has its fads and fashions, just like everything else human, and morphology has accordingly gone in and out of style as an analytic tool at various points down through the years. The same rule applies to other fields of scholarship where morphology can be used. History is among the classic examples. There's a long tradition of morphological thinking in history, because the causes of historical change are generally hidden from scholars by the lapse of time and the sheer complexity of the past. Giambattista Vico, Oswald Spengler and Arnold Toynbee are among the most important historians who put civilizations side by side in order to trace out common patterns of rise and fall.

These days, that approach has fallen out of fashion, and other analytic tools get much more of a workout in historical scholarship, but the method remains useful in making sense of the past and, in certain situations, of the future as well. That's the secret, or one of the secrets, of morphological thinking. If you've learned to recognize the shape of a common sequence of events, and you see the first stages of that sequence get under way, you can predict the outcome of the sequence, and be right far more often than not.

That's what I was doing, though I didn't yet know the formal name for it, when I considered the tech stock bubble, compared it to the stock market bubble of the mid-1980s and to previous examples of the same species, and predicted that it would end in a messy crash and a wave of bankruptcies — as of course it did. That's also what I'm attempting to do in this book, by placing today's popular faith in the inevitability and beneficence of progress side by side with other civil religions and, more broadly, with theistic religions as well.

Now of course any attempt at comparison between the modern faith in progress and those belief systems more generally regarded as religions falls afoul of deeply rooted presuppositions. Most of those either openly or implicitly assume, as already noted, that religion is a specific, concrete thing that includes some characteristic that faith in progress doesn't have: for example, that faith in progress can't be a religion because religions by definition believe in things that can't be proved to exist. Now of course it's worthwhile to ask where such definitions come from, and how well they actually fit the facts on the ground, but there's another point at issue here.

Human beliefs, practices and institutions rarely come into existence with the words "this is a religion" stamped on them. People whose cultures and languages have the category "religion" among their higher-order abstractions are generally the ones who make that judgment call. All the judgment call means, in turn, is that in the eyes of the people making it, the things gathered together under the label "religion" have enough morphological traits in common that it makes sense to talk about them as members of a common category.

When we talk about individual religions — Christianity, Druidry, faith in progress, or what have you — we're still talking about abstract categories, though they're abstractions of a lower order, reflecting constellations of beliefs, practices, institutions and the like that can be observed together in specific instances in the real world: this person in this building praying to this deity in words drawn from this scripture, for example. Those specific instances are the concrete realities that make the abstractions useful tools for understanding. Now of course it might be claimed that a given abstraction can't be used to see some specific concrete reality clearly, but it's hardly reasonable to do so in advance of making the experiment.

Thus I'd like to ask my readers to bear with me, whether or not the thought of faith in progress as a civil religion makes any obvious sense at first glance, and try the experiment of seeing the modern faith in progress through the abstract category of religion, using the same sort of morphological thinking I've discussed above. I grant freely that a porpoise doesn't look much like a bat, and tech stocks are not the same thing as no-doc mortgages. If you put the bones of the porpoise's flipper next to the bones of the bat's wing, or the rise and fall of the tech stock bubble next to the rise and fall of the real estate bubble, it becomes possible to learn things that are much easier to miss in any other context — and some of these, I'd like to suggest, are things of immense importance.

Part of that importance in the case at the heart to this book comes from the raw power that religions of every kind have as sources of human motivation. Though religions routinely have subtle and closely reasoned intellectual dimensions, those are arguably secondary growths; what gives religions their real power is that they reach right down into the deepest places of the human heart and draw on powerful and unreasoning passions rooted there. Civil religions and theist religions alike have motivated believers to die for their faith and to kill for it, to make tremendous sacrifices and commit appalling crimes. Not many human motivations can equal religion as a driving force, and I don't know of any that reliably surpass it. When people push past the limits of ordinary humanity in any direction, whether good or evil, if it's not a matter of the love or hate of one human being for another, odds are that what drives them onward is either a theist faith or a civil one.

This is among the reasons why it's essential to pay attention to religion at this stage of history, and why it's especially important to pay close attention to the most distinctive feature of the religious landscape of our time: the way that belief in the invincibility and beneficence of progress has come to serve a religious role in the modern world, permeating the collective conversations of our time. Any such exploration, though, will necessarily have to contend with some of the more problematic dimensions of the contemporary faith in progress — notably the historical mythology that underlies it, and the distortions it imposes on nearly all of our society's assumptions about the future.

It's important, to begin with, to pay attention to the ambiguities wrapped up in the modern conception of progress. When people think or talk about progress, by that name or any of its common euphemisms, there are at least three different things they can mean by it. All three share the common presupposition that history has an inherent and invincible tendency to move in a particular direction, that movement in that direction is a good thing and that human beings can and should contribute to that forward movement toward the good; it's the dimension of human life in which the movement is believed to be taking place that marks the distinction between these different meanings of progress.

One of these meanings is *moral progress*. That meaning centers on the claim that history's inherent tendency is toward increasingly ethical human relationships and social forms. These days, especially on the leftward end of society, this version of progress is usually framed in political terms, but its moral thrust is impossible to miss, as its proponents inevitably frame their arguments in terms of moral absolutes, virtues and vices.

At its best, the ethical stance of the contemporary mainstream Left in America and Europe is one of the few really original moral philosophies to develop in modern times, with a distinctive focus on the virtues of equality, social justice and kindness, all understood and pursued primarily on a collective rather than an individual level. At its worst — like all philosophies, it has its less impressive side — it becomes a self-righteous cant, by turns saccharine and shrill, in the service of the craving for unearned power that's the besetting sin of so many modern moralists. The faith in moral progress becomes visible any time people insist that some proposed social change is an advance, a move forward, away from the ignorance and injustice of the benighted past.

Even when this sort of talk is cheap manipulative rhetoric, as of course it so often is, it's the faith in moral progress that gives the manipulation power and allows it to work. Think about the implications of "forward" and "backward" as applied to social changes, and you can begin to see how deeply the mythology of progress pervades contemporary thought: only if history has a natural direction of moral change does it make any kind of sense to refer to one set of social policies as "progressive" and another as "retrograde," say, or to describe the culture or laws of one of the flyover states despised by the coastal literati as "stuck in the 1950s." It's the faith that history moves in the direction set out by a specific definition of moral progress that gives these very common metaphors their meaning.

That's only one of the three things that faith in progress can choose as its focus, though. Another is *scientific and technical progress*, which centers on the claim that history's inherent tendency is toward increasingly complete human knowledge and domination of the cosmos. In theory, it might be possible to conceive of scientific progress without a corresponding increase in technical power, or vice versa. In practice, at least in the minds of those who interpret progress along these lines, the two are rarely separated. As Francis Bacon argued in the first gray dawn of the scientific revolution,[3] the value of knowledge concerning nature is the power that results from that knowledge; investment in the production of scientific knowledge is almost universally justified by talking about what the resulting knowledge will let humanity do to the world.

To see the core features of a religion in starkest terms, it's often useful to look at its most extreme forms, and the faith in scientific and technical progress is no exception. The example I have in mind here is the Singularitarian movement, which claims that sometime soon — Singularitarian prophet Ray Kurzweil has set the date as 2045[4] — the unstoppable onward march of progress, bootstrapped by the creation of artificial intelligences far more powerful than any human mind, will accelerate to infinity. All the dreams of science fiction, from starflight through immortality to virtual sex with Marilyn Monroe, will become realities, and humanity will achieve something like godhood — unless the hyperintelligent computers decide to exterminate us all instead, that is.

There are plenty of things worth discussing about the Singularitarian religion, but the one that's relevant to the present theme is the wild misunderstanding it imposes on the nature of scientific knowledge. A large portion of the discoveries of science, including many of its

greatest achievements, can be summed up neatly by the words "you
can't do that." If an all-wise supercomputer could be created at all —
and it's far from certain that one can be — it's entirely possible that it
would sort through the sum total of human science and technology
and say to us, "For beings of such modest mental capacities, you've
done a good job of figuring out what can be done with the resources
available to you. Here are some technical tricks you haven't worked out
yet, but starflight, immortality, sex with this Marilyn Monroe person?
Sorry, those aren't possible; you'll have to go on living without them."
What's more, it's entirely possible that it would be right.

Even outside the Singularitarian faith, though, you can count on
either blank incomprehension or furious disagreement if you suggest
that the law of diminishing returns applies to scientific and technological progress just as firmly as it does to almost everything else, and that as
a result there might be things that scientific and technological progress
simply can't achieve. I would encourage any of my readers who doubt
this to try to suggest to their friends and neighbors that betting the future
on infinite resource extraction from a finite planet is not a bright idea.
Nearly always, the response is some variation on "Oh, I'm sure they'll
come up with something." The "they" in this overfamiliar sentence are
of course scientists and engineers, and the mere fact that "they" have
been trying to come up with something in this particular case for well
over a century, and success is still nowhere in sight, does nothing to dent
the blind faith that today's popular culture places in their powers.

Scientific and technical progress, then, plays a massive role in
the modern mythology of progress. Its role in contemporary life,
though, is equaled if not exceeded by the third kind of progress, *economic progress.* This third form of progress centers on the claim that
history's inherent tendency is toward ever greater levels of economic
abundance, however that abundance may happen to be distributed.
The belief that unlimited exponential economic growth is normal and
beneficent, and that anything else is abnormal and destructive, is perhaps the most widely accepted form of the mythology of progress in

contemporary life, not least because most people like to imagine that they themselves will benefit from it.

Open the business section of any newspaper, turn the pages of any economics textbook, scan the minutes of any meeting of any business corporation in contemporary America or almost anywhere else in the modern world, and you'll get to see a faith in economic progress as absolute and unthinking as any medieval peasant's trust in the wonder-working bones of the local saint. In the mythic world portrayed by the prophets and visionaries of that faith, economic growth is always good and comes as a reward to those who obey the commandments of the economists. The fact — and of course it is a fact — that obeying the commandments of the economists has by and large brought more di-saster than prosperity to the industrial world's economies for decades somehow rarely enters into these reverential thoughts.

In recent years, to be sure, faith in economic progress — that is, growth — has come under fire from two sides. On the one hand, there's the small but gradually expanding body of ecologists, econ-omists and other scholars who point out the absurdity of perpetual economic expansion on a finite planet and document some of the ways that an obsession with growth for its own sake produces a bumper crop of problems.[5] On the other, there's the less coherent but far more widespread sense that economic progress doesn't seem to be happen-ing the way it's supposed to, that standards of living for most people are declining rather than improving and that economic policies that have been sold to the public as ways to fix a troubled economy are having exactly the opposite effect.

Even so, most of the critiques coming out of this latter awareness, and no small number of those belonging to the former class, assume that growth is normal and fixate on how that supposedly normal state got derailed. Here as elsewhere in the contemporary world, faith in the inevitability and beneficence of progress retains an immense emotion-al power even when history fails to cooperate.

Moral progress, scientific and technological progress, and economic progress: those are the three forms that progress takes in the minds of those who put their faith in it: if you will, the three persons of the triune deity of the Church of Progress. It's crucial to keep in mind, though, that these three visions of progress often intertwine in the minds of believers with a complexity that rivals Christian theologies of the Trinity. To many liberals in late twentieth-century America, for example, it was axiomatic that the onward march of science and technology would bring boundless prosperity, which would make it possible to abolish poverty, provide equal opportunity for all and fulfill the hopes of moral progress without requiring the already privileged to give up any of the benefits the existing order of things conferred on them.

So complete a fusion of the three modes of progress was once standard. Read any of the vast supply of self-congratulatory literature on progress churned out by popular presses in nineteenth-century Britain or America, for example, and you can count on finding all three twisted tightly round one another, with the supposed moral superiority of Anglo-Saxon civilization serving as the linchpin of arguments that claimed to explain the limitless progress of technology and also to justify the extremely uneven distribution of the benefits of economic growth. The twentieth century's ghastly history made such moral claims a good deal harder to make with a straight face, and so versions of the faith in progress popular in recent decades very often drop the moral dimension and focus on the other two forms of progress.

These days, as a result, the most common American version of faith in progress fixates on the supposedly unstoppable feedback loop between scientific and technological progress, on the one hand, and economic growth on the other, while moral progress has been consigned to bit parts here and there. It's mostly on the left that faith in moral progress retains its former place in the blend — one of the many ways in which the leftward end of the American political landscape is significantly more conservative, in the strict sense of the word, than those who call themselves conservative these days — and even there, it's increasingly a fading hope, popular among the older generation of activists and among those who have moved toward the fringes of society and mixed their faith in progress with an ample helping of its antireligion, the faith in apocalypse.

It's from this unstable mix that we get an assortment of well-publicized claims that the morally better world will arrive once evil powers, and most of the planet's population, are blown to smithereens. I've long since lost track of the number of times that someone has suggested to me that if industrial civilization continues down the well-worn track of overshoot and decline, the silver lining to that very dark cloud is that the rigors of the decline will force the survivors to become better people — "better" being defined variously as more ecologically sensitive, more compassionate, or what have you, depending on the personal preferences of the speaker.

Now of course when civilizations overshoot their resource base and start skidding down the arc of decline toward history's compost bin, a sudden turn toward moral virtue of any kind is not a common event. The collapse of social order and a good many of the other concomitants of decline and fall tend to push things hard in the other direction. Still, faith in progress dominates the collective imagination of our time so completely that some way has to be found to make the future look better than the present. If a future of technological advancement and economic growth is no longer an option, then the hope for moral betterment becomes the last frail reed to which believers in progress cling with all their might.

To many of my readers, this may seem like a good idea; many others may consider it inevitable. I'm far from convinced that it's either one. How many times have we all heard the claim that economic growth was going to take care of resource depletion and environmental degradation, or that scientific and technical advances were going to take care of them, or that moral progress of one kind or another — call it the rise of planetary consciousness, or some other popular buzzword, if you wish — was going to take care of them? As it turned out, of course, none of those things took care of them at all, and since so many people relied on progress to spare them the trouble of doing something, nothing else took care of them, either.

Nor, for that matter, is faith in progress hardwired into the human psyche. It's a specific belief system rooted in the unique historical experience of the modern Western world, and most other people in most other places and times have had beliefs about the future that contradicted it in every particular. There have been many cultures in which history was believed to move steadily downhill, from a Golden Age in the past to a wretched end off somewhere in the future, and the strategy that made sense was to cling to what was left of the glorious past as long as possible. Nor are these the only options; there have, for example, been many cultures that saw time as a circle, and many more for whom time had no direction at all.

It's quite common for people raised in a given culture to see its view of things as normal and natural, and to scratch their heads in bewilderment when they find that people in other places and times saw things in very different ways. Modern industrial civilization, for all its self-described sophistication, is no more exempt from this custom than any other human society.

To make sense of the future closing in on us, though, it's going to be necessary to get past our habitual assumptions about reality, to recognize that the contemporary faith in progress is a culturally specific product that emerged in a highly unusual and self-terminating set of historical circumstances, and to realize that while it was highly adaptive in those circumstances, it's become lethally maladaptive now. To grasp these things, in turn, it's going to be necessary to grapple with one of the basic cognitive frameworks our society uses to make sense of the inkblot patterns of the cosmos. For want of a better label, we'll call this framework "the shape of time."

The shape of time is so pervasive and so central to our thought that trying to have a conversation about it — to make use of an apt if familiar metaphor — is rather like discussing the nature of water with fish. That's a common difficulty whenever the core presuppositions of our experience come up for discussion. The ideas that play the largest part in shaping our experience of the world and of ourselves are so deeply woven into the act of perception itself that we rarely if ever notice them until we run face first into their limits.

Even the recognition that ideas play a role in the process of perception requires an uncommon degree of attention to the way the human mind works. Most people, most of the time, think and act as though the things that they experience with their senses and sort with their thoughts are objective realities "out there," and pay no attention to the generations of careful research that's shown that what we perceive is a cooperative project in which external stimuli, the biologically defined structures of our sense organs and nervous systems, and the culturally and individually defined contents of our minds all have roles to play.

There's good reason for that lack of awareness. Patterns of thinking, like patterns of action, are most efficient when they don't require conscious attention. Just as you can't really become good at playing a musical instrument until you no longer have to consciously move every finger into position on the keys or strings, you can't really use a way of thinking about the world until it slips below the surface of the mind and starts to structure how you experience other things.

Pay attention to what happens when you wake in dim light in an unfamiliar room, and the vague shapes around you take time to turn into recognizable furniture, and you'll get a sense of the way that your thinking affects your awareness of the world. Learn some cognitive skill such as plant identification, and notice the shifts in perception as foliage changes from a vague green blur to a galaxy of legible patterns, and you'll get a sense of the same process from a different angle. To borrow a useful term from philosopher Owen Barfield, the mental process at work in both cases is *figuration*:[6] the act of assembling the data provided by the senses into meaningful forms that can be known by the mind.

Figuration plays an essential, if usually unnoticed, role in all mental activity. Its strength and its weakness comes from the simple and subtle fact that the framework onto which your mind fits the evidence of the senses is provided by the perceiving mind, not by the things being perceived. More precisely, the framework of your figurations is partly given you by inherited patterns hardwired into human neurology over the course of our species' evolutionary past, partly by culturally specific notions that are so much a part of your thinking that you normally don't notice their existence at all, and partly by personal ideas and experiences that have been absorbed just as completely into the background of your thinking.

The invisibility of figurative patterns is necessary to their functioning, for obvious reasons. If you had to decide moment by moment which mental pattern to use to make sense of any given set of sensory data, your conscious mind would be too busy to do anything else. The invisibility of the patterns only becomes a problem when the unnoticed ideas you're using to frame your experience of the world no longer tell you what you most need to know about the world.

Wilderness tracker Tom Brown Jr. tells a story about a group of senior students who were skilled at plant identification, and who were out with Brown on an herb walk. Brown stopped them at one point along the trail, pointed to a plant, and said, "What do you see?" The students all correctly named the plant. "Get closer and take another look," Brown said. The students did so, and confirmed that it was, in fact, the plant they'd named. After several repetitions, they were almost on top of the plant, and it wasn't until then that the rabbit that was nibbling on the plant leaves bounded away, startling the students. They had been paying so much attention to plants that they hadn't seen the rabbit at all.[7]

The same thing happens in far less innocuous ways, when the unnoticed ideas aren't simply the product of a weekend workshop's focus, but the culturally transmitted presuppositions that provide basic frameworks for the experiences and the thinking of an entire society. The cognitive framing that I've called the shape of time is a case in

point. Most people, most of the time, don't notice that all their thinking about past, present and future is shaped by some set of unnoticed
assumptions about time and history. Those assumptions usually come
out of some fusion of culturally valued narratives and recent experience — not a bad idea, all things considered, unless events begin to
move in ways that our culturally valued narratives no longer explain.

⚜

It's easiest to understand this by taking an example that's as different as possible from the commonplaces of contemporary thinking.
Fortunately, the history of ideas has no shortage of those. The one I
want to introduce here comes to us courtesy of Hesiod, one of the very
first ancient Greek poets whose works still survive. He lived in the
eighth century BCE in the harsh and beautiful hill country of Boeotia,
halfway down the eastern side of the Greek peninsula. He wrote two
major poems that survive, *Theogony* and *Works and Days*, and the latter
of these sketches out a vision of the shape of time that would have an
immense influence long after Hesiod's day.[8]

It's a vision of relentless decline. For Hesiod, the zenith of human
happiness lay in the distant past, in the Golden Age when the old
wise god Kronos ruled and the earth produced crops by itself without
human labor. Since then, age after age, it's been all downhill: the Silver
Age of folly and ignorance, the Bronze Age of merciless warfare, the
Age of Heroes immediately before Hesiod's time and finally the bitter
Iron Age, when misery and hard labor are humanity's lot. In his vision,
it's not going to get any better, either: eventually the last frail scraps of
goodness will go whistling down the wind, and infants will be born
with their hair already gray. Then Zeus will destroy the humanity of the
Iron Age as he destroyed the inhabitants of the previous four ages, and
the story ends. If the Golden Age was scheduled to return after that,
Hesiod doesn't mention it.

To some extent Hesiod's model simply echoes the human life cycle,
seen from the perspective of an old man looking back on life in a hard

age: happiness in infancy, folly in childhood, war and passion in adolescence, hard productive labor in adulthood and finally the miseries
of old age and death. Still, there's more to it than that, because Hesiod's
vision of the shape of time was a tolerably good reflection of the history his corner of the world had experienced in the centuries before he
was born.

Two thousand years before Hesiod, prehistoric Greece had been the
home of a lively assortment of village cultures making the slow transition from polished stone tools to bronze. On that foundation more
complex societies rose, borrowing heavily from contemporary high
cultures in the Middle East, and culminating in the monumental architecture and literate palace bureaucracies of the Mycenean age. Those of
my readers who have some sense of the ecological rhythms of history
will already know what followed: too much clearcutting and intensive
farming, made worse by the importation of farming methods better
suited to flat Mesopotamian valleys than easily eroded Greek hills,
triggered an ecological crisis. Most of the topsoil of Mycenean Greece
ended up at the bottom of the Aegean Sea, where it can still be found
in core samples; warfare, migration and population collapse followed
in the usual manner, as Mycenean society stumbled down the curve of
its own Long Descent.[9]

That's the past that defined Hesiod's vision of the present and the
future. Those of my readers who are up for a challenge might consider
trying, for a few moments, to fit their minds around that vision — to
try to sense what it would have been like to see history as a long and
bitter descent, and to imagine that view of things not as an interesting
speculation or a theory, but simply as the way things are, the way they
have always been and will always be. Think about the way the world
would look to you if humanity's best years were in the distant past, the
future held nothing but a long trajectory of decline ending in extinction and your chances of achieving some degree of happiness in your
life depended on being smart, tough and intensely aware of the downside risks in every choice you made.

Hope is not a virtue in such a world. Whether or not Hesiod invented the story of Pandora's box, he's the source from which every later version derives,[10] but there's a detail you'll find in modern versions of the tale that is not in his account. In today's versions, when all the plagues and curses in the box flew out to afflict humanity, Hope remained behind as a kind of consolation prize. In Hesiod, it's not a consolation prize; it's the nastiest of the curses that Zeus put in the box, the enticing delusion that things will get better when they won't. Greek poets liked to use fixed adjective-noun pairs — the rosy-fingered dawn, the wine-dark sea, and so on. When the word "hope" appears in ancient Greek poetry, the adjective normally assigned to it was "blind."

The attitude expressed in that phrase neatly defines the world in which Hesiod lived. The point that too many of his modern interpreters don't grasp is that his attitude, and the practical implications of that attitude which filled the verses of *Works and Days* — distrust the new, rely on traditional wisdom, aim for modest goals, keep a year's supply of grain on hand so you don't starve — were better suited to his world than, for example, our faith in the limitless potential of the future would have been. In an impoverished tribal society scrabbling for survival amid the ruins of a far more complex culture and the long-term impacts of ecological collapse, accepting the reality of decline and the likelihood of further trouble to come was a better strategy than any of the alternatives; in the language of evolutionary ecology, it was adaptive. It's unlikely to be an accident that visions of time like Hesiod's are very common in the hard times that follow the collapse of major civilizations.

Now of course Hesiod's bleak vision is far from the only alternative to the vision of progress that defines the shape of time to most people in today's industrial world. For another alternative, consider the distinctive way of thinking about time that's common to a great many tribal societies around the world. In this vision of the shape of time, everything important took place *in illo tempore* — in the Dreamtime, as the Australian aboriginal term has it, the time when animals lived and spoke like people and the powers who defined the cosmos traced out the patterns that humanity would follow ever after.

In this way of thinking about time, all of the history that mattered happened in an other-time that is simultaneously long ago and happening right now in parallel to ordinary time. Its changes are chronicled in the mythic narratives that the elders recite to children so that they will know the right way to live. Each event since then, whether it's part of the cycle of the year, the cycle of a human life, or what have you, simply reiterates and reflects some feature of that original time. This shape of time doesn't go anywhere at all — not up, not down, not around in circles. It stays put, an eternal pattern reflected endlessly in the happenings of everyday existence.

Our modern industrial sensibility is profoundly hostile to this way of experiencing time. When I was growing up, as one measure of that hostility, there were any number of children's novels set in "primitive societies" — that is, cultures that experienced time in the way I've just outlined — which focused obsessively on some imaginary individualist who turned his (or, very rarely, her) back on tribal custom via one triumphant innovation after another. Those stories were very flattering to the tender feelings of readers in modern industrial cultures, to be sure, but they missed nearly everything relevant to the tribal cultures in question. By the time a society following a hunter-gatherer or village horticulture ecology has inhabited a given bioregion for a few thousand years, after all, it's a safe bet that the people in that culture will have tried all the available options, figured out which ones work and which ones don't and enshrined that hard-won knowledge in stories, customs and taboos, the normal technologies for passing knowledge down through the generations in societies that don't have writing.

In such a context, innovation is rarely a good idea. The resource base that would be necessary to deal with subsistence failure or ecological instability simply isn't available — the ability to store food over the long term doesn't usually come in until the invention of grain agriculture, so nothing as substantial as Hesiod's year of stockpiled grain stands between a hunter-gatherer or village horticultural society and starvation. The innovator who introduces the bow and arrow to a people used to hunting with spears thus might be dooming them to starve to death when the new technology proves too successful at killing game and wipes out the herds. In that ecological setting, an understanding of time that wards off such potentially lethal possibilities is adaptive, while one that fosters innovation is not.

Another shape of time, different from Hesiod's implacable descent and the Dreamtime's stasis, is common to most literate urban civilizations once they're past their adolescence and start paying attention to the traces of earlier civilizations around them. There are dozens of examples; one worth close study is the traditional Chinese version, which guided historical thought in China from archaic times straight through to the twentieth century.

The basic theory of the Chinese science of time is that events are guided by many different cycles, some faster and some slower, some influencing one dimension of human life and some shaping another. The cycle of the seasons was one of these; the cycle of human life was another; the cycle of the rise and fall of dynasties was a third; there were many more, each with its own period and typical sequence of events. Just as no two years had exactly the same weather on exactly the same days, no two repetitions of any other cycle were identical, but common patterns allowed the events of one repetition to be more or less predicted by a sufficiently broad knowledge of earlier examples.

On a much broader scale, all cycles of every kind could be understood as expressions of a single abstract pattern of cyclic change, which was explored in the classic Chinese textbook of time theory, the I Ching — in English, the Book of Change. Most people in the Western world who are familiar with the I Ching at all think of it as a fortune-telling book, full of obscure oracles accessed by flipping Chinese coins or, for the cognoscenti, sorting bundles of yarrow stalks. Back in the day, that was the kindergarten level of I Ching practice.[11]

The masters of the Book of Change recognized that each of the 64 hexagrams was an abstract representation of a particular stage in the unfolding of a cyclic pattern; each hexagram could turn into any other hexagram under the right conditions; and the goal of study was to be able to contemplate any given sequence of events, identify what pattern was in process just then, figure out where it was going next and get there first. This wasn't a purely philosophical pursuit by any means — certain Chinese martial arts rely on the I Ching as a basis for strategy, and "getting there first" to them means bringing a fist or a foot up hard against the opponent's vulnerable spots.[12]

Like the other shapes of time we've discussed so far, the vision of time as a matrix of cycles is highly adaptive in its own historical context. It tends to emerge, as I've already noted, in mature literate civilizations that have access to the records and ruins of older societies. Whether it's Chinese scholars pondering the rise and fall of dynasties, Chaldean priests mulling over the fates of the kingdoms of the Mesopotamian plain, Roman Stoics sketching out the rhythms in which Greek city-states flourished and fell, or early twentieth-century European historians recognizing familiar patterns in the historical events of their own time, students of the cycles of history recognize that the past has lessons to offer the present and use a sense of cyclic change to guide their efforts to understand those lessons and put them to work.

Does that make cyclical cosmologies more accurate than the others we've just considered? Is the circle the true shape of time? It's hard to see any way in which those questions could mean anything. What I've called the shape of time is an abstraction, a convenient model that doesn't contradict what's known about past, present and future, and sums up the way that events seem to unfold from the standpoint of particular people in a particular historical situation. Abstractions of this kind are tools, not truths — you might as well ask if a hammer is factually accurate.

It's nonetheless true that different tools are better suited, more adaptive, to different situations. If you live in a society struggling to endure in the wake of cultural and ecological collapse, Hesiod's vision may be your best bet; if you live in a society that has a stable relationship with its bioregion but very few resources on which to fall back in time of trouble, the Dreamtime cosmology will likely be a better choice; if you live in a society that has a literate historical tradition and want to use that resource to help you duck some of the troubles that overwhelmed earlier societies, the cyclical approach is the tool you need. Other situations have other tools better suited to them — the handful of shapes of time I've outlined here are only a few of the many options that have been tried, with more or less success, over the span of recorded history.

One of the others is of particular importance to this book's theme. If you happen to live in a society that has stumbled across an energy source of unparalleled abundance and concentration, a source so rich that the major economic challenge faced over the course of three centuries is that of finding enough clever ways to use it to replace human muscle power and the other, far more limited energy sources of less lavishly supplied eras, then a vision of time as endless progress is going to be your most adaptive choice. That's arguably the main reason why belief in progress has become so deeply entrenched in the collective imagination of the industrial world: for more than three hundred years, much more often than not, it worked. During that era, those people, companies and nations that gambled on progress by and large did much better than those that bet their money and other resources on stasis or decline.

As the fine print says, though, past performance is no guarantee of future results, and a shape of time that was highly adaptive to some particular set of historical conditions can become maladaptive when the conditions suddenly change. Ancient Greece went through such a shift, beginning a century or so after Hesiod's time, as the reopening of trade routes closed since Mycenae's fall made it profitable for Greek farmers to turn hillside acreage over to olive orchards and vineyards for the export trade.[13]

By the beginning of the sixth century, as Greek wine and oil flooded markets across the eastern Mediterranean and brought a corresponding flood of hard currency and imported goods back home, Hesiod's harsh but functional views stopped being relevant, though it was many years more before that lack of relevance was really processed by the Greeks. Another millennium passed before the old pattern repeated itself, and the civilization of classical Greece stumbled down the curve of decline and fall toward a dark age that Hesiod would have recognized at once.

A central theme of this book, in turn, is that the same sort of transformation is happening in our own time, but in the other direction. The shape of time that governs nearly all contemporary thinking in the industrial world, the vision of perpetual progress, was adaptive back when ever more abundant energy supplies were being extracted out of mines and wells and poured into the project of limitless industrial expansion. The end of the age of cheap abundant energy and the depletion of most of the other resources on which industrial civilization depends, though, make that shape of time hopelessly maladaptive, and a galaxy of assumptions and ideas founded on faith in progress are thus well past their pull date.

Since most people in the modern industrial world aren't even aware of the role that faith in progress plays in their thinking, their chances of adapting to the end of progress are not good — and certain habits of thought that the civil religion of progress has inherited from older theist religions make the necessary adaptations even harder than they have to be.

Three

The Rock By Lake Silvaplana

ONE OF THE MOST IMPORTANT AND LEAST POPULAR LESSONS taught by the history of ideas is that every attempt to answer the big questions — where did we come from, why are we here, where are we going and so forth — gets whatever support it has from two distinct sources. The first of these is the factual evidence, if any, that backs it. The second is the emotional appeal, if any, that it offers to those who embrace it. Habits of thinking hardwired into contemporary culture treat the first of those as though it's the only thing that matters, and react to any mention of the second with the same sort of embarrassed silence that might greet a resounding fart at a formal garden party. Since human beings aren't passionless bubbles of intellect, though, the second source of support is usually the more important and the more revealing of the two.

The flurry of apocalyptic predictions that surrounded December 21, 2012, makes as good an example as any. The factual evidence supporting the idea that anything unusual would happen on that date was — well, to call it dubious is charitable. The entire furor was based on misinterpretations of the Mayan calendar that wouldn't have survived 15 minutes of unbiased research, but which were accepted as gospel and padded out by industrious true believers into a magpie's nest of arbitrary speculations, misquoted or invented prophecies and scientific hypotheses that were yanked out of context and hammered into shape to support the preexisting 2012 narrative.[1] Those of my readers who tried to question that narrative will recall the reaction from believers: talk about the facts and you'd get a stream of justifications for belief; talk about the narrative, its parallels in previous apocalyptic fads and the tangled emotional drives that all too clearly lay behind it, and you'd get a furious insistence that bringing up such matters was irrelevant and unfair.

Questioning the modern faith in progress is a good way to observe a similar species of handwaving in its native habitat. The concept of progress has no content of its own, no single measurement by which it stands and falls; all three of the competing versions of progress discussed in Chapter Two are vague enough to give believers in progress as much wiggle room as any would-be prophet could desire. No matter how many things are pretty clearly regressing — and these days, the list of things that are regressing is getting quite long — believers can always find something or other that appears to be progressing and use that to defend the narrative.

When that fails in turn, as it generally does, there's always something else, even if that turns out to be no more than the pious hope that the regress will turn out to be a temporary hurdle over which, as the myth of progress demands, humanity will sooner or later leap. Move the discussion to the narrative of progress, its parallels among other triumphalist narratives and the emotional drives that lie behind it, though, and you'll get the same sort of angry denunciation that came from believers in the 2012 narrative when confronted with similar questions about the nonrational underpinnings of their apocalyptic faith.

It's going to be necessary to risk that reaction, and a variety of other unhelpful responses, in order to get past the present paired fixations on the straight line of perpetual progress and the sudden stop of apocalypse that heralds the cataclysmic arrival of the New Jerusalem, however renamed. The route past those overly familiar alternatives requires attention to the emotional dimensions of the shapes we give to the inkblot patterns of time, and in particular, to a distinctive emotional payoff that the narratives of progress and apocalypse share in common.

Call it provisional living: the belief that life will become what it's supposed to be once x happens. What x might be varies as wildly from case to case as the diversity of human psyches will permit. Among individuals, it might be losing 20 pounds, being promoted to that supervisor's position you've always wanted, getting a divorce, or what have you, but it always has two distinctive features. The first is that x serves as an anchor for a flurry of unrealistic fantasies about the future that will supposedly arrive once x happens; the second is that x never happens and is more or less chosen — subconsciously or otherwise — with that outcome in mind.

It's precisely the fact that x never happens that makes provisional living so tempting. Most of us are aware on one level or another that the choices we prefer to make don't reflect the values and beliefs we claim to hold and aren't going to bring us the lives we think we ought to have. Confront that reality head on, and the message that the statue of Apollo gave to Rainier Maria Rilke[2] — "you must change your life" — becomes hard to ignore. The avoidance of that reality is therefore the cornerstone on which most dysfunctional lives are built.

Provisional living is among the most popular ways to engineer that avoidance. The pounds you can't lose, the promotion you won't get, the divorce papers you never quite get around to filing, or some other x factor becomes the villain you can blame for the failure of your choices to reflect your ideals and bring you the life you think you should have. Meanwhile the dreams that pile up on the other side of the change that never happens can get as gaudy as you like, since they never have to face the gray morning light of reality. Not all those dreams are happy ones; people are almost as likely to put fantasies about suffering and death on the far side of x as they are to stock that imaginary space with wealth, power and plenty of hot sex. It all depends on the personal factor.

The mythic narratives of progress and apocalypse, in turn, offer the same payoff on a collective scale. The imagined world of the future, whether it's the product of business as usual or of the cataclysmic repudiation of business as usual, becomes a dumping ground for every kind of fantasy, and those fantasies never have to stand up to the test of reality because the x event that's supposed to make them real never quite gets around to happening. This allows believers in progress and apocalypse, like other practitioners of provisional living, to put a wholly imaginary world at the center of their emotional lives. It also makes it relatively easy for them to ignore the depressingly ordinary world in which they actually live and, more to the point, the role of their own choices in making that world exactly what it is.

The imaginary future worlds conjured up by the mythologies of progress and apocalypse, in turn, are pallid reflections of an older and more robust conception, the belief in a heaven of immortal bliss to which the souls of true believers ascend after death. That belief is one of the most distinctive traits of the last two thousand years or so of Western and Middle Eastern religion — other cultures and ages have their own conceptions of the afterlife, and most of these differ sharply from the heaven-concept standard in the faiths familiar to most people in the West. To what extent that heaven-concept is simply one more form of provisional living is a matter for theologians to discuss, but it's certainly filled that role quite often in popular culture.

It's indicative here that when the concept of reincarnation came back into circulation in alternative circles in the Western world in the nineteenth century, it was at first denounced in incandescent terms.[3] What made it "disgusting" and "repulsive," to note only two of the heated labels applied to reincarnation in that long-forgotten debate, was precisely the suggestion that human souls after death would cycle right back to the same existence they had just left and be forced to live in the world their own choices had helped shape.

It's at this point that we return to Nietzsche, for one of the central themes of his philosophy was an edgy analysis of the creation of imaginary "real worlds" by the human mind as a way of devaluing the world we actually inhabit.[4] That was an even bigger issue in his time than it is in ours, since the society he saw around him was full to the choking point with the sort of Christian piety which claimed that the proper response to every injustice was to wait patiently for payback in heaven, and the sort of philosophies in which airily abstract speculations about the Absolute had all but replaced meaningful attention to the realities of human existence. The phrase "provisional living" wasn't in Nietzsche's vocabulary, but the practice was central to the social morality of the Victorian era, and that habit was among the principal targets of Nietzsche's grand project for a revaluation of all values that would take life itself as its touchstone.

That project had for its core theme the affirmation of existence as it actually is — in Nietzsche's own phrase, a yes-saying to life that would counter more than two thousand years of naysaying morality, philosophy and spirituality. As he developed his critique of the conventional wisdom of his time, his insistence on saying yes to life as it is became increasingly forceful. That journey reached its final destination in August of 1881 on a walk around Lake Silvaplana in the Alps, at a roughly pyramidal mass of stone that still stands beside the lake: "six thousand feet beyond man and time," as Nietzsche wrote excitedly on a scrap of paper shortly thereafter.[5]

If, as Nietzsche thought, the only ideas that matter are those conceived while walking, it may be useful to spend a few moments strolling along the path that led up to his formula of affirmation. A classical philologist by training, Nietzsche applied a specialist's familiarity with ancient Greek thought to the more immediate problems of philosophy and Western culture that concerned him in his major works. Many of his core conceptions can thus be traced back at least in part to one particular school of Greek and Roman philosophers, the one such school that affirmed life as it is with as much verve as Nietzsche himself: the old Stoics.

Mention the word "Stoic" to most people these days and you might, if you're lucky, get some sort of vague sense of gritted teeth and unwillingness to crumple under the impact of pain. Off past that dim misunderstanding lies one of the most challenging adventures in human thought, a sustained effort to sort out human life on the basis of what we actually know about the world.[6] The Stoic school of philosophy was founded around 300 BCE by Zeno of Citium and became one of the primary schools of classical thought, remaining a living tradition until the long night of the dark ages closed in.

Its core insight was that human beings can control only two things — their own choices of action and inaction and their own assessments of the things they experience — and that sanity consists of recognizing this fact and refusing to make any emotional investment in those things that aren't subject to the individual will. In any situation, said the Stoics, the job assigned to human beings is to recognize the good and act accordingly. Nothing else matters, and the point of Stoic spiritual practice is to get to the point where, in fact, nothing else matters.

The radical affirmation of the world as it is was one standard element of the Stoic training. From the Stoic perspective, the world is what it is, and though the Stoic may freely choose to fling himself into a struggle to change some part of it for the better and unhesitatingly lay down his life in that struggle, no power in heaven or earth can make him whine about it.

The Stoics took that formula of radical acceptance to an extreme that few later thinkers have ever been willing to contemplate. Most philosophers in the classical world accepted the astrological theory that the motions of the planets and stars shaped events on Earth and speculated that after an immense length of time, the heavens will repeat the same patterns of movement and bring about a corresponding repetition below. Stoic philosophers embraced that theory and built up a worldview in which the whole universe moved through endlessly repeated cycles from one *ekpyrosis* — "Big Bang" would not be an inaccurate translation of this bit of technical Greek — to the next, with every single event duplicated down to the last detail in each repetition.

It's one thing to accept the present moment and another to accept the whole of your life. It's quite another thing again to imagine that same life repeated endlessly through infinite time and accept that as a whole, without wishing a single thing to be different. That's the state to which the most extreme Stoics aspired — and that was the vision that came crashing into Nietzsche's mind as he stood beside the rock by Lake Silvaplana.

Suppose, he said, we engage in a thought experiment. Scientists tell us that there is a fixed quantity of matter and energy in the cosmos and no sign that the universe has a beginning or an end. (This was all generally accepted scientific opinion in the late nineteenth century; the Big Bang theory was still decades away.) Given a finite amount of matter and energy and a fixed set of natural laws working over infinite time, every event any of us experiences here and now must have happened an infinite number of times before, and will happen an infinite number of times again, in an eternal recurrence that admits of no variation. As you consider your life, past, present and to come, can you face the prospect of infinite repetitions of that same life? Can you joyously affirm that prospect? Can you *will* it?

It's hard to imagine a more all-out assault on provisional living, or a more forceful challenge to live up to one's ideals. As he passed through his few remaining years of sanity, though, Nietzsche seems to have convinced himself that his thought experiment was in fact a reality, that every moment of his life had in fact happened countless times before and would be repeated countless times again. I sometimes wonder if that's what finally pushed him over the edge into madness. Like most thinkers whose work makes a fetish of ruthlessness, Nietzsche was obsessively kind and gentle in his personal life. As he stood there on the Piazza Carlo Alberti, hearing the thump of the teamster's stick and the terrified cries of the horse, growing more agitated by the moment, it's all too easy to imagine the voice whispering in his mind: can you joyously affirm *this*, over and over again, from eternity to eternity?

A moment later he was sprinting across the piazza, flinging himself between the drover and the horse. It was a classically Stoic thing to do, and I suspect that if he'd known that what was left of his sanity wouldn't survive the moment, he'd have done it anyway. *Fiat justicia, ruat caelum*, said the old Stoics: let justice be done, even if it brings the sky crashing down. That it was his own mental sky that came crashing down was, as the Stoics also liked to say, a matter of indifference.

It was Nietzsche's great misfortune and a central flaw of his philosophy that he never quite managed to grasp that the opposite of a bad idea is very often another bad idea. To challenge oneself with the vision of eternal recurrence as a thought experiment is one thing, and I recommend it to my readers as a useful exercise. If that vision were in fact the literal truth, could you give the rest of your life a shape and a purpose that would give sufficient meaning and value to everything you have already been and done and suffered, so that when you add it all up, you can joyously affirm the whole pattern — and what would the rest of your life need to become in order for you to do so?

To pass beyond that, though, and to try to inhabit a cosmos in which everything is fixed by fate, in which everything revolves through the same series of events endlessly from eternity to eternity, and in which the only freedom open to the will is to affirm that sequence joyously or vainly reject it, is to court Nietzsche's fate for no good reason. To be even more precise, insisting on a cosmos in which everything is fated to repeat endlessly is as useless, in practical terms, as insisting that one fine day in the not too distant future, the march of progress or the arrival of apocalypse will transform the cosmos into whatever you think it ought to be.

The eternal recurrence, though, lacks the emotional payoffs that give the religion of progress and its antireligion of apocalypse their appeal. In both these civil religions, the future functions as a surrogate for heaven and hell alike, the place where the wicked will finally get the walloping they deserve and the good will be granted the promised benefits that the present never quite gets around to providing them. The fading out of living religious belief as a significant force in public life that Nietzsche colorfully described as the death of God left people across the Western world flailing for something to backstop the sense of moral order in the cosmos they once derived from religious faith. Over the course of the nineteenth century, as already noted, a great many of them found what they wanted in one or another civil religion that projected utopia onto the future.

It's crucial not to underestimate the emotional force of the resulting beliefs. The future of perpetual betterment promised by the faith in progress, and the utopia on the far side of cataclysm promised with equal fervor by the faith in apocalypse, are no less important to their believers than heaven is to the ordinary Christian, and for exactly the same reason. Every human society has its own conception of the order of the cosmos and its own way of relating that conception to human knowledge; the distinctive concept of cosmic order that became central to the societies of Europe and the European diaspora envisioned a moral order that could be understood, down to the fine details, by human beings.

Since everyday life pretty clearly fails to follow any such order, there had to be some offstage location where everything would balance out, whether that location took the form of heaven, humanity's glorious future among the stars, a society of equality and justice come the Revolution, or what have you. Discard that imagined place and, for a great many people in the Western world, the cosmos ceases to have any order or meaning at all.

It was precisely against this sense of moral order that Nietzsche declared war. Like any good general, he sent his forces into action along several routes at once; the assault relevant to our theme was aimed at the belief that the arithmetic of morality would finally add up in some other place or time. He rejected the idea of a utopian world of past or future just as forcefully as he did the concept of heaven itself. That's one of the things his doctrine of eternal recurrence was intended to do:

by revisioning the past and the future as endless repetition, Nietzsche did his level best to block any attempt to make the past or the future fill the role once filled by heaven.

Here, though, he overplayed his hand. Strictly speaking, a cycle of eternal return is just as imaginary as any golden age in the distant past, or for that matter the glorious future come the Revolution when we will all eat strawberries and cream. In a philosophy that presents itself as a Yes-saying to life exactly as it is, his reliance on a theory of time just as unprovable as those he assaulted was a massive problem. Nietzsche's madness, and the resolute effort on the part of most European intellectuals of the time not to think about any of the issues he tried to raise, left this point, among many others, hanging in the air.

It would take a later thinker, drawing on Nietzsche's insights but avoiding his habit of countering one extreme by going to the other, to trace out a shape of time that does a better job of reflecting the world of human experience — or, more specifically, the world experienced by human beings who happen to be living at the peak of modern industrial civilization and have begun to glimpse the long road down on the peak's other side. His name was Oswald Spengler.

⁂

Spengler was in his own way as eccentric a figure as Nietzsche, though it was a more stereotypically German eccentricity than Nietzsche's fey Dionysian aestheticism. A cold, methodical, solitary man, he spent his entire working life as a schoolteacher and all his spare time — he never married — with his nose in a polymath's banquet of books from every corner of scholarship. Old Kingdom Egyptian theology, traditional Chinese landscape design, the history of the medieval Russian church, the philosophical schools of ancient India, the latest discoveries in early twentieth-century physics: all these and more were grist for his highly adaptable mill.

In 1914, as the impending fall of the British Empire was sweeping Europe into a vortex of war, he started work on the first volume of *The*

Decline of the West. It appeared in 1918, and the second volume followed it in 1922. The books became immediate bestsellers in German and several other languages — this despite a world-class collective temper tantrum on the part of professional historians. *Logos*, one of the most prestigious German scholarly journals of the time, ran an entire special issue on him in which historians engaged in a frenzy of nitpicking about Spengler's historical claims. (Spengler, unperturbed, read the issue, doublechecked his facts, released a new edition of his book with corrections and pointed out that none of the nitpicking addressed any of the major points of his book; he was right, too.)

One study of the furor around Spengler noted more than four hundred publications, most of them hostile, discussing *The Decline of the West* in the decade of the 1920s alone. Interest in Spengler's work peaked in the 1920s and 1930s and faded out after the Second World War; some of the leading figures of the Beat generation used to sit around a table reading *The Decline of the West* out loud, and a few other figures of the 1950s drew on his ideas, but thereafter silence closed in. There's an ironic contrast here to Nietzsche, who provided Spengler with so many of his basic insights; Nietzsche's work was almost completely unknown during his life and became a massive cultural presence after his death; with Spengler, the sequence ran the other way around.

The central reason why Spengler was so fiercely if inconclusively attacked by historians in his own time and so comprehensively ignored since then is the same reason why he's relevant to this book. At the core of his work stood the same habit of morphological thinking discussed earlier. Johann Wolfgang von Goethe, who launched the study of comparative morphology in the life sciences in the eighteenth century, remained a massive cultural presence in the Germany of Spengler's time, and so it came naturally to Spengler to line up the great civilizations of history side by side and compare their histories, in the same way that a biologist might compare a dolphin's flipper to a bat's wing to see the common patterns of deep structure that underlie the surface differences.

Such comparisons are surprisingly unfashionable in modern historical studies. Most other fields of study rely on comparisons as a matter of course: the astronomer compares one nebula to another, just as the literary critic compares one experimental novel to another, and in both fields it's widely accepted that such comparisons are the most important way to get past irrelevancies to an understanding of what's really going on. There are historical works that compare, say, one revolution to others, or one feudal system to another, but they're in the minority.

More often, historians consider the events of some corner of the past by themselves, without relating them to comparable periods or events, and either restrict themselves to storytelling or propose assorted theories about the causes of those events — theories that can never be put to the test because it's all but impossible to test a hypothesis when you're working with a sample size of one. The reason why this is so popular, I've come to think, is precisely that a sample size of more than one turns up patterns that next to nobody these days wants to see.

By placing past societies side by side with the modern industrial West, Spengler thus found that all the great historical changes that our society sees as uniquely its own have exact equivalents in older societies. Each society emerges out of chaos as a decentralized feudal society, with a warrior aristocracy and an epic poetry so similar that an enterprising bard could have recited the Babylonian tale of Gilgamesh in an Anglo-Saxon mead hall without anyone present sensing the least incongruity. Each then experiences corresponding shifts in social organization: the mead halls and their equivalents give way to castles, the castles to fortified towns, the towns to cities, and then a few of the cities outgrow all the others and become the centers in which the last stages of the society's creative life are worked out.

Meanwhile, in the political sphere, feudal aristocrats become subject to kings, who are displaced by oligarchies of the urban rich, and these latter eventually fall before what Spengler calls *Caesarism*, the emergence of charismatic leaders who attract a following from the urban masses and use that strength to seize power from the corrupt institutions of an oligarchic state. In the intellectual sphere, while these political shifts are proceeding, traditional religions rich in myth give way to rationalist philosophies as each society settles on the intellectual projects that will define its legacy to the future — logic and philosophy in the classical world, for instance, or natural science in ours.

Out of the diverse background of folk crafts and performances, similarly, each culture selects the set of art forms that will become the focus of its creative life, and these evolve in ever more distinctive ways. Gilgamesh and Beowulf could just as well have swapped swords and fought each other's monsters, for example, but the briefest glance at plays from the mature drama of ancient Greece, India, China and the Western world shows a wholly different dramatic and aesthetic language at work in each. The same is true of every cultural phenomenon in Spengler's view: diversification, not progress, is the keynote of cultural history.

All this might have been forgiven Spengler, but the next step in the comparison passes into territory that makes most people in the modern West acutely uncomfortable. Spengler argued that the creative potential of every culture is subject to the law of diminishing returns. Sooner or later, everything worth bothering with that can be done with Greek sculpture, Chinese porcelain, Western oil painting, or any other creative art has been done; sooner or later, the same exhaustion occurs in every other dimension of a culture's life — its philosophies, its political forms, its sciences and technologies, or what have you. At that point, in the terms that Spengler used, a culture turns into a civilization, and its focus shifts from creating new forms to sorting through the output of its creative centuries, choosing a selection of political, intellectual, technical religious, artistic and social patterns that will be sustainable over the long term, and repeating those thereafter in much the same way that the director of a classical orchestra in the modern West picks and chooses out of the same repertoire of standard composers and works.

As that last example suggests, furthermore, Spengler didn't place the transition from Western culture to its subsequent civilization at some conveniently far point in the future. According to his chronology, that transition began in the nineteenth century and would be complete by 2000 or so. The traditional art forms of the Western world would stagnate, while political ideologies would turn into empty slogans providing an increasingly sparse wardrobe to cover the naked quest for power.

Western science, having long since exhausted the low-hanging fruit in every field, would wind down into a repetition of existing knowledge, and most forms of technology would stagnate, while a few technological fields capable of yielding grandiose prestige projects would continue to be developed for a while until they, too, reached and passed the point of diminishing returns. Rationalism would be preserved in intellectual circles, while popular religious movements riddled with superstition would rule the mental life of the bulk of the population. Progress in any Western sense of the word would be over forever, for future cultures would choose their own directions in which to develop, as different from ours as ours is from the traditional Chinese or the Mayans.

Spengler didn't leave these projections of the future in so abstract a form, for that matter. He turned them into detailed predictions about the near future, and those predictions have by and large turned out to be uncomfortably correct. He was wrong in thinking that Germany would become an imperial state that would unite the Western world the way Rome united the classical world, the kingdom of Qin united China and so on, though it's fair to say that Germany's two efforts to fill that role came uncomfortably close to succeeding. Other than that, his aim has proved remarkably good.

He argued, for example, that the artistic forms that defined Western creativity up to the late nineteenth century were dead and would survive thereafter only as museum-pieces repeated in increasingly stylized forms — a judgment that has proven far more insightful than not, as a visit to art museums and concert halls shows clearly enough.[7] In the political sphere, he suggested that the history of the twentieth and twenty-first centuries would be dominated by a prolonged struggle pitting charismatic national dictators against a globalized oligarchy of high finance lightly concealed under a mask of democracy, a struggle that the financiers would eventually lose.[8] There, though the jury's still out on the final outcome, the struggle itself is splashed over the news on a daily basis.

All these events took place in other times and places, Spengler claimed, and will take place in future societies, each in its own way. What distinguishes contemporary Western society from earlier urban civilizations, according to Spengler's view, is not that it's "more advanced," "more progressive" — such distinctions are meaningless between cultures, since every society goes in a different direction and proceeds along that route until the same law of diminishing returns cuts in — but simply that it happened to take mastery of matter and energy as its special project, and in the process stumbled across the buried carbon we're burning so extravagantly just now.

It's hard to think of any historical vision less flattering to the inherited egotism of the modern industrial West. It deprives us of our imagined role as the cutting edge of humanity in its grand upward march toward the stars and plops us back down to earth as just one civilization among many, rising and falling along with the rest.

⚜

It's in this way that Spengler proved to be Nietzsche's heir. Where Nietzsche tried to challenge the imaginary utopia at the end of history with an equally imaginary vision of eternal return, Spengler offered a vision that was *not* imaginary, but rather rested on a foundation of historical fact. Where Nietzsche's abandonment of a moral order to the cosmos left him staring into an abyss in which order and meaning vanished once and for all, Spengler presented an alternative vision of cosmic order in which any given culture's morality is not a guiding principle, but simply a socially constructed form that comes and goes with the tides of history. Life was as much Spengler's banner as it was Nietzsche's, life in the full biological sense of the word, unreasoning, demanding and resistant to change over less than geological time scales. The difference was that Nietzsche saw life as the abyss, while Spengler used it to found his sense of an ordered universe and ultimately his values as well.

It's among the richest ironies of Spengler's project that among the things that he relativized and set in a historic context was Nietzsche's philosophy. Nietzsche liked to imagine himself as a figure of destiny, poised at the turning point of the ages, though this was admittedly a common occupational disease of nineteenth-century philosophers. Spengler noted his debts to Nietzsche repeatedly in *The Decline of the West*, but kept a sense of perspective the older man lacked and found room for Nietzsche himself in that perspective. In the table of historical parallels that finishes the first volume of Spengler's book, Nietzsche is noted down as one more symptom of the late, "Winter" phase of Western culture, one of many figures participating in the final disintegration of traditional religious thought at the hands of skeptical intellectuals proposing new systems of philosophical ethics.

When Nietzsche announced the death of God, in other words, he was filling a role familiar in other ages, announcing an event that occurs on schedule in the life of each culture. The Greek historian Plutarch had announced the death of Pan some 18 centuries earlier, around the time that the classical world was settling firmly into the end-state of civilization; the people of ancient Crete, perhaps recalling some similar event even further back, used to scandalize Greek tourists by showing them the grave of Zeus. Every literate urban society, Spengler argued, followed the same trajectory from an original folk religion rich in myths, through the rise of intellectual theology, the birth of rationalism, the gradual dissolution of the religious worldview into rational materialism and then the gradual disintegration of rational materialism into a radical skepticism that ends by dissolving itself. Thereafter ethical philosophies for the intellectuals and resurgent folk religion for the masses provide the enduring themes for the civilization to come.

In drawing these conclusions, Spengler was to some extent covering ground that had been broken for him centuries earlier. Back in 1725, as the industrial revolution was just getting under way, the Italian philosopher Giambattista Vico traced out "the course the nations run" — the phrase is his — in the pages of his masterpiece, *Principles of a New Science Concerning the Common Nature of Nations* (for obvious reasons, scholars these days shorten this to *The New Science*). Since then, it's been rare for more than a generation to go by without some historian or philosopher pointing out to readers that every previous society has followed the familiar arc of rise and fall, and ours seems to be doing exactly the same thing.

Spengler was thus contributing to an established tradition, rather than breaking wholly new ground, and there have been important works since his time — most notably Arnold Toynbee's sprawling *A Study of History*, 12 hefty volumes packed with evidence — that carried the same tradition further. Vico spent his whole career laboring in obscurity, but Spengler and Toynbee were both major public figures in their day as well as bestselling authors whose ideas briefly became part of the common currency of thought in the Western world. They and their work, in turn, were both consigned to oblivion once it stopped being fashionable to think about the points they raised, and you can read any number of hefty studies of the philosophy of history and never find either man mentioned at all.

What makes this disappearance fascinating is that very few critics ever made a serious attempt to argue the facts that Spengler and his peers discussed. There was never any shortage of disagreement, to be sure, but nearly all of it remained weirdly detached from the issues the theorists of historical cycles were attempting to raise. There was a great deal of quibbling about details, a great deal of handwaving about fatalism and pessimism, and whole armies of straw men were lined up and beaten with gusto, but next to nobody tried to show that the basic concept of cyclic history doesn't work — that the patterns traced by the history of China, let's say, contradict those displayed by the history of ancient Egypt — and the few attempts that have been made in this direction were embarrassingly weak.

By and large, those who disputed Vico, Spengler, Toynbee, et al. either brushed aside the entire question of patterns of historical change, or conceded that, well, of course, those other civilizations of the past might have followed a shared trajectory, but ours? Never. That's still the predictable response to any suggestion that the past might have anything useful to say about the future: in words made famous in any number of speculative bubbles, "it's different this time."

There's a wry amusement to be had by thinking through the implications of this constantly repeated claim. If our society was in fact shaking off the burdens of the past and breaking new ground with every minute that goes by, as believers in progress like to claim, wouldn't it be more likely that every time the theory of historical cycles appeared, it would be challenged by dazzlingly new, innovative responses that no one had ever imagined before? Instead, in an irony Nietzsche would have relished, the claim that history can't repeat itself endlessly repeats itself, in what amounts to an eternal recurrence of the assertion that there is no eternal recurrence.

What's more, those who claim that it's different this time seem blissfully unaware that anyone has made the same claim before them, and if this is pointed out to them, they insist — often with quite some heat — that what they're saying has nothing whatsoever to do with all the other times the same argument was used to justify the same failed claims to uniqueness down through the years. There are deep patterns at work here, but it's probably necessary to tackle the different-this-time argument on its own terms first.

Of course there are differences between contemporary industrial civilization and those older societies that have already traced out the completed arc of rise and fall. Each of those previous civilizations differed from every other human society in its own unique ways, too. Each human life, to use an analogy Spengler liked to cite, differs from every other human life in a galaxy of ways, but certain processes — birth, infancy, childhood, puberty and so on through the life cycle to old age and death — are hardwired into the basic structure of being human and will come to every individual who lives out a normal lifespan. The talents, experiences and achievements that fit into the common sequence of life will vary, often drastically, from person to person, but those differences exist within a common frame. The same thing, the theorists of cyclic history suggest, is true of human societies, and they offer ample evidence to support that claim.

Furthermore, these same scholars point out, modern industrial civilization has already passed through all the normal stages of social existence appropriate to its age. It emerged out of a feudal setting all but indistinguishable from those that provided the cradle for past civilizations; out of that background, it developed its own unique view of the cosmos, expressed first in religious terms and later in the form of a rationalist philosophy; it passed through the normal political, economic and social changes in the usual order, and at the same broad time intervals, as other civilizations; its current political, economic and cultural condition has precise parallels in older civilizations as far back as records reach. Given that the uniqueness of modern industrial civilization has so far failed to nudge it off the standard trajectory, it's hard to find any valid reason to insist that our future won't continue along the same track.

Claims that it's different this time usually rest on one of three foundations. The first is that this is the first global civilization on record. A difference of scale, though, does not necessarily equal a difference of kind; the trajectory we're discussing appears in Neolithic societies limited to a single river basin and continental empires with thriving international trade networks as well as every scale in between. While it might be argued that the greater size of contemporary industrial society amounts to a difference in kind, that claim would have to be backed up with evidence rather than merely asserted — as, so far, it generally has been. Furthermore, when the slower speed of earlier transportation technologies is taken into account, the "worlds" inhabited by older societies were effectively as large as ours; if your speediest means of transport is a horse-drawn chariot, for example, ancient China is a very big place.

The second foundation for claims of our uniqueness is, of course, the explosive growth of technology made possible over the last three centuries by the reckless extraction and burning of fossil fuels. It's true that no other civilization has done that, but the differences have had remarkably little impact on the political, cultural and social trends that shape our lives and the destinies of our communities. The corruption of mass politics in the modern industrial world, for example, is following point for point the same patterns traced out by equivalent phenomena in ancient Greece and Rome; the weapons of war have changed, similarly, but the downward spiral of a failing empire trying to cling to fractious but strategically vital borderlands is the same for the United States in Afghanistan as it was for the Babylonians in the Elamite hill country in 1000 BCE. Our technology has given us new means, but by and large we've employed them for the same ancient purposes and reaped the same consequences.

The third foundation is newer and appears these days mostly in those corners of the blogosphere where various apocalyptic beliefs have become articles of faith. This is the claim that the global disasters that are about to wallop industrial civilization go so far beyond anything in the past that there's no basis for comparison. Now of course that argument is very often based on the well-worn tactic of heaping up an assortment of worst-case scenarios, insisting that the resulting cataclysm is the only possible outcome of current trends and using that imagined future as a measuring rod with which to dismiss what really happened in the past.

What tends to be missed by such claims, though, is that ecological disasters of the sort we're facing featured repeatedly in the collapse of earlier civilizations. Surveys of ecological history such as Clive Ponting's *A Green History of the World* and Sing C. Chew's *World Ecological Degradation* are helpful correctives for this myopia. There

have been dozens of previous civilizations destroyed by their misman-
agement of their relationships with the biosphere, and most of the
factors that bid fair to bring modern industrial civilization down —
depletion of essential resources, topsoil degradation, climate change
and more — have exact parallels in the fate of these earlier societies.

To judge by past examples, the downfall of a civilization normally takes between one and three centuries and involves the loss of
irreplaceable cultural treasures and scientific knowledge, the abandon
ment of cities and population declines of anything up to 95 percent of
the pre-collapse peak. It's by no means impossible, or even unlikely, that
the decline and fall of modern industrial civilization could take place in
this same way. Believers in perpetual progress and believers in imminent apocalypse, of course, both reject this suggestion out of hand. It
is a source of wry fascination to me that this suggestion — based as it
is on the one source of useful evidence we've got, the experience of
many previous societies going through equivalent processes — should
be dismissed by the one as too pessimistic, and by the other as too
optimistic.

It's exactly this twofold dismissal that points to the deeper, non-ra-
tional dimension underlying any discussion of possible futures in the
contemporary world. The belief in progress and the equal and opposite belief in apocalypse are narratives about the unknowable. Both
claim that the past has nothing to say about the future, that something
is about to happen that has never happened before and that can't be
judged on the basis of any previous event. Whether the thing that's
about to happen is a shining new age of wonder or a sudden end of history, it refutes everything that has come before. This is what lies behind
the endlessly repeated (and just as repeatedly disproved) insistence,
on the part of believers in both narratives, that it's different this time: if
it's not different this time, if the lessons of the past reveal the shape of
the future, then both belief systems come crashing down at once.

That is to say, the belief in progress and in apocalypse are both matters of faith, not fact. Now of course the same is true of every set of beliefs about the future, or about anything else for that matter. No system of logical inferences, however elaborate and exact, can prove its own presuppositions. Dig down to the foundations and you'll find that the structure rests on assumptions about the nature of things that have to be taken on faith.

It probably has to be pointed out that this is just as true of rationalist beliefs as it is of the most exotic forms of mysticism. To say, as science does, that statements about the universe ought to be based on observation assumes, and indeed has to assume, that what we observe tells us truths about the universe — an assumption that the old Gnostics would have considered laughably naive. To claim that there are many gods, a few gods, only one god, or no gods at all is to insist on something about which human beings have no independently verifiable source of information whatsoever.

It's tolerably common these days, outside of the surviving theist religions, for people to affect to despise faith, and you'll find plenty of people who insist that they take nothing on faith at all. Of course they're quite wrong. None of us can function in the world for five minutes without taking a galaxy of things on faith, from the solidity of the floor in front of us, through the connection between another person's words and their thoughts, to the existence of places and times we will never experience. Gregory Bateson pointed out, in a series of papers that have vanished as thoroughly from the literature of psychology as Spengler and Toynbee have from that of history, that an unwillingness to take anything on faith is at the core of schizophrenia. That's what lies behind the frantic efforts of the paranoiac to find the hidden meaning in everything around him and the catatonic's ultimate refusal to have anything to do with the world at all.[9]

Faith is, among other things, the normal and necessary human response to those questions that can't be answered on the basis of any form of proof, but have to be answered in one way or another in order to live in the world. The question that deserves discussion is why different people, faced with the same unanswerable question, put their faith in different propositions. The answer is as simple to state as it is sweeping in its consequences: every act of faith rests on a set of values.

The difference between facts and values is straightforward, though the simplicity of the distinction unfolds into a galaxy of implications. Facts, as the word implies, are *facta*, "things made" by the process of figuration discussed in Chapter Two; they belong to the senses and the intellect, and they're objective, at least to the extent that any human being with an ordinarily functioning nervous system and sensorium and no reason to prevaricate can say, "yes, I see it too." Values, by contrast, are a matter of the heart and the will, and they're irreducibly subjective; to say "this is good" or "this is bad," or any other statement of value, doesn't communicate an objective fact about the thing being discussed, but always expresses an irreducibly individual point of view.

More than half the confusions of contemporary thought result from attempts to treat personal value judgments as though they were objectively knowable facts — to say, for example, "x is better than y" without addressing such questions as "better by what criteria?" and "better for whom?" The prejudices of modern industrial culture encourage these confusions by claiming a higher status for facts than for values.

Listen to atheists and Christians talking past each other, as they normally do, and you have a classic example of the result. The real difference between the two, as the best minds on both sides have grasped, is a radical difference in values that defines equally profound differences in basic assumptions about humanity and the world. Behind the atheist vision of humanity as a unique but wholly natural phenomenon, in the midst of a soulless universe of dead matter following natural laws, stands one set of value judgments about what counts as right and true. Behind the Christian vision of humanity as the adopted child of divine omnipotence, placed temporarily in the material universe as a prologue to eternal bliss or damnation, stands a completely different set. The difference in values is the heart of the matter, and no amount of bickering over facts can settle a debate rooted in that soil.

In the classical world, in an age when values were given at least as high a status as facts, debates of this sort were conducted on their natural ground, and systems of thought appealed to potential followers by presenting their own visions of the Good and calling into question the values presented by competing systems. Nowadays, such clarity is rare, and indeed it's embarrassingly common to hear people insist that there's no way to judge among competing value claims. It's true that a value can't be disproved in the same way as a fact, but values don't exist in a vacuum. Any statement of value has implications and consequences, and it's by assessing these that each of us can judge whether a value is consistent with the other values we happen to hold and with the universe of fact that we happen to experience.

We all know this, at least in practice. The reason why doctrines of racial inequality are widely and rightly dismissed by most people in the modern industrial world, for example, has little to do with the shoddy intellectual basis offered for such doctrines by their few defenders, quite a bit to do with lynch mobs, ethnic cleansing, concentration camps and other well-known consequences of value systems that deny the humanity of other ethnic groups, and at least as much to do with the conflict between the values expressed in these consequences and other values, such as fairness and compassion, that most people embrace. This is an extreme example, but the same principle applies more generally: when a statement is made about the unprovable, it's always wise to ask what the consequences of believing that statement have been in the past and what other values are consistent or inconsistent with the claim.

We can thus apply the same logic to the faith in perpetual progress and imminent apocalypse. One consequence of accepting these beliefs and embracing the values that underlie them is clear enough: both reliably yield false predictions about the future. Believers in progress like to claim the opposite, but you have to read descriptions of the future from before 1970 or so — the days when it was axiomatic that soon we would all commute in flying cars, vacation on the Moon and live for more than a century, if not forever — to grasp just how few the hits have always been compared to the flops. For all its failures, though, the faith in progress has a better track record than the faith in apocalypse. Across the centuries, whenever anyone has insisted that the world was about to end, he or she has always been dead wrong. Aside from speculative bubbles or the quest for perpetual motion, it's hard to name a more reliable source of utter hogwash.

For faiths that focus on the future as intently as these do, this inability to foresee the future is not exactly encouraging. It's possible to go further, though, by noticing the values embodied in the progressive and apocalyptic faiths. Both of them insist that the world we know must shortly be swept away to be replaced by some better era or annihilated in some grand final judgment. Both of them anchor their entire sense of meaning and value on an imaginary future and disparage the present by contrasting it with the nonexistent. Both faiths are thus founded on a passionate rejection of the world as it actually exists.

To borrow one of Nietzsche's phrases, both are naysayings to life, attempts to posit an unreal "real world" (the shining future of progress, the world after apocalypse) against which life as it actually is can be judged, condemned and sentenced to death. The mere fact that the executioners never do their job, though it's an inconvenience to the believers on either side, does nothing to alter the furious zeal with which, over and over again, the sentence is handed down.

The religion of progress and its antireligion of apocalypse are by no means alone in their Nay-saying to life. The same world-condemning attitude has had a pervasive role in most of the historic branches of Christianity, the theist faith from which these secular religions covertly derive a good many of their ideas and images. The attitude derives from a particular sensibility, one that predates Christianity by some centuries and has shaped nearly all the theist and secular religions of the Western world to one degree or another. In a later chapter, I'll discuss the way that this sensibility in its many forms has helped send contemporary industrial society slamming face first into the wall of crises that shape today's headlines and will be defining our history for a good many years to come.

For the moment, though, I'd like to encourage my readers to grapple with this reflection: what would it mean to found a set of values and a corresponding set of presuppositions about the world on life exactly as it is? The process of opening that can of worms and getting the worms inside it more comfortably situated in their proper soil will begin the process of circling in toward the question at the center of this book — the quest for a sensibility, a philosophy of life and perhaps even a spirituality that can make sense of the human experience in a world after progress.

Four

A Peculiar Absence of Bellybones

WHEN YOU THINK ABOUT IT, it's really rather odd that so many people nowadays should be so hostile to the suggestion that history tends to move in circles. Central to the rhetoric that celebrates industrial civilization's supposed triumph over the ignorant and superstitious past is the notion that our beliefs about the world are founded on experience and tested against hard facts. Since the cyclic theory of history gave Oswald Spengler the basis for accurate predictions about the future — predictions, mind you, that contradicted the conventional wisdom of his time and ours, and proved to be correct anyway — wouldn't it be more reasonable to consider the suggestion that his theory applies to our civilization too?

Reasonable or not, of course, that's not what generally happens. Suggest that industrial civilization is following the same arc of rise and fall that all previous civilizations have traced through time, and that it shows every sign of completing the rest of that trajectory, and outside of a few circles of intellectual heretics on the fringes of contemporary culture, what you'll get in the way of response is an angry insistence that it just ain't so. The overfamiliar claim that this time it really is different, that modern industrial civilization will either keep soaring ever higher on the wings of some glorious destiny or plunge overnight into some unparalleled catastrophe, is wedged so tightly into the collective imagination of our age that not even repeated failure seems to be able to break it loose.

That last comment is anything but hyperbole. The repeated failures have happened, and are continuing to happen, without having the least effect on the claims just mentioned. A glance back over the last century or so of prophecies of progress, as noted in Chapter Three, displays an extraordinarily large number of abject flops. From domed cities and vacations on the Moon, through fusion power and household robots who can cook your dinner and do your laundry for you, to the conquest of poverty, disease and death itself, how many advances have been proclaimed as imminent and inevitable by scientists and the media, only to end up in history's wastebasket when it turned out that they couldn't be done after all? Of all the dozens of great leaps forward that were being announced so confidently in my youth, only a few — notably the computer revolution — actually happened, and even there the gap between what was predicted and what we got remains vast.

Meanwhile, the litany of failed apocalyptic prophecies — the Tweedledoom to the Tweedledee of failed predictions of progress — mounts up even faster than the litany of failed predictions of technological marvels. Year after weary year, the same grandiose visions of destiny and disaster get dusted off for one more showing; they resemble nothing so much as a rerun of a television show that originally aired when your parents were on their first date, and yet audiences across the industrial world sit there and do their best to forget that they've watched the same show so often they could close their eyes and plug their ears and still recall every tawdry detail.

While these prophecies were being proclaimed as the unstoppable wave of the future, furthermore, a very different story has been unfolding across the industrial world. Cheap, easily accessible deposits of the vital resources on which industrial civilization depends have been exhausted and have had to be replaced with increasing difficulty by more expensive substitutes, at steadily rising costs in money, labor, energy and other resources. Here in the United States, but not only here, national infrastructures and the natural environment have both been drawn into an accelerating spiral of malign neglect; standards of living for most people have been sliding steadily, along with most measures of public health and meaningful education; constitutional rights and the rule of law have taken a beating, administered with equal enthusiasm by all major parties, who seem incapable of agreeing on anything else even when the welfare of the nation is obviously at stake.

In other words, while one set of true believers has been waiting hopefully for the arrival of a bright new golden age of scientific and technological progress, and another set of true believers has been waiting just as hopefully for the arrival of the vast catastrophe that will prove to their satisfaction just how wrong everyone else was, history ignored them both and brought what it usually brings at this season of a civilization's life: that is to say, decline.

Even so, our collective fixation on those two failed narratives shows few signs of slipping. It's uncomfortably easy to imagine an America a century from now, in which half the sharply reduced population lives in squalid shantytowns without electricity or running water, tuberculosis and bacterial infections are the leading causes of death, cars and computers are luxury goods assembled from old parts and reserved for the obscenely rich, and space travel is a distant memory — and in which one set of true believers still insists that the great leap upward into a golden age of progress will get going any day now, another set insists just as passionately that some gaudy cataclysm is about to kill us all, and only a few intellectual heretics on the fringes of society are willing to talk about the hard facts of ongoing decline or the destination toward which that decline is pretty obviously headed.

There's no shortage of irony here, because modern industrial culture's fixation on fantasies of progress and apocalypse and its irritable rejection of any other possibilities have contributed mightily to the process of decline that both sets of fantasies reject out of hand. Since the Reagan-Thatcher counterrevolution of the early 1980s, when the industrial world turned its back on the promising beginnings of the previous decade and slammed the door on its best chance of a smooth transition to sustainability, every attempt to bring up the limits to growth or propose a useful response to the impending mess has been assailed by partisans of both fantasies.

The rhetoric of progress — "I'm sure they'll come up with something," "There are no limits to the power of technology," and so on — has been precisely balanced by the rhetoric of apocalypse — "Jesus will come soon so we don't have to worry about that," "It's too late to save humanity from inevitable extinction" and so on. Thirty years on, the breakthroughs have proven just as elusive as the catastrophes, but the rhetoric still plods onward.

Behind both sides of that rhetoric is the sensibility and the style of thought mentioned toward the end of Chapter Three — the habit of postulating an imaginary "real world" that contains some set of desirable features the actual world lacks, and then condemning the actual world for its failure to measure up to the imaginary one. It's a surprisingly pervasive mental tic in contemporary industrial culture. Few corners of modern thought have escaped that habit of thinking, and fewer still have avoided being harmed by it.

Take politics, which used to be the process of finding acceptable compromises among the competing needs and wants of members of a community. These days that process has been all but swamped by supporters of an assortment of fictive worlds — consider the heavily fictionalized pre-1960s America that features so heavily in Christian fundamentalist rhetoric, in which Christian faith was universal, happy families all prayed together on Sunday mornings, and gays, atheists and other deviant types were safely quarantined in New York City, for example. For that matter, consider the assorted utopias of political correctness to be found on the other end of the political spectrum.

People who are struggling to make the actual world conform to some imaginary one are rarely prepared to accept the compromises, the negotiations and the quest for common ground that make for functional politics, and the result is the stalemate between entrenched factions that pervades politics on nearly all levels today.

From public health to personal ethics, from dietary choices to the management of the economy, the words are different but they're all sung to the same overfamiliar tune. Abstract theories about how the world ought to work are treated as descriptions of how the world actually works, and heaven help you if you suggest that the theories might be judged by comparing them to the facts on the ground. All the contortions of cognitive dissonance then come into play when, as so often happens, measures that are supposed to improve public health make it worse, moral stances intended to improve the world cause more harm than good, diets that are supposed to make people healthy actually make them sick, economic programs proclaimed as the key to lasting prosperity run one economy after another straight into the ground and so on.

What's the alternative? Simply put, it involves setting aside our own desires, preferences and sense of entitlement, and paying attention to the way things actually happen in the world.

It's important not to overthink what's being said here. Philosophers since ancient times have pointed out, and quite rightly, that human beings have no access to absolute truth. The world as we experience it comes into being out of the interaction between raw sensory data and the structures of the individual consciousness through the process of figuration, the arrangement of sensory inputs into meaningful patterns that can be known to the human mind. The world of fact, as noted in Chapter Three, is the world of figurations we share with other human beings. In that world, some things happen reliably, other things happen unpredictably and still other things never seem to get around to happening at all — and it's not hard, even across cultural and linguistic barriers, to find common ground concerning which things belong in which of these categories.

That quest for common ground among the vagaries of individual experience is among other things the basis of modern science. The theory of gravitation is an elegant mathematical way of summing up the fact that billions of individual human beings have had the experience of watching something fall, and each one of those experiences had important features in common with all the others, as well as with such apparently unconnected things as the apparent movements of the Sun in the sky. The kind of knowledge found in the theory of gravitation and the whole range of other scientific theories is not absolute truth; it's always at least a little tentative, subject to constant testing and reformulation as more data comes in; but it was good enough to put human bootprints on the Moon, and it was gained by setting aside narratives that played on the preferences of the individual and collective ego in order to listen to what Nature herself was saying.

Suggest that this attentiveness to what actually happens is a good idea when dealing with falling rocks, and you'll get little debate. It's when you suggest that the same approach might be usefully applied to falling civilizations that the arguments spring up. Even so, the principle is the same in both cases.

Over the last five thousand years or so, scores of societies have risen and fallen, and their trajectories through time, like those of falling rocks, have had important features in common. It's easy to insist that because contemporary industrial society differs from these other societies in various ways, those common features have nothing to say to our future, but what follows this claim? Inevitably, it's yet another weary rehash of the familiar, failed narratives of perpetual progress and imminent apocalypse. If the present case really is unprecedented, wouldn't it make more sense either to suggest some equally unprecedented model for the future, or simply to shrug and admit that nobody knows what will happen? Both these responses would make more sense than trotting out scraps of secondhand theology that have been dolled up repeatedly in secular drag since the market for religious prophecy turned south in the eighteenth century.

I'd like to suggest that it's high time for both narratives to be put out to pasture. No, I'll go further than that. I'd like to suggest that it's high time for all our narratives about the world and ourselves to be tested against the yardstick of what actually happens and chucked into the compost if they can't meet that test.

What I'm suggesting here needs to be understood with a certain amount of care. Knowledge about the world takes two broad forms, and the connection between them is rather like the connection between a pile of bricks and lumber, on the one hand, and the house that will be built out of the bricks and lumber on the other. The first form of knowledge is history in the broadest sense of the world — a sense that includes what used to be called "natural history," the careful collection of observed facts about the world of nature. Before Isaac Newton could sit down in his Cambridge study and work out the theory of gravitation, hundreds of other investigators had to note down their own observations about how things fall, and tens of thousands of astronomers down the centuries had to look up into the sky and notice where the little moving lights they called "wanderers" — *planetoi* in Greek — had turned up that night.

That was the gathering of the bricks and the milling of the lumber that would eventually be used to build the elegant structure of Newton's gravitational theory. Long before Newton got to work, though, his brick-hauling and lumber-gathering predecessors had picked up quite a bit of relevant knowledge about how rocks fall, how planets move, and a range of similar things, and could explain in quite some detail what these things did and didn't do. The theoretical models they used to explain these regularities of behavior weren't always that useful — I'm thinking here especially of those medieval mystics who were convinced that rocks were head-over-heels in love with the Earth and would fling themselves in the direction of their beloved whenever other forces didn't prevent them from doing so — but the regularities themselves were well understood.

That's the kind of knowledge that comes from a close study of history. Once enough historical data has been gathered, that empirical knowledge can often be summarized and replaced by a coherent theory — often, but not always. If the subject is complex enough, the number of examples is small enough, or any of an assortment of other problems gets in the way, a meaningful theory may remain out of reach. In that case, though, the empirical knowledge is well worth having, since it's the only real knowledge you have to go on.

The trajectory of human civilizations over time is an immensely complex subject, and the scores of societies that have risen and fallen during recorded history provide a small enough data set that strict theoretical models may be premature. That leaves the empirical knowledge gathered from history. It's impossible to prove from that knowledge that the same patterns will continue to happen, just as it was impossible for one of the medieval mystics I mentioned to disprove the claim that now and then a rock might have a lover's quarrel with the Earth and fall straight up into the sky to get away from her. Still, when known patterns are already at work in a given society, it's reasonable to accept that they're likely to continue to their normal end, and when a given theory about the future has failed every time it's been proposed, it's just as reasonable to dismiss it from consideration and look for alternatives that work better in practice.

This is what I'd like to ask my readers to do. Each of us carries around an assortment of narratives about what the future might be like, most of them derived from one or another corner of popular culture or from various older traditions and writings. Each of us uses those narratives, consciously or otherwise, as templates into which scraps of information about the future are fitted by means of the process of figuration, and very often this is done without paying attention to what history has to say about the narratives themselves — about their origins, their histories and their success rate in predicting events that haven't happened yet.

I'd like to suggest, in place of this casual acceptance of these narratives, that it's worth taking a hard look at them whenever they surface
and checking them against the evidence of history. Has anything like
this happened before, and if so, what results followed? Has anyone ever
believed something like this before, and if so, how did that belief work
out in practice? These are the kinds of questions I encourage my readers to ask. I'm aware that this is a heavy burden — much heavier than
it may seem at first glance because it involves discarding some of our
most cherished cultural narratives, including some that have woven
their way into a great many modern religious traditions.

That act of questioning will be helped by a glance at an innocuous
layer of stone in the Canadian Rockies called the Burgess shale. Unlike
the Marcellus shale, the Barnett shale and the other geological for-
mations at the heart of the fracking boom as I write these words, the
Burgess shale doesn't contain any appreciable amounts of oil or natural
gas. What it does contain is a vast number of delicate fossils from the
Cambrian period.[1] It's been argued that your ancestors and mine are
there in the Burgess shale, in the form of a tiny, wriggling whatsit called
Pikaia, which has a little strip of cartilage running down its back, the
first very rough draft of what eventually turned into your backbone.

There are plenty of other critters there that are unlike anything else
since that time, and it's perfectly plausible to imagine that they, rather
than *Pikaia*, might have left descendants who evolved into the readers of this book. That's not what happened, though. Intelligent beings
descended from five-eyed, single-tentacled *Opabinia* were possible;
they could have happened, but they didn't, and once that was settled,
a whole world of possibilities went away forever. There was no rational
reason for that exclusion. It just happened that way.

Let's take a closer look at *Pikaia*, though. Study it closely, and you
can just about see the fish that its distant descendants will become. The
strip of cartilage runs along the upper edge of its body, where fish and

all other vertebrates have their backbones. It didn't have to be there; if *Pikaia* happened to have cartilage along its lower edge, then fish and all the other vertebrates to come would have done just as well with a bellybone in place of a backbone, and you and I would have the knobbly bumps of vertebrae running up our abdomens and chests. Once *Pikaia* came out ahead in the struggle for survival, that possibility went wherever might-have-beens spend their time. There's no logical reason why we don't have bellybones. It simply turned out that way, and the consequences of that event still constrain us today.

Fast forward 200 million years or so, and a few of *Pikaia's* putative descendants were learning to deal with the challenges and possibilities of muddy Devonian swamps by wriggling up out of the water and gulping air into their swim bladders to give them a bit of extra oxygen. It so happens that these fish had four large fins toward the underside of their bodies. Many other fish at the time had other fin patterns instead, and if the successful proto-lungfish had happened to come from a lineage with six fins underneath, then amphibians, reptiles, birds and mammals would have six limbs today instead of four.

A six-limbed body plan is perfectly viable — ask any insect — but the vertebrates that ventured onto land had four, and once that happened, the question was settled. Nothing makes six-legged mammals impossible, but there aren't any and never will be. In an abstract sense, they can happen, but in the real world, they don't, and it's only history that explains why.

Today, another 400 million years later, most of the possible variables shaping life in this planet's biosphere are very tightly constrained by an intricate network of ecological pressures rooted in the long history of the planet. Those constraints, among other things, drive convergent evolution — the process by which living things from completely different evolutionary lineages end up looking and behaving like each other.

One hundred million years ago, when the Earth had its normal hothouse climate and reptiles were the dominant vertebrates, the icthyosaurs, a large and successful family of seagoing reptiles, evolved what we now think of as the basic dolphin look. When they went extinct and a cooling planet gave mammals the edge, seagoing mammals competing for the same ecological niche gave us today's dolphins and porpoises. The ancestors of those dolphins and porpoises, by the way, looked like furry crocodiles, and for good reason. If you're going to fill a crocodile's niche, as the protocetaceans did, the pressures that the rest of the biosphere brings to bear on that niche pretty much require you to look and act like a crocodile.

The lesson to be drawn from these examples, and countless others, is that evolution isn't free to do everything that, in some abstract sense, it could possibly do. Between the limits imposed by the historically determined genetics of the organism struggling to adapt, and the even stronger limits imposed by the historically determined pressures of the environment within which that struggle is taking place, there are only so many options available. On a planet that's had living things evolving on it for two billion years or so, most of those options will have already been tried out at least once.

Even when something new emerges, as happens from time to time, that doesn't mean that all bets are off. It simply means that familiar genetic and environmental constraints are going to apply in slightly different ways. That means that there are plenty of living things that theoretically could appear that never will appear, because the constraints that define the biosphere haven't left room for them to occur.

That much is uncontroversial, at least among students of evolutionary ecology. Apply the same point of view to human history, though, and you can count on a firestorm of protest. Nonetheless, that's one of the things I'm trying to do in this book — to point out that historical change is subject to limits imposed by the previous trajectories of societies struggling to adapt, and the even stronger limits imposed by the pressures of the environment within which that struggle is taking place; worse, to point out that societies have an equivalent of convergent evolution, which can be studied by the morphological trick of putting different societies side by side and comparing their historical trajectories; worse still, to show that this reveals otherwise untraceable constraints and thus allows meaningful predictions to be made about the future of our own civilization.

Each of those proposals offends several of the most basic assumptions with which most people nowadays approach the future. The resulting quarrels have enlivened any number of discussions I've had in an equally wide assortment of forums.

Whether we're talking about 2012 or near-term human extinction or the latest claim that some piece or other of energy-related vaporware will solve the world's increasingly intractable energy and resource shortages, my critics say, "It could happen!" and I reply, "Yes, but it won't." They proceed to come up with elaborate scenarios and arguments showing that, in fact, whatever it is could possibly happen, and get the imperturbable answer, "Yes, I know all that, but it still won't happen." Then it doesn't happen, and the normal human irritation at being wrong gets thrown in the blender with a powerful sense of the unfairness of things — after all, that arrogant so-and-so of an archdruid didn't offer a single solitary reason why whatever it was couldn't possibly happen! — to make a cocktail that's uncommonly hard to swallow.

There's a reason, though, why these days the purveyors of repeatedly disproved predictions, from economists through fusion-power proponents to believers in the current end of the world du jour, so constantly use arguments about what *can* happen and so consistently ignore what *does* happen. It's a historical reason, and it brings us a substantial step closer to the heart of this book's exploration.

When Nietzsche proclaimed the death of God to a mostly uninterested nineteenth century, he was convinced that he was doing something utterly unprecedented — and he was wrong. If he'd been a little more careful about checking his claims against what he'd learned as a classical philologist, he would have remembered that the gods also died in ancient Greece in the fourth century BCE, and that the rationalist revolt against established religion in the Greek world followed the same general course as its equivalent in western Europe and the European diaspora two millennia or so later. Put the materialist philosophers of the Greek Enlightenment side by side with the corresponding figures in its European equivalent, or line up the skeptical barbs aimed at Homer's portrayal of the gods and goddesses of Greece with those shot at the Bible's portrayal of the god of Christianity — by Nietzsche among others! — and the similarities are hard to miss.

What's more, the same thing has happened elsewhere. India went through its rationalist period beginning in the sixth century BCE, giving rise to full-blown atomist and materialist philosophies as well as an important school of logic, the Nyaya; it's indicative of the tone of that period that the two great religious movements founded then, Buddhism and Jainism, in their earliest documented forms were wholly uninterested in gods. The equivalent period in ancient China began about a century later, with its own achievements in logic and natural science and its own dismissal of formal religion — sacrifices and rites are important for social reasons, Confucius argues, but to busy oneself excessively with them shows that one is ignorant and unreasonable.

This is a standard element of the trajectory of literate civilizations through time. Every human society comes out of the shadows of its origins well equipped with a set of beliefs about what does happen. Since most human societies in their early phases are either wholly innocent of writing, or have lost most of a former tradition of literacy in the collapse of some previous civilization, those beliefs are normally passed down by way of the oldest and most thoroughly proven system of information storage and transfer our species has invented — that is to say, mythology: a collection of vivid, colorful stories, usually in verse, that can be learned starting in early childhood and remembered letter-perfect into advanced old age.

Since the information storage capacity of myths is large but not limitless, each myth in a mature mythology is meant to be understood and interpreted on several levels, and learning how to unpack the stories is an essential part of education as an adult in these societies. For human societies that rely on hunter-gatherer, nomadic pastoral, or village horticultural economies, mythology is amply suited to their information storage and transfer needs, and it's rare for these to go looking for other options. Those societies that take to field agriculture and build urban centers, though, need detailed records, and that usually means writing or some close equivalent, such as the knotted cords of the old Incas.

Widespread public literacy seems to be the trigger that sets off the collapse of mythic thinking. Where literacy remains the specialty of a priesthood jealous of its privileges, as it was among the ancient Maya or in Egypt before the New Kingdom, writing is simply a tool for data storage and ceremonial proclamations, but once it gets into general circulation, rationalism of one kind or another follows in short order: an age of faith gives way to an age of reason. That transformation has many dimensions, but one of the more important is a refocusing from what does happen to what can happen.

At the time, that refocusing is a very good thing. Literacy in an age of faith tends to drive what might be called the rationalization of religion; myths get written down, scribes quarrel over which versions are authentic and what interpretations are valid, until what had been a fluid and flexible oral tradition stiffens into scripture, while folk religion goes through a similar hardening into an organized religion with its own creed and commandments. That process of rigidification robs oral tradition of the flexibility and openness to reinterpretation that gives it much of its strength and helps feed the building pressures that will eventually tear the traditional religion to shreds.

It's the rise of rational philosophy that allows people in a literate civilization to get out from under the weight of a mummified version of what does happen and start exploring alternative ideas about what can happen. That's liberating, and it's also a source of major practical advantages, as life in a maturing urban civilization rarely fits a set of mythic narratives assembled in an older and, usually, much simpler time. It becomes possible to ask new questions and speculate about the answers and to explore a giddy range of previously unexamined options.

That much of the story is hardwired into the historical vision of contemporary Western culture. It's the next part of the story, though, that leads to our present predicament. The wild freedom of the early days of the rationalist rebellion never lasts for long. Some of the new ideas that unfold from that rebellion turn out to be more popular and more enduring than others and become the foundations on which later rationalists build their own ideas. With the collapse of traditional religions, in turn, people commonly turn to civil religions as a source of values and meaning, and popular civil religions that embrace some form of rationalist thought, as most do, end up imbuing it with their own aura of secondhand holiness.

The end result of the rationalist rebellion is thus a society as heavily committed to the supposed truth of some set of secular dogmas as the religion it replaced was to its theological dogmas. What's more, those secular dogmas turn out to be just as much of an obstacle to necessary change as their theological equivalents were in their day. Crucially, rationalist ideologies reliably fail to make room for the awkward realities that rationalism has its own limits, that there are dimensions of human experience that are not well managed by purely rational means, and that a set of beliefs about the world can be perfectly rational and perfectly consistent and still leave out factors that are crucial for individual and collective survival.

Those realities are among the most pervasive social facts of our time, as they were in comparable times in the trajectories of previous civilizations. Yet when they're discussed at all — which is rarely — they're inevitably crammed into the mythology of progress and turned into speeches meant to be uttered in doleful tones by the losing side. By doing so, modern industrial society has blinded itself to crucial sources of feedback that might otherwise save it from a galaxy of disastrous mistakes. That, again, is a common feature, and it leads to the inevitable sequel, which is a reaction against the failures of rationalism.

You know that this point has arrived when the rebellion starts running in reverse, and people who want to think ideas outside the box start phrasing them, not in terms of rational philosophy, but in terms of some new or revived religion. The rebellion of rationalism thus eventually gives rise to a rebellion against rationalism, and this latter rebellion packs a great deal more punch than its predecessor, because the rationalist pursuit of what can happen has a potent downside: it can't make accurate prediction of the phenomena that matter most to human beings because it fixates on what can happen rather than paying attention to what does happen.

It's only in the fantasies of extreme rationalists, after all, that the human capacity for reason has no hard limits. The human brain did not evolve for the purpose of understanding the universe and everything in it. It evolved to handle the considerably less demanding tasks of finding food, finding mates, managing social interactions with fellow hominids and driving off the occasional leopard. We've done some remarkable things with a brain adapted for those very simple purposes, to be sure, but the limits imposed by our ancestry are still very much in place.

Those limits show most clearly when we attempt to understand processes at work in the world. There are some processes in the world that are simple enough and sufficiently insulated from confounding variables that a mathematical model that can be understood by the human mind is a close enough fit to allow the outcome of the process to be predicted. That's what physics is about, and chemistry, and the other "hard" sciences: the construction of models that copy, more or less, the behavior of parts of the world that are simple enough for us to understand. The fact that some processes in the world lend themselves to that kind of modeling is what gives rationalism its appeal.

The difficulty creeps in, though, when those same approaches are used to try to predict the behavior of phenomena that are too complex to conform to any such model. You can make such predictions with fairly good results if you pay attention to history because history is the product of the full range of causes at work in comparable situations, and if A leads to B over and over again in a sufficiently broad range of contexts, it's usually safe to assume that if A shows up again, B won't be far behind. Ignore history, though, and you throw away your one useful source of relevant data; ignore history, come up with a mental model that says that A will be followed by Z and insist that since this can happen, it will happen, and you're doomed.

≈≈≈

Human behavior, individual as well as collective, is sufficiently complex that it falls into the category of things that rational models divorced from historical testing regularly fail to predict. So do many other things that are part of everyday life, but it's usually the failure of rational philosophies to provide a useful understanding of human behavior that drives the revolt against rationalism.

Over and over again, rational philosophies have proclaimed the arrival of a better world defined by some abstract model of how human beings ought to behave, some notion or other of what can happen, and the actions people have taken to achieve that better world have resulted in misery and disaster. The appeal of rationalism is potent enough that it normally takes a few centuries of repeated failures for the point to be made, but once it sinks in, the age of reason is effectively over. What replaces it, to borrow one of Spengler's terms, is the Second Religiosity, a renewal of religion as a source of meaning and value in the wake of rationalism's failure.

That doesn't mean that the intellectual tools of rationalism go away. Quite the contrary; the rise of the Second Religiosity involves sweeping transformations of religion and rational philosophy alike. More precisely, it demands the abandonment of extreme claims on both sides and the recognition of what it is that each does better than the other. What comes after the age of reason isn't a new age of faith — not right away, at least; that's further down the road — but an age in which the claims of both contenders are illuminated by the lessons of history: an age of memory.

That's why, a few centuries after the rationalists of Greece, India and China had denounced or dismissed the gods, their heirs quietly accepted a truce with the new religious movements of their time, and a few centuries further on, the heirs of those heirs wove the values taught by the accepted religion into their own philosophical systems. That's also why, over that same time, the major religions of those cultures quietly discarded claims that couldn't stand up to reasonable criticism. Where the Greeks of the Archaic period believed in the literal truth of the Greek myths, and their descendants of the time of Socrates and Plato were caught up in savage debates over whether the old myths had any value at all, the Greeks of a later age accepted Sallust's neat summary — "Myths are things that never happened, but always are"[2] — and saw no conflict at all between pouring a libation to Zeus the Thunderer and taking in a lecture on physics in which thunderbolts were explained by wholly physical causes.

That state of mind is very far from the way that most people in the contemporary industrial world, whether or not they consider themselves to be religious, approach religious beliefs, narratives and practices. I'd like to suggest, though, that some such understanding defines the most likely shape for the religious future of a declining industrial world, and that it also offers the best hope we've got for getting at least some of the achievements of the last three centuries or so through the difficult years ahead.

I'm aware that this poses a stark challenge to most existing faiths. Those of my Christian readers who believe that their scriptures predict a total overturning of the order of history in their lifetimes, for example, may feel that challenge more sharply than most. To them, I would point out that the belief in an imminent and literal apocalypse is only one of several ways that devout Christians have interpreted the scriptures. A great many believers in Christ, for example, have seen his words on the Mount of Olives as a prophecy of the destruction of Jerusalem by the Romans, which happened, as he predicted, within the lifetime of some of those who were there to hear his message.

In the same way, many Christians have understood the Book of Revelations as a prophecy, put in symbolic terms to get past Roman censors, of the impending decline and fall of the Roman Empire. That was, after all, an event of far more importance to its first-century readers than some cosmic catastrophe in the distant twenty-first century, or for that matter the thirty-first or ten thousand and first — for what is the insistence that the end of everything must happen in our own lifetimes but one more manifestation of the modern world's overdeveloped sense of its own importance?

My atheist readers will have an easier time of it in one sense but, in at least some cases, as hard a time in others. To believe that the universe is mere matter and energy without purpose or consciousness, that humanity is simply one more biological species to which evolution has granted a few unusual gifts and that nobody is peering anxiously down from the sky to observe our species' foibles and bail it out from its mistakes, might seem to offer few obstacles to the sort of realism I'm proposing.

Still, I've met an embarrassingly large number of atheists who accord humanity the same privileged status and glorious destiny that prophetic religions claim for their believers. It might seem odd to portray humanity as the Chosen Species while denying that there's anybody to do the choosing, but such is the nature of the return of the repressed. To those of my atheist readers who indulge in such imaginings, I would encourage attention to the presuppositions of their own beliefs and a particularly close study of past claims of progress and apocalypse that didn't happen to include a god as one of the stage properties.

To those of my readers who share my Druid faith, or any of the other movements in today's inchoate but lively field of nature-centered spirituality, I hope I may speak even more frankly. For those who recognize the ways of Nature as a revelation of the powers that create and sustain the cosmos, as Druidry does, the notion that the world will abandon her normal ways and jump through hoops like a trained seal to satisfy our sense of entitlement or our craving for revenge is really pretty absurd.

To study nature from a Druid perspective is to learn that that limitation is the first law of existence, that what looks like a straight line to us is merely part of a circle too large to see at a single glance, that every movement generates and is balanced by a corresponding countermovement, that what systems theory calls negative feedback and an older way of thought calls the Royal Secret of equilibrium governs all things and all beings, with or without their conscious cooperation. In such a cosmos — and all things considered, a strong case can be made that this is the kind of cosmos we live in — there's no room for the paired fantasies of perpetual progress and imminent apocalypse, except as exhibits in a display of the odd things human beings talk themselves into believing from time to time.

Other faiths face their own challenges in dealing with the task I've proposed. I hope that at least some of my readers will be willing to attempt that revaluation, though, because the consequences of that act are far less abstract than they might seem at first. Such a revaluation has practical applications that bear directly on the hard work of preparing for the difficult future ahead. To pay attention to what actually happens in the world of our experience, and to set aside even the most emotionally attractive narratives if they fail to check out against the world of fact, is essential in order to avoid getting blindsided by utterly predictable events. As we'll see shortly, furthermore, it also offers some surprising benefits in making sense of the basic claims of religious faith.

Five

The God with the Monkeywrench

ONE RELIABLE CONSEQUENCE OF A FIXATION on what can work, instead of what does work, is a tendency to pursue policies that should work in theory but never manage to do so in practice. That's become a pervasive feature of life in contemporary industrial society. Open a copy of today's newspaper or the online equivalent, and it's a safe bet that you'll find at least one op-ed piece calling enthusiastically for the adoption of some political, military, or economic policy that's failed every single time it's been tried. It's hard, in fact, to think of any broadly accepted policy in any dimension of public life today that can't be accurately described in those terms.

Arnold Toynbee, whose sprawling study of historical cycles has been mentioned already, pointed out quite some time ago that this process of self-inflicted failure is one of the standard ways that civilizations write their own obituaries.[1] In his formulation, societies thrive so long as the creative minority that leads them can keep on coming up with new responses to the challenges the world throws their way — a process that normally requires the regular replacement of the society's leadership from below, so that new leaders with new ideas can rise to the top.

When that process of replacement breaks down, and the few people who still rise into the ruling class from lower down the pyramid are selected for their willingness to go along with the status quo rather than for their commitment to new ideas that might just work, what was once a creative minority degenerates into a dominant minority, which rules by coercion because it can no longer inspire by example. You can tell that this has happened to a society when every crisis gets met with the same stereotyped set of responses, even when those responses clearly don't work. That happens because dominant minorities identify themselves with certain policies and with the social roles and narratives that go with those policies, and it takes much more than mere failure to shake those obsessions loose.

The resulting one-track thinking can go very far indeed. The ideology of the Roman Empire, as noted above, copied the theological vision of Roman Pagan religion and projected it onto the world of politics. Roman Pagans saw the universe as a realm of primal chaotic powers that had been subjected to the benevolent rule of a cosmic paterfamilias by way of Jove's thunderbolts. Roman social thought understood history in the same way, as a process by which an original state of chaos was bashed into obedience by Rome's legions and subjected to the benevolent rule of the emperor. For much of Rome's imperial history, that model even made a certain amount of sense, as substantial parts of the Mediterranean world that had been repeatedly ravaged by wars beforehand experienced an age of relative peace and prosperity under Roman rule.

The problem was simply that this way of dealing with problems had little relevance to the pressures that gutted the Roman Empire in its final years, and trying to apply it anyway very quickly turned into a massive source of problems in its own right. The endless expansion of the Roman military required by increasingly drastic attempts to hammer the world into obedience imposed crippling tax burdens across

Roman society, driving whole economic sectors into bankruptcy, and the government responded to this by passing laws requiring every man to practice the same profession as his father, whether he could afford to do so or not. Across the dying empire, whenever one extension of centralized imperial authority turned into a costly flop, some even more drastic act of centralization was the only thinkable option, until finally the whole system fell to pieces.[2]

Modern industrial civilization is well on its way to this same destination, following the same road that Toynbee sketched out in such detail. Across the board, in politics, in economics, in energy policy, in any other field you care to name, the enthusiastic pursuit of repeatedly failed policies has become one of the leitmotifs of contemporary life. I'd like to focus on one of those briefly, partly because it's a classic example of the kind, partly because it shows with rare clarity the thinking that underlies the whole phenomenon. The example I have in mind is the ongoing quest for fusion power.[3]

Scientists in the United States and something like a dozen other countries have been busy at that quest since the 1950s. In the process, they've discovered something well worth knowing about fusion power: if it can be done at all, on any scale smaller than a star — and the jury's still out on that one — it can't be done at a price that any nation on Earth can possibly afford. The current state of the art in fusion research, the internationally funded ITER facility currently under construction in southern France, is the poster child for this awkward fact; years behind schedule, with total costs currently estimated at $17 billion and rising, and a completion date that keeps receding into the far future, it will at best bring the dream of fusion power one inconclusive step closer.

The reason all this money is being plowed into the ITER facility is simple enough: all the less expensive methods for producing commercially viable fusion power have already been tried and have failed. No one is even talking yet about the gargantuan investment that would be needed to build commercial power plants using some similar technology on any kind of scale. The dream of limitless cheap fusion power that filled the pages of gosh-wow newspaper articles and science fiction stories in the 1950s and 1960s is thus as dead as a sack full of doornails. Has this stopped the continuing flow of billions of dollars of grant money into round after futile round of gargantuan fusion-power projects? Surely you jest.

Thus fusion researchers are stuck in a self-defeating loop. They're approaching the situation in a way that prevents them from learning from their mistakes, no matter how many times the baseball bat of failure whacks them upside the head. In the case of the fusion scientists, what drives that loop is evident enough: the civil religion of progress and, in particular, the historical mythology at the core of that religion. By and large, scientists in the fusion industry see themselves as figures standing at the cutting edge of technological progress. Given their training, their history and the cultural pressures that surround them and define their work, it's all but impossible for them to do anything else. That's what has them boxed into a dead-end with no easy exits, because the way progress is conceptualized in contemporary culture is fatally out of step with the facts on the ground.

Progress, as the word literally means, is continued forward motion in one direction. To believers in the civil religion of progress, that's the shape of history: whatever it is that matters — moral improvement, technological prowess, economic expansion, or what have you — marches invincibly onward over time, and any setbacks in the present will inevitably be overcome in the future, just as equivalent setbacks in the past were overcome by later generations. To join the marching legions of progress, according to the myth, is to enlist on the side of history's winners and to help the inevitable victory come about just that little bit sooner, just as to oppose progress is to fight valiantly in a misguided cause and lose.

That's the myth that guides contemporary industrial society, just as the myth of Jupiter clobbering the Titans and imposing the rule of law on a fractious cosmos was the myth that guided Roman society. In the broadest sense, whether any given change is "progressive" or "regressive" has to be settled by good old-fashioned politics, since changes don't arrive with these labels branded on their backsides. Once a group of people have committed themselves to the claim that a change they're trying to bring about is progressive, though, they're trapped; no matter what happens, the only action the myth allows them to consider is that of slogging gamely onwards under the conviction that the obstacles will inevitably give way if they just keep at it. Thus the fusion research community is stuck perpetually pushing on a door marked PULL and wondering why it won't open.

Of course fusion researchers also have deeply pragmatic reasons for their refusal to learn the lessons of repeated failure. Careers, reputations and government funding all depend on keeping up the pretense that further investment in fusion research has a chance of producing something more than a collection of vastly overpriced laboratory curiosities, and the field of physics is so specialized these days that shutting down fusion research programs would leave most fusion researchers with few marketable job skills relevant to anything this side of flipping burgers. Thus the charade goes on, funded by granting agencies just as committed to that particular corner of the myth of progress as the researchers whose salaries they pay, and continuing to swallow vast amounts of money, resources and intellectual talent that might accomplish quite a bit if they could be applied to some less futile task.

The fusion research community, in effect, is being held hostage by the myth of progress. I've come to think that a great deal of contemporary science is caught in the same bind. By and large, the research programs that get funding and prestige are those that carry forward existing agendas, and the law of diminishing returns — which applies to scientific research as it does to all other human activities — means that the longer an existing agenda has been pursued, the fewer useful discoveries are likely to be made by pursuing it further. Yet the myth of progress has no place for the law of diminishing returns; in terms of the myth, every step along the forward march of progress must lead to another step, and that to another still.

This is why, to glance briefly at another example, efforts to craft a unified field theory out of Einsteinian relativity and quantum physics still get ample funding today, despite a century of total failure, while scores of research projects that might actually yield results go unfunded. It's also why certain enduring conundrums remain wedged in place in contemporary scientific culture, even though they have straightforward solutions once the mythology of progress is set aside. The example I have in mind here is Fermi's paradox.

As the name suggests, that conundrum was first posed by the famous nuclear physicist Enrico Fermi. One summer day in 1950, at the nuclear laboratory at Los Alamos, Fermi and several of his fellow nuclear scientists were chatting over lunch about the prospects for interstellar travel, when Fermi suddenly asked: "Where *is* everybody?" After a series of the rapid calculations for which he was famous, Fermi had noticed a drastic problem with the usual logic surrounding the idea of extraterrestrial civilizations.

His paradox is easy to state. The Milky Way galaxy has been in existence for around 14 billion years and has some 400 billion stars in it. Even if only a very small fraction of stars have planets orbiting them, only a very small fraction of planets have life forms on them, only a very small fraction of planets with life develop intelligent life, and only a very small fraction of those intelligent life forms go in for the kind of science and technology that results in spacecraft, the logical result given so much space and time would be a galaxy teeming with inhabited planets — and in that case there would be some trace of extraterrestrial civilizations recognizable from Earth, whether the evidence consisted of anomalous radiation patterns from distant worlds, say, or spaceships landing on the White House lawn. Neither the spaceships nor the radiation, nor any other trace of extraterrestrial life, have been detected — so where are the aliens?

Any number of solutions to Fermi's paradox have been proposed and widely discussed — Stephen Webb's useful 2002 survey *Where Is Everybody?* lists fifty of them — but all of them require a bit (or more than a bit) of special pleading here, an ad hoc hypothesis or two there and so on. This is all the more interesting in that there's a simple, straightforward explanation that requires nothing of the kind and follows directly from well-known principles that are utterly uncontroversial when applied to any other subject you care to name. The solution is that technological progress, like so many other phenomena, is subject to the law of diminishing returns, and for this reason, interstellar travel is well past the point that any species' technology will actually reach.

Ironically, Webb mentions this possibility in his book, but only in passing, in what amounts to a footnote to another of his options. His sole argument against it? "This suggestion seems unduly pessimistic, at least to me."[4] In a book that provides detailed and well-reasoned arguments for and against the other proposals Webb considers, the omission of any more relevant response to this possibility seems distinctly odd. More precisely, it seems odd so long as the role of progress as a surrogate deity in modern industrial society is left out of the picture.

⚜

One of the things that makes the end of progress so difficult for many people to accept today, more generally, is the way that it drives a wedge between science and what has often been called scientism. Science, at its core, is simply a method of practical logic that tests hypotheses against experience. Scientism, by contrast, is the ideology that insists that the questions the scientific method can answer are the most important questions human beings can ask, and that the answers yielded by science provide a more valuable model of reality than those provided by any other means. Science and scientism are not the same, but it's one of the most common habits of modern thought to assume their identity — more precisely, to wrap up scientism in the borrowed garb of science and fail to notice anything odd in the awkward fusion that results.

This is not a new thing; most sets of intellectual tools have given rise to their own worldview and values, and as often as not these remained all but invisible to their believers, redefined as plain common sense or simply as the way things were. Classical logic followed the same trajectory. Greek and Roman philosophers took logic as their basic toolkit, defined reality as whatever could be reduced to verbal statements and analyzed by logical means, and consigned the rest to the *apeiron*, the realm of the formless and unknowable. The results predetermined most of the successes and failures of the ancient world's intellectual history. It's easy enough to condemn the old philosophers for their failures — the debates about justice, for example, that never quite stopped to ask if there might be something wrong with the ancient world's economic dependence on slavery — but of course equivalent blind spots pervade modern thinking as well.

What verbal statements were to classical logic, quantification is to the scientific method. Phenomena that can't be expressed in numbers usually can't be investigated by the scientific method. Many scientists have reacted by consigning anything that can't be quantified to their own version of the *apeiron*. Recognizing this bad habit is not a condemnation of science, or even of scientism; rather, it is simply an acknowledgment of the fact that no tool is suited for every job.

Still, the natural tendency of a small child with a hammer to believe that everything is in need of a good whacking isn't the only factor at work here. The scientific method itself very often becomes an obstacle in the way of clarity. Meaning, value and purpose, after all, are among the things the scientific method handles most poorly — it's very hard to quantify a value judgment — and this problem becomes particularly serious when the scientist tries to think clearly about the meanings, values and purposes that have been assigned to science itself.

No controlled double-blind experiment could possibly prove, for example, that truths revealed by science are more important than those uncovered by other means, much less that the scientific method is the best hope for the human future. The fact that scientists have made these claims doesn't make them scientific; rather, they're among the value judgments that are at the core of scientism.

The same point can be made with even more force about humanity's supposed "conquest of nature," perhaps the most distinctive concept of scientism and one that has been welded into the rhetoric of the civil religion of progress. A military metaphor that defines humanity as nature's enemy, mind you, is an odd way to understand our relationship with the systems that sustain our lives; still, scratch today's attitudes toward the natural world and the hackneyed image of Man the conqueror of Nature is rarely far below the surface. Even the narratives of modern environmentalism, far from rejecting this view, reinforce it; most of them glorify human power, in fact, by embracing the claim that humanity has become so almighty that it can destroy the Earth and itself in the bargain.

The conflict between these beliefs and the hard realities of our age could not be more stark. Human limits, not human power, define the situation we face today, because the technological revolutions and economic boom times that most modern people take for granted resulted from a brief period of extravagance in which we squandered half a billion years of stored sunlight. The power we claimed was never really ours, and we never conquered Nature. Instead, we stole as many of her carbon assets as we could reach and spent most of them. Now the bills are coming due, the balance left in the account won't meet them, and the only question left is how much of what we bought with all that carbon will still be ours when Nature's foreclosure proceedings finish with us.

Such perspectives are impossible to square with most contemporary attitudes about Nature and humanity's place in it, and they conflict just as sharply with the Enlightenment conviction that reason is the door to a better world. From the perspective of that faith, it's axiomatic that anything unsatisfactory is a problem in need of a solution and that a solution can be found for it. The suggestion that deeply unsatisfactory conditions cannot be solved but, rather, have to be lived with, is unthinkable and offensive to a great many people. Yet if human life is subject to hard ecological limits, the narrative of human omnipotence falls, and a popular and passionately held conception of humanity's nature and destiny falls with it.

It's easy to turn scientism into the villain of this particular piece, but scientism is simply a recent example of the human habit of using a successful technique to define the universe. Hunting and gathering peoples see the animals they hunt and the plants they gather as the building blocks of the cosmos; farming cultures see their world in terms of soil, seed and the cycle of the year; the efforts of classical civilization to inhabit a wholly logical world, and those of modern industrial civilization to build a wholly scientific one, are simply two more examples.

Nor was scientism always as maladaptive as it is today. During the heyday of the Industrial Age, it directed human effort toward what was, at that time, a successful human ecology. In retrospect, scientism's limitless faith in the power of human reason turned out to be a case study in what the ancient Greeks called *hubris*, which may usefully be defined as the overweening pride of the doomed. At the time, though, this wasn't obvious at all, and there's a valid sense in which scientism has become problematic today simply because its time of usefulness is over.

Still, the cultures and ways of thought that will arise in a world on the far side of progress will have to embrace an attitude toward nature differing sharply from scientism: an attitude that starts from humility rather than hubris, remembering that "humility" shares the same root as "humus," the soil on which we depend for the food that keeps us alive. That attitude offers few justifications for today's arrogant notions about humanity's place in Nature. Still, just as Greek logic was pulled out of the rubble of the classical world and put to use in a string of successor civilizations, the scientific method is worth hauling out of the wreckage of the Industrial Age and could function just as well in a culture of environmental humility as it does in today's culture of environmental hubris. My guess, for what it's worth, is that the environmental sciences offer the most likely meeting ground for such a project of rescue.

Every culture draws on the techniques it finds most useful to provide it with its worldview. Industrial civilization thus drew most of
the ideas of scientism, and even more of its symbolism and emotional
appeal, from the world revealed by Galileo and Newton in the seventeenth century and embodied in the first wave of industrial technology
a century later. In the same way, the crucial role ecological knowledge
will likely play in the wake of the Industrial Age makes the emergence
of a broader way of thinking modeled on ecological science a near-cer-
tainty over the centuries immediately ahead of us.

Call that way of thinking *ecosophy*: the wisdom (*sophia*) of the
home, as distinct from — though in no sense opposed to — the "speaking about the home" that is ecology, or the "craft (*techne*) of the home"
that is ecotechnics. Ecosophy isn't a science, any more than scientism
is, nor is it a religion. Rather, ecosophy is a philosophy and a value system that gives meaning to ecology and ecotechnics, and makes sense
of human life not in terms of some imagined conquest of nature, but
in terms of our species' dependence on and participation in the wider
circle of the biosphere.

Some elements of ecosophy already exist, and others will evolve
gradually as the twilight of the age of cheap energy makes environmental realities impossible to ignore. Still, there is also a point in sketching
at least some of the outlines of an ecosophic worldview here and now.
The Christian worldview of the Middle Ages appeared in the writings of
theologians such as Augustine of Hippo long before it rooted itself in the
imagination of the medieval world. In the same way, founders of modern science from Galileo to Darwin explored the worldview of scientism
in their writings, and from there it spread into popular consciousness.

Elements of ecosophy have been sketched out in greater or lesser
detail in the writings of the great biologists and ecologists of the last
two and a half centuries or so, and in a great many other writings that
broke with the civil religion of progress and reached toward a philosophy and an ethic of humanity as inseparable parts of the living Earth.
The sciences, and particularly ecology and its related life sciences, have

a crucial role to play in the formation of an ecosophy suited to the needs of a world after progress. The great barrier that stands in the way of that important project is the widespread commitment on the part of scientists and scientific institutions alike to ideologies tightly bound to faith in progress.

⚒

It does no good to science, in other words, to be imprisoned within the myth of endless linear progress. I've wondered more than once what modern science would look like if some philosophical SWAT team were to kick down the doors of the temple of Progress and liberate the hostages held inside. My best guess is that, freed from the myth, science would look like a tree, rather than a road leading into infinite distance: rooted in mathematics and logic, supported by the strong trunk of the scientific method and extending branches, twigs and leaves in all directions, some of which would thrive while others would inevitably fail. Its leaves would spread out to catch as much of the light of truth as the finite nature of the tree allowed, but if one branch — the one called "fusion research," let's say — strayed into a lightless zone, the tree of science would direct its resources elsewhere and let that branch turn into a dry stick.

Eventually, the whole tree would reach its maximum growth, and after a lifespan of some centuries or millennia more, it would weaken, fail and die, leaving its remains as a nurse log to nurture a new generation of intellectual saplings. That's the way that Greek logic unfolded over time, and modern science started out its existence as one of the saplings nurtured on classical logic's vast fallen trunk. More generally, that's history's way with human intellectual, cultural and artistic systems of all kinds. Only the blinders imposed by the myth of progress make it impossible for most people in today's industrial world to see science in the same terms.

That same logic is not restricted to science, either. If some force of philosophers packing high-caliber syllogisms and fallacy-piercing ammunition ever does go charging through the door of the temple of Progress, quite a few people may be startled by the identity of some of the hostages who are led out blinking into light and freedom. It's not just the sciences that are tied up and blindfolded there; nearly all the Western world's religious denominations share the same fate.

It's important to recognize here that the myth of progress provides two potential roles for those who buy into its preconceptions. As noted earlier, they can join the winning side and enlist in the marching legions of progress, or they can join the losing side, struggle against the irresistible march of progress and heroically fail. Both those roles are necessary for the enactment of the myth, and the raw power of the pressure exerted by popular culture can be measured in the ease with which nearly every religious tradition in the Western world has been pushed into one role or the other. The major division is of course that between liberal and conservative denominations: the former have by and large been reduced to the role of cheerleaders for progress, while the latter have by and large been assigned the corresponding role as cannon fodder for the side that's destined to lose.

We can begin with the spectacularly self-defeating behavior of most liberal Christian denominations in the English-speaking world in the decades that followed the Second World War. In those years, a series of wildly popular books — John A.T. Robinson's *Honest to God*, Pierre Berton's *The Comfortable Pew* and others of the same kind — argued that, in order to be properly progressive, modern and relevant, Christian churches ought to surrender their historic beliefs and commitments, revise their traditional narratives to fit the myth of progress and accept whatever diminished role they might then be assigned by secular society.

Some of these books, such as Robinson's, were written by churchmen. Others, such as Berton's, were not, but all of them were eagerly received by what was then the liberal Christian mainstream in North America and elsewhere. The case of *The Comfortable Pew* is particularly intriguing, as the Anglican Church of Canada hired a well-known Canadian atheist to write a book about what was wrong with their church and what they should do about it. They then gamely took his advice with disastrous results. Other denominations were not quite so forthright in expressing a death wish, but the results were broadly similar.

Across the board, liberal churches thus reworked seminary programs to imitate secular liberal arts degrees, abandoned instruction in religious practice, took up the most radical forms of scriptural criticism and redefined their clergy as amateur social service providers and progressive social activists with a sideline in rites of passage. Since most people who go to church are there to worship God, not to provide their clergy with an admiring audience for political monologues and lectures on fashionable agnosticism, this shift was promptly followed a steep plunge in attendance and church membership the liberal denominations and their replacement in the cultural mainstream by conservative denominations.

Here again, though, the logic of progress made it all but impossible for church leaders to learn the lessons taught by failure. Because the changes in question were packaged and sold to liberal churches under the label of progress, heroic efforts have been made to insist that the changes must have been the right thing to do and to find other reasons to blame for the death spiral that resulted. They remain trapped by the same double bind that has the fusion research community by the throat: once some project has been assigned the label "progressive," the mythology of progress insists that it must be both good and inevitable, and believers in that mythology keep on thinking of the project in those terms no matter how disastrous it turns out to be in practice.

Meanwhile, conservative denominations were busy demonstrating that the opposite of one bad idea is usually another bad idea. Panicked by the global expansion of Communism — you rarely heard that latter term in American public discourse in the 1950s and 1960s without the word "godless" tacked onto its front end — and the sweeping social changes triggered by postwar prosperity, the conservative denominations moved as eagerly as their liberal counterparts to embrace the role that the myth of progress offered them. Along with William F. Buckley and the other architects of postwar American pseudoconservatism, the conservative denominations redefined themselves in opposition to the self-proclaimed "progressive" agenda of their time, and never seemed to notice that they were so busy standing against this, that and the other that most of them forgot to stand *for* anything at all.

The social pressure to conform to the stereotypes of the myth of progress and resist progress in every sense drove the weirdest dimension of late twentieth century American Christian conservatism, the holy war against Darwinian evolution. Nowhere in the Bible does it say that the luminous poetry of the first chapter of Genesis ought to be treated as a geology textbook, nor is a literal reading of Genesis mandated by any of the historic creeds of the Christian churches. Nonetheless an enormous number of Christian conservatives managed to forget that the Bible is about the Rock of Ages, not the age of rocks. "Thou shalt not evolve" got turned into an ersatz 11th Commandment, and devout believers exercised their ingenuity to the utmost to find ways to ignore the immense and steadily expanding body of evidence from geology, molecular biology, paleontology and genetics that backed Darwin's great synthesis.

The crusade against Darwin, together with such sideshows as the effort to insist on the historical reality of the Noah's ark story despite conclusive geological evidence disproving it, made it all but impossible for conservative Christian denominations to reach out effectively to audiences that didn't already share their preconceptions, in much the same way that a mindless embrace of secular ideologies made it all but impossible for the liberal denominations to hang onto more than a fraction of the audience whose spiritual needs they once addressed. The conservatives never quite managed to discard their historic beliefs, practices and commitments with the same enthusiasm shown by their liberal counterparts, preferring to maintain them in mummified form while political activism and pseudoscience took center stage; still, the result was much the same.

Today, the spokespersons for conservative religious denominations in America speak and act as though reinstating the scientific beliefs of the Middle Ages and the social mores of 1950s middle America have become the be-all and end-all of their religion. In response, many former parishioners of conservative denominations have withdrawn into the rapidly growing home church movement, in which families meet in living rooms with their neighbors to pray and study the Bible together. If that trend accelerates, as it appears to be doing, today's conservative megachurches may soon turn into cavernous spaces visited once a week by a handful of retirees, for all the world like the once-bustling liberal churches across the road.

The hijacking of religious institutions by the competing civil religion of progress has thus turned out to be a disaster on both sides of the liberal-conservative divide. The distortions imposed on religion, once it was taken hostage by the myth of progress, thus correspond closely to the distortions imposed on science during its own imprisonment by the same myth. As the civil religion of progress begins to lose its grip on the imagination of our time, in turn, both science and religion thus will have to undergo a difficult process of reappraisal, in which many of the mistaken commitments of recent decades will need to be renegotiated or simply abandoned.

Harrowing as that process may be, it may just have an unexpected benefit — a negotiated truce in the pointless struggle between science and religion, or even a creative rapprochement between these two distinct and complementary ways of relating to the universe. The potential for such a rapprochement can be seen most clearly in the religious dimensions of evolution, one of the core flashpoints of the pointless struggle just mentioned. As a major hot-button issue in the tangled relationship between science and religion, the quarrel over evolution highlights the way that this relationship has gotten messed up and thus will have to be sorted out as the civil religion of progress comes unraveled and its believers have to find some new basis for their lives.

Mind you, I also have a personal stake in settling the quarrel over evolution. It so happens that I'm a religious person who accepts the validity of Darwin's theory of evolution. That's not despite my religion — quite the contrary, it is part of my religion. The traditions of Druidry, the faith I that follow, embraced the concept of biological evolution even before Darwin provided a convincing explanation for it. Here's part of a ritual dialogue from the writings of Edward Williams (1747–1826), one of the major figures of the early Druid Revival:

> "Q. Where art thou now, and how camest thou to where thou art?"
>
> "A. I am in the little world, whither I came, having traversed the circle of Abred, and now I am a man at its termination and extreme limits."
>
> "Q. What wert thou before thou didst become a man in the circle of Abred?"
>
> "A. I was in Annwn the least possible that was capable of life, and the nearest possible to absolute death, and I came in every form, and through every form capable of a body and life, to the state of man along the circle of Abred."[5]

Like most eighteenth-century ritual texts, this one goes on for a good long while, but the passage just cited is enough to give the flavor and some of the core ideas. Abred is the realm of incarnate existence and includes "every form capable of a body and life," from what used to be called "infusoria" (single-celled organisms, nowadays) all the way up the scale of biological complexity and diversity, through every kind of living thing, including you and me. What the dialogue is saying is that we all, every one of us, embody all these experiences in ourselves. When Taliesin in one of his great songs of triumph said, "I have been a multitude of shapes,"[6] this is what we believe he was talking about.

There are at least two ways in which all this can be taken. It might be referring to the long biological process that gave rise to each of us, and left our bodies and minds full of traces of our kinship with all other living things. It might also be referring to the transmigration of souls, which was a teaching of the ancient Druids and is fairly broadly accepted in the modern tradition as well: the belief that there is a center of consciousness that survives the death of one body to be reborn in another, and that each such center of consciousness, by the time it first inhabits a human body, has been through many other forms, slowly developing the complexity that will make it capable of reflective thought and wisdom.

You'll find plenty of Druids on either side of this divide. What you won't find — at least I've yet to encounter one — are Druids who insist that the existence of a soul is somehow contradicted by the evolution of the body. Yet you can't bring up the idea of evolution in today's America without being besieged by claims that Darwinian evolution is inherently atheistic.

Creationists insist on this notion just as loudly as atheists do, which is really rather odd, considering that it's nonsense. By this I don't simply mean that an eccentric minority faith such as Druidry manages to combine belief in evolution with belief in divinity. I mean that the supposed incompatibility between evolution and the existence of one or more gods rests on the failure of religious people to take the first principles of their own faiths seriously.

Let's cover some basics first. First of all, Darwin's theory of natural selection may be a theory, but evolution is a fact. Living things change over time to adapt to changing environments. We've got a billion years of fossil evidence to show that, and the thing is happening right now — in the emergence of the Eastern coyote, the explosive radiation of cichlid fishes in East Africa and many other examples. The theory attempts to explain why this observed reality happens. A great deal of creationist rhetoric garbles this distinction and tries to insist that uncertainties in the explanation are proof that the thing being explained doesn't exist, which is bad logic. The theory, furthermore, has proven itself solidly in practice — it does a solid job of explaining things for which competing theories have to resort to ad hoc handwaving — and it forms the beating heart of today's life sciences.

Second, the narratives of the Book of Genesis, if taken literally, fail to match solidly proven facts about the origins and history of the Earth and the living things on it. It's been shown beyond reasonable doubt, for example, that the Earth came into being billions of years before 4004 BCE, that animals and plants didn't evolve in the order given for their creation in the first chapter of Genesis, that no flood large enough to put an ark on Mount Ararat happened during the chronological window the Bible allows for the Noah story and so on. It was worth suggesting back in the day that the narratives of the Book of Genesis might be literally true, but that suggestion has been put to the test; the hypothesis failed to fit the data, and insisting that the facts must be wrong if they contradict a cherished theory is not a useful habit.

Third, the value of the Bible — or of any other scripture, for that matter — does not depend on whether it makes a good geology textbook any more than the value of a geology textbook depends on whether it addresses the salvation of the soul. I don't know of any religion in which faith and practice center on notions of how the Earth came into existence and got its current stock of living things. Certainly the historic creeds of Christianity don't even consider the issue worth mentioning. The belief that God created the world does not require believing any particular claim about how that happened; nor does it say anywhere in the Bible that the Biblical account of creation has to be taken in the most pigheadedly literal of senses, or that the Bible deals with questions of geology or paleontology at all.

What's happened here is that a great many devout Christians in America have been suckered by the civil religion of progress into playing a mug's game. They've put an immense amount of energy into something that does their religion no good and plays straight into the hands of their opponents.

It's a mug's game, to begin with, because the central strategy that creationists have been using since well before Darwin's time guarantees that they will always lose. It's what historians of science call the "God of the gaps" strategy — the attempt to find breaks in the evolutionary process that scientists haven't yet filled with an explanation, and then to insist that only God can fill them. Back in Darwin's own time, the usual argument was that there weren't any transitional forms between one species and another; in response to the resulting talk about "missing links," paleontologists spent the next century and a half digging up transitional forms, so that nowadays there are plenty of evolutionary lineages — horses, whales and human beings among them — where every species is an obvious transition between the one before it and the one after.

As those gaps got filled in, critics of evolution retreated to another set, and another, and another. These days, they've retreated all the way to fine details of protein structure, and when that gap gets filled in — as it will be — it'll be on to the next defeat. The process is reliable enough that I've come to suspect that biologists keep an eye on the latest creationist claims when deciding what corner of evolutionary theory gets intensively researched next.

Still, there's a much deeper sense in which it's a mug's game, and explaining that deeper sense is going to require attention to some of the basic presuppositions of religious thought. To keep things in suitably general terms, we'll talk here about what philosophers call classical theism, defined as the belief that the universe was created out of nothing by a unique, perfect, eternal, omnipotent and omniscient being. There's more to classical theism than that — you can find the details in any good survey of philosophy of religion — but these are the details that matter for our present purposes. I've argued elsewhere that classical theism isn't the best explanation of human religious experience,[7] but we'll let that go for now; it corresponds closely to the beliefs of most American creationists, and it so happens that arguments that apply to classical theism here can be applied equally well to nearly all other theist beliefs.

Of the terms in the definition just given, the one that gets misused most often these days is "eternal." That word doesn't mean "lasting for a very long time," as when we say that a bad movie lasts for an eternity; it doesn't even mean "lasting for all of time." What it means instead is "existing outside of time." (Connoisseurs of exact diction will want to know that something that lasts for a very long time is diuturnal, and something that lasts for all of time is sempiternal.) Eternal beings, if such there be, experience any two moments in time the way you and I experience two points on a tabletop — distinct but simultaneously present. It's only beings who exist in time, as you and I do, who have to encounter those two moments sequentially, or as we like to say, "one at a time."[8]

That's why, for example, the endless arguments about whether divine providence contradicts human free will are barking up the wrong stump. Eternal beings don't have to foresee the future — they simply see it, because to them, it's not in the future. An omniscient eternal being can know exactly what you'll do in 2025, not because you lack free will, but because there you are, doing it right out in plain sight, as well as being born, dying and doing everything else in between. An eternal being could also see what you're doing in 2025 and respond to it in 2015, or at any other point in time from the Big Bang to whatever final destiny might be waiting for the universe billions of years from now. All this used to be a commonplace of medieval philosophy, and it's no compliment to modern thought that a concept every undergraduate knew inside and out in 1200 has been forgotten even by people who think they believe in eternal beings.

Now of course believers in classical theism and its equivalents don't just believe in eternal beings in general. They believe in one, unique, perfect, eternal, omnipotent and omniscient being who created the universe and everything in it out of nothing. Set aside for the moment whether you are or aren't one of those believers, and think through the consequences of the belief. If it's true, then everything in the universe — without a single exception — is there either because God deliberately put it there, or because he created beings with free will in the full knowledge that they would put it there. Everything that wasn't done by one of those created beings with divine permission, in turn, is a direct manifestation of God's will. Gravity and genetics, photosynthesis and continental drift, the origin of life from complex carbon compounds and the long evolutionary journey since then grant the presuppositions of classical theism, and these are, and can only be, how beings in time perceive the workings of the eternally creative will of God.

Thus it's a waste of time to go scrambling around the machinery of the cosmos, looking for scratches left by a divine monkeywrench on the gears and shafts. That's what the "God of the gaps" strategy does in practice. Without ever quite noticing it, that strategy accepts the purely mechanistic vision of the universe that's promoted by atheists, and then tries to prove that God tinkers with the machinery from time to time. Accept the principles of classical theism and you've given up any imaginable excuse for that way of thinking, since an eternal, perfect, omniscient and omnipotent deity leaves no scratches and doesn't need to tinker. It's not even a matter of winding up the gears of the cosmos and letting them run from there, in the fashion of the "clockmaker God" of the eighteenth-century Deists; to an eternal divine being, all of time is present simultaneously, every atom is doing exactly and only what it was put there to do and what looks like machinery to the atheist can only be, to the believer in classical theism or its equivalents, the action of the divine will in eternity acting upon the world in time.

Such a universe, please note, doesn't differ from the universe of modern science in any objectively testable way, and this is as it should be. The universe of matter and energy is what it is, and modern science is the best toolkit our species has yet discovered for figuring out how it works. The purpose of theology isn't to bicker with science over questions that science is much better prepared to address, but to relate the material universe studied by science to questions of ultimate concern — of value, meaning and purpose — which science can't and shouldn't address and are instead the proper sphere of religion.

To return to a point made earlier, not everything that matters to human beings can be settled by an objective assessment of fact. There are times, many of them, that you have to decide on some other basis which of several different narratives you choose to trust. Step beyond questions of fact, that is, and you're in the territory of faith — a label that properly includes the atheist's belief in a purely material cosmos just as much as it does the classical theist's belief in a created cosmos made by an infinite and eternal god, the traditional polytheist's belief in a living cosmos shaped by many divine powers and so on, since none of these basic presuppositions about the cosmos can be proven or disproven.

How do people decide between these competing visions, then? As noted in Chapter Four, when that choice is made honestly, it's made on the basis of values. Values are always individual, always relative to a particular person in a particular context. They are not a function of the intellect, but of the heart and will — or to use an old and highly un-fashionable word, of character. Different sets of presuppositions about the cosmos speak to different senses of what values matter; which is to say that they speak to different people, in different situations.

This, of course, is what a great many religions have been saying all along. In most of the religions of the West, and many of those from other parts of the world, faith is a central theme, and faith is not a mat-ter of passing some kind of multiple choice test; it's not a matter of the intellect at all; rather, it's the commitment of the whole self to a way of seeing the cosmos that can be neither proved nor disproved rationally, but has to be accepted or rejected on its own terms. To accept any such vision of the nature of existence is to define one's identity and relation-ship to the whole cosmos; to refuse to accept any such vision is also to define these things, in a different way; and in a certain sense, you don't make that choice — you *are* that choice. Rephrase what I've just said in the language of salvation and grace, and you've got one of the core concepts of Christianity; phrase it in other terms, and you've got an important element of many other religions, Druidry among them.

It's important not to ignore the sweeping differences among these different visions of the nature of existence — these different faiths, to use a far from meaningless idiom. Still, there's a common theme shared by many of them, which is the insight that human beings are born and come to awareness in a cosmos with its own distinctive order, an order that we didn't make or choose, and one that imposes firm limits on what we can and should do with our lives.

Different faiths understand that experience of universal order in radically different ways — call it Dharma or the Tao, the will of God or the laws of Nature, or what have you — but the choice is the same in every case: you can apprehend the order of the cosmos in love and awe, and accept your place in it, even when that conflicts with the cravings of your ego, or you can put your ego and its cravings at the center of your world and insist that the order of the cosmos doesn't matter if it gets in the way of what you think you want. It's a very old choice: which will you have, the love of power or the power of love?

What makes this particularly important just now is that we're all facing that choice today with unusual intensity, in relation to part of the order of the cosmos that not all religions have studied as carefully as they might. Yes, that's the order of the biosphere, the fabric of natural laws and cycles that keep all of us alive. It's a teaching of Druidry that this manifestation of the order of things is of the highest importance to humanity, and not just because human beings have messed with that order in remarkably idiotic ways over the last three hundred years or so.

Your individual actions toward the biosphere are an expression of the divide just sketched out. Do you recognize that the living Earth has its own order, that this order imposes certain hard constraints on what human beings can or should try to do, and do you embrace that order and accept those constraints in your own life for the greater good of the living Earth and all that lives upon her? Or do you shrug it off, or go through the motions of fashionable eco-piety, hop into your SUV lifestyle and slam the pedal to the metal?

Science can't answer that question, because science isn't about values. (When people start claiming otherwise, what's normally happened is that they've smuggled in a set of values from some religion or other — most commonly from the civil religion of progress.) Science can tell us how fast we're depleting the world's finite oil supplies and how quickly the signs of unwelcome ecological change are showing up around us; it can predict how soon this or that or the other resource is going to run short and how rapidly the global climate will start to cost us in blood; it can even tell us what actions might help make the future less miserable than it will otherwise be and which ones will add to the misery — but it can't motivate people to choose the better of these, to decide to change their lives for the benefit of the living Earth rather than say with a shrug, "I'm sure they'll think of something" or "I'll be dead before it happens" or "We're all going to be extinct soon, so it doesn't matter," and walk away.

That's why it's so crucial just now to understand the role of faith in progress as a civil religion and to come to terms with the implication of its failure as a source of values. Religion is the dimension of human culture that deals most directly with values, and values are the ultimate source of all human motivation. It's for this reason that I feel it's crucial to find a common language that will bridge the gap between religion and science, to get both parties to settle down on their own sides of the border that should properly separate them — and to show that there's a path beyond the misguided struggle between them.

The pointless debate over evolution just surveyed, after all, has any number of equivalents in contemporary industrial culture. Pick a topic, any topic, and it's a pretty safe bet that the collective imagination of the modern industrial world defines it as an irreconcilable divide between two and only two points of view, one of which is portrayed as realistic, reasonable, progressive, hard-headed and triumphant, while the other is portrayed as sentimental, nostalgic, inaccurate, emotionally appealing and certain to lose — that is to say, as a microcosm of the mythology of progress.

According to that mythology, after all, every step of the heroic on-ward march of progress came about because some bold intellectual visionary or other, laboring against the fierce opposition of a majority of thinkers bound by emotional ties to outworn dogmas, learned to see the world clearly for the first time and in the process deprived hu manity of some sentimental claim to a special status in the universe. That's the way, for example, you'll find the emergence of the theory of evolution described in textbooks and popular nonfiction to this day. Darwin's got plenty of company, too: all the major figures of the history of science from Copernicus through Albert Einstein get the same treatment in popular culture. It's a remarkably pervasive bit of narrative, which makes it all the more remarkable that, as far as history goes, it's essentially a work of fiction.

I'd encourage those of my readers who doubt that last point to read evolutionary biologist and science writer Stephen Jay Gould's fascinating book *Time's Arrow, Time's Cycle.* Gould's subject is the transformation in geology that took place in the late eighteenth and early nineteenth centuries, when theories of geological change that centered on Noah's flood gave way to the uniformitarian approach that's dominated geology ever since. Pick up a popular book on the history of earth sciences and you'll find the narrative I've just outlined: the role of nostalgic defender of an outworn dogma is assigned to religious thinkers such as Thomas Burnet, while that of heroic pioneer of reason and truth is conferred on geologists such as James Hutton.

What Gould demonstrates in precise and brutal detail is that the narrative can be imposed on the facts only by sacrificing any claim to intellectual honesty. It's simply not true, for example, that Burnet dismissed the evidence of geology when it contradicted his Christian beliefs, or that Hutton reached his famous uniformitarian conclusions in a sudden flash of insight while studying actual rock strata — two claims that have been endlessly repeated in textbooks and popular literature. More broadly, the entire popular history of uniformitarian geology amounts to a "self-serving mythology" — those are Gould's words, not mine — that's flatly contradicted by every bit of the historical evidence.

Another example? Consider the claim, endlessly regurgitated in textbooks and popular literature about the history of astronomy, that the geocentric theory — the medieval view of things that put the Earth at the center of the solar system — assigned humanity a privileged place in the cosmos. I don't think I've ever read a popular work on the subject that didn't include that factoid. It seems plausible enough, too, unless you happen to know the first thing about medieval cosmological thought.

The book to read here is *The Discarded Image* by C.S. Lewis — yes, *that* C.S. Lewis; the author of the Narnia books was also one of the most brilliant medievalists of his day and the author of magisterial books on medieval and Renaissance thought. What Lewis shows, with a wealth of examples from the relevant literature, is that nobody in the Middle Ages thought of the Earth's position as any mark of privilege, or for that matter as centrally placed in the universe. To the medieval mind, the Earth was one notch above the rock bottom of the cosmos, a kind of grubby suburban slum built on the refuse dump outside the walls of the City of Heaven. Everything that mattered went on above the sphere of the Moon; everything that *really* mattered went on out beyond the sphere of the fixed stars where God and the angels dwelt.

The one scrap of pride left to fallen humanity was that, even though it was left to grub for a living on the dungheap of the cosmos, it hadn't quite dropped all the way to the very bottom. The very bottom was Hell, with Satan trapped at its very center; the Earth was a shell of matter that surrounded Hell, the same way that the sphere of the Moon surrounded that of Earth, the sphere of Mercury that of the Moon and so on outwards to Heaven. Physically speaking, in other words, the medieval cosmos was diabolocentric, not geocentric — again, the Earth was merely one of the nested spheres between the center and the circumference of the cosmos — and the physical cosmos itself was simply an inverted reflection of the spiritual cosmos, which had God at the center, Satan pinned immovably against the outermost walls of being and the Earth not quite as far as you could get from Heaven.

Thus the Copernican revolution didn't deprive anybody of a sense of humanity's special place in the cosmos. Quite the contrary, eminent thinkers at the time wondered if it wasn't arrogant to suggest that humanity might be privileged enough to dwell in what, in the language of the older cosmology, was the fourth sphere up from the bottom! It takes only a little leafing through medieval writings to learn that, but the fiction that the medieval cosmos assigned humanity a special place until Copernicus cast him out of it remains glued in place in the conventional wisdom of our time. When the facts don't correspond to the mythology of progress, in other words, too bad for the facts.

⁂

Other examples could be multiplied endlessly, starting with the wholly fictitious flat-earth beliefs that modern writers insist on attributing to the people who doubted Columbus,[9] but these will do for the moment, not least because one of the authors I've cited was one of the twentieth century's most thoughtful evolutionary biologists and the other was one of the twentieth century's most thoughtful Christians. The point I want to make is that the conventional modern view of the history of human thought is a fiction, a morality play that has nothing to do with the facts of the past and everything to do with justifying the distribution of influence, wealth and intellectual authority in today's industrial world. That's relevant here because the divide sketched out a few paragraphs ago — the supposedly irreconcilable struggles between a way of knowing the world that's realistic, progressive and true, and a received wisdom that's sentimental, nostalgic and false — is modeled on the narrative we've just been examining and has no more to do with the facts on the ground than the narrative does.

The great difference between the two is that neither medieval cosmographers nor late eighteenth-century geologists had the least notion that they were supposed to act out a morality play for the benefit of viewers in the early twenty-first century. Here in the early twenty-first century, by contrast, a culture that's made the morality play in question the center of its collective identity for more than 300 years is very good at encouraging people to act out their assigned roles in the play, even when doing so flies in the face of their own interests.

Christian churches gain nothing by accepting the loser's role in the ongoing squabble over evolution. The huge amounts of time, effort and money that have gone into the creationist crusade could have been applied to something relevant to the historic creeds and commitments of the Christian religion, rather than serving to advance the agenda of their enemies. That this never seems to occur to them is a measure of the power of the myth.

Those of my readers who have an emotional investment in the environmental movement might not want to get too smug about the mistakes of the creationists, mind you, because their own movement has been drawn into filling the same role with equally disastrous consequences. It's not just that the media consistently likes to portray environmentalism as a sentimental, nostalgic movement with its eyes fixed on an idealized prehuman or pretechnological past, though of course that's generally true. It's that a great many of the public spokespersons for environmental causes also speak in the same terms, either raging against the implacable advance of progress or pleading for one or another compromise in which a few scraps are tossed nature's way as the engines of progress go rumbling on.

According to the myth of progress, those are the sort of speeches that are assigned to the people on history's losing side, and environmentalists in recent decades have done a really impressive job of conforming to the requirements of their assigned role. When was the last time, for example, that you heard an environmentalist offer a vision of the future that wasn't either business as usual with a coat of green spray paint, a return to an earlier and allegedly greener time, or utter catastrophe? As recently as the 1970s, it was quite common for people in the green end of things to propose enticing visions of a creative, sustainable, radically different future in harmony with nature,[10] but that habit got lost in the next decade, about the time the big environmental lobbies sold out to corporate America. Now of course once a movement redefines its mission as begging for scraps from the tables of the wealthy and influential, as mainstream environmentalism has done, it's not going to get any benefit from dreaming big dreams.

Still, there's a deeper pattern at work here. The myth of progress assigns the job of coming up with bold new visions of the future to the winning side — which means in practice the side that wins the political struggle to get its agenda defined as the next step of progress — and assigns to the losing side instead the job of idealizing the past and uttering doleful warnings about the dreadful catastrophes that are sure to happen unless the winners relent in their onward march. Teach people to believe implicitly in a social narrative, and far more often than not they'll fill their assigned roles in that narrative, even at great cost to themselves, since the alternative is a shattering revaluation of all values in which the unthinking certainties that frame most human thought have to be dragged up to the surface and judged on their own potentially dubious merits.

Such a revaluation, though, is going to happen anyway in the not too distant future, because the onward march of progress is already failing to live up to the prophecies that have been made in its name. As noted earlier, civil religions are vulnerable to sudden collapse because their kingdom is wholly of this world. Believers in a theist religion can console themselves in the face of continual failure with the belief that their sufferings will be amply repaid in heaven, but the secular worldview common to civil religions slams the door in the face of that hope.

The civil religion of Communism thus imploded when it became impossible for people on either side of the Iron Curtain to ignore the gap between prophecy and reality, and there's good reason to think that the civil religion of Americanism may go the same way in the decades ahead of us. The civil religion of progress, though, is at least as vulnerable to that species of sudden collapse. So far, the suggestion that progress might be over is something you'll encounter mostly in the writings of intellectual heretics far enough out on the cultural fringes to be invisible to the arbiters of fashion; so far, "they'll think of something" remains the soothing mantra du jour of the true believers in the great god Progress.

Nonetheless, history points up the reliability with which one era's unquestioned truths become the next era's embarrassing memories. To return to a point raised earlier, the concept of progress has no content of its own, and so it's been possible so far for believers in progress to pretend to ignore all the things in American life that are blatantly retrogressing and to keep scrabbling around for something, anything, that will still prop up the myth.

In today's America, living standards for most people have been falling for decades, along with literacy rates and most measures of public health. The nation's infrastructure has been ravaged by decades of neglect, its schools are by most measures the worst in the industrial world, and even the most basic public services are being cut to Third World standards or below. The lunar landers scattered across the face of the Moon stare back blindly at a nation that no longer has a manned space program at all and, despite fitful outbursts of rhetoric from politicians and the idle rich, almost certainly will never have one again. None of that matters — yet.

Another of the lessons repeatedly taught by history, though, is that sooner or later these things *will* matter. Sooner or later, some combination of events will push cognitive dissonance to the breaking point, and the civil religion of progress will collapse under the burden of its own failed prophecies. That's almost unthinkable for most people in the industrial world these days, but it's crucial to recognize that the mere fact that something is unthinkable is no guarantee that it won't happen.

Thus it's important for those of us who want to be prepared for the future to try to think about the unthinkable — to come to terms with the possibility that the future will see a widespread rejection of the myth of progress and everything connected to it. That wasn't a likely option in an age when economic expansion and rapid technological development were everyday facts of life, but we no longer live in such an age, and the fading memories of the last decades when those things happened will not retain their power indefinitely.

Imagine a future America where the available resources don't even suffice to maintain existing technological systems, only the elderly remember sustained economic growth, and the new technological devices that still come onto the market now and then are restricted to the very few who are wealthy enough to afford them. At what point along that curve do the promises of progress become so self-evidently absurd that the power of the civil religion of progress to shape thought and motivate behavior breaks down completely?

It's ironic but entirely true that actual technological progress could continue, at least for a time, after the civil religion of progress is busy pushing up metaphorical daisies in the cemetery of dead faiths. What gives the religion of progress its power over so many minds and hearts is not progress itself, but the extraordinary burden of values and meanings that progress is expected to carry in our society. It's not the mere fact that new technologies show up in the stores every so often that matters, but the way that this grubby commercial process serves to bolster a collective sense of entitlement and a galaxy of wild utopian dreams about the human future. If the sense of entitlement gives way to a sense of failure or, worse, of betrayal, and the dreamers wake up and recognize that the dreams were never anything more than delusions in the first place, the backlash could be one for the record books.

One way or another, the flow of new products will eventually sputter to a halt, though at least some of today's technologies will stay in use for as long as they can be kept functioning in the harsh conditions of an age of resource scarcity and ecological payback. A surprisingly broad range of technologies can be built and maintained by people who have little or no grasp of the underlying science, and thus it has happened more than once — as with the Roman aqueducts that brought water to medieval cities — that a relatively advanced technology can be kept running for centuries by people who have no clue how it was built. Over the short and middle term, in a world after progress, we can probably expect many current technologies to remain in place for a while, though it's an open question how many people in the industrial world will still be able to afford to use them for how much longer.

Ultimately, that last factor may be the Achilles' heel of most modern technologies. In the not-too-distant future, any number of projects that might be possible in some abstract sense will never happen, because the energy, raw materials, labor and money that are still available are already committed twice over to absolute necessities, and nothing can be spared for anything else. In any age of resource scarcity and economic contraction, that's a fairly common phenomenon, and it's no compliment to contemporary thinking about the future that so many of the grand plans being circulated in the sustainability scene ignore the economics of contraction so completely.

Still, the relevant point here has to do with the consequences of a collective loss of faith in the civil religion of progress — consequences that aren't limited to the realm of technology but spill over into economics, politics and nearly every other dimension of contemporary life. The stereotyped debates introduced at the beginning of this post and discussed in more detail toward the middle will be abandoned, and their content will have to be reframed in completely different terms, once the myth of progress, which provides them with their basic script, loses its hold on the collective imagination.

The historical fictions also discussed earlier will be up for the same treatment. It's hard to think of any aspect of modern thought that hasn't been permeated by the myth of progress. When that myth shatters and has to be replaced by other narratives, an extraordinary range of today's unquestioned certainties will be up for grabs.

Six

On the Far Side of Progress

Wᴴᴇɴ Nɪᴇᴛᴢsᴄʜᴇ ᴘʀᴏᴄʟᴀɪᴍᴇᴅ ᴛʜᴇ ᴅᴇᴀᴛʜ ᴏꜰ Gᴏᴅ, he saw that event as a turning point in human history, a shattering and liberating transformation that would open the road to the Overman. That hope turned out to be misplaced, as noted in an earlier chapter, and it's worth keeping in mind that whatever grandiose claims might be made about the consequences of the death of progress will likely face the same kind of disappointment.

Even so, the collapse of the civil religion of progress marks a significant shift, as important in our time as the event Nietzsche announced was in his. Like its forerunner, the death of progress promises to kick the props out from under a great deal of today's conventional wisdom and poses serious challenges to some of the industrial world's most central institutions. The example I have in mind here is modern science, and in particular the impressively large and expensive institutional forms that have been built up around the scientific project over the last century or so. Those forms were achievable only because a widely shared faith in progress made resources and funding available for them, and their continued existence depends just as directly on the survival of that same faith.

A specific example may be helpful here, so let's consider the future of astronomical observatories. An observatory big and high-tech enough to contribute significantly to the advance of astronomy can be a very expensive proposition — the Palomar observatory outside San Diego, for example, costs more than \$10,000 a night to operate — and the ebbing tide of prosperity in the industrial world is starting to make those costs hard to cover. Here in the US, most astronomical observatories are facing funding cuts or closure, as part of a quiet but very broad retrenchment that is leaving few scientific fields unscathed.

Observatories are particularly vulnerable in this context because they don't earn money for anybody. At a time when computer science and molecular biology departments at many universities increasingly operate as commercial enterprises, churning out patentable products to line the pockets of professors and university administrators alike, astronomers have got to be feeling like the red-headed stepchildren of academe. No matter how excited they and their colleagues may be about discovering a new type of quasar or what have you, the discovery's not going to make them or their university any money, and the university administration is just as aware of this difference as the astronomers are.

These days, as a result, the sciences are being sorted out into two camps, those that produce technologies useful to government and business and those that don't. I'm sure my readers need no help figuring out which of those camps is getting the lion's share of research dollars these days and which is being left to twist in the wind.

At this point I'd like to take the discussion in a deliberately improbable, even whimsical direction. It so happens that astronomers do have another source of income available to them — a funding source that could probably support many if not most of the existing observatories in the style to which they've become accustomed, and would be independent of government grants and the whims of university administrations alike. It would require a certain number of grad students to get some additional training, but all the necessary work could be done with equipment that can be found in any observatory. What's more, it was the funding source for several of history's most important astronomical projects, so there's even a tradition behind it.

It's as simple as it is elegant, really. All that would be required is that observatory staff would have to learn how to cast and interpret horoscopes.

Yes, I'm well aware that that's not going to happen, and in a moment we'll talk about the reasons why, but let's set the real world aside for a moment and consider the thing in the abstract. Despite the fulminations and wishful thinking of the rationalists among us, astrology's not going to go away any time soon. It's been a living tradition for well over two millennia in close to its current form and is as lively now as it's ever been. The rationalist crusade against astrology has been a resounding flop, having failed to make the least dent in its popularity. Today the astrological community is by many measures in better financial health than the astronomers who despise it; it supports its own economic sector of publishers, computer firms, annual conferences, correspondence schools and many other businesses, not to mention thousands of professional astrologers who make a living casting birth charts, annual progressions, horary charts and other astrological readings for a large and enthusiastic clientele.

Not only could astronomers tap into this market, it actually takes a continuing effort on their part to avoid doing so. I've been told by astronomer friends that observatories in the US routinely field calls from people who are a little confused about the difference between astronomy and astrology, and want someone to cast their horoscopes. Put a new message on the answering machine, teach the receptionist how to take down birth data and that difficulty's out of the way. The biggest and most prestigious observatories would have the most to gain — what Hollywood pop icon, for example, could resist the temptation to drop five figures on a genuine horoscope from the Palomar

Observatory, complete with a glossy star field photo of the second or
so of arc that was rising on the ecliptic when he or she was born?

Nor would this be anything new in the history of astronomy. While
Johannes Kepler was working out the laws of planetary motion, he paid
the bills by casting horoscopes; Claudius Ptolemy did the same thing
more than a millennium earlier while he was writing the *Almagest*.
(Granted, neither man was in it just for the money; Ptolemy also wrote
the most influential treatise on astrology ever penned, the *Tetrabiblos*,
while Kepler was a brilliant innovator in astrology — the Keplerian
aspects are very nearly as important in the history of modern astrology
as the laws of planetary motion are in that of modern astronomy.) For
that matter, the roots of modern astronomy reach deep into the traditions of the astronomer-priests of Sumeria and Babylonia, who made
the first known systematic records of planetary movements and, not
coincidentally, cast the first known horoscopes.

Much more could be said along these lines, but it's probably better
to stop here, so that my rationalist readers don't fling themselves at this
book in a purely reflexive attempt to leap through the pages and wring
my neck. Of course the modest proposal I've just offered has about
as much chance of being taken seriously as Jonathan Swift's famous
suggestion that the Irish ought to support themselves by selling their
infants for meat, and it was made in much the same spirit.

We can take it as given that in today's America, astronomers will
embrace astrology on the same day that Sam Harris and Richard
Dawkins fall on their knees together and accept Jesus as their lord and
savior. Nor, for that matter, am I interested in rehashing the weary debates over the validity of astrology. The issue I want to raise here is why
the suggestion that astronomers might consider taking up astrology
summons up so violent and visceral a reaction on the part of so many
people these days.

It's important to get past the standard rhetoric that surrounds the
subject — the insistence on the part of rationalists that astrology is un-
acceptable because it's irrational, medieval and just plain wrong. Sports

fandom, for example, is arguably well up there on the scale of irratio-nality, and yet it's perfectly acceptable for astronomers to be rabid fans of the local baseball team. Reenactment groups such as the Society for Creative Anachronism are about as medieval as you can get, and yet an astronomer who belongs to such a group faces no criticism. As for just plain wrong, your average economist has astrologers beat three falls out of three. You'll never catch an astrologer claiming that the sun will rise in the west tomorrow morning and then never set again, while it's par for the course for economists to insist that the speculative bubble du jour will never pop, that the laws of economics can trump the laws of physics and geology and so on. Yet it's remarkably rare to hear sci-entists denouncing economics as the crackpot pseudoscience that it arguably is.

What puts astrology outside the pale for today's astronomers and the rest of the scientific community, rather, is that the collective imagi-nation of the modern world assigns it to the dismal past from which the surrogate messiah of progress is forever saving us. Like the Christianity from which it drew a great many of its central metaphors, the civil re-ligion of progress has a very wide streak of moral dualism; there's the side of the angels in white — or, rather, the researchers in white lab coats — and then there's the side of the devils in some infernal equiv-alent of Madras plaid. In contemporary culture, there's no question about the side of the border on which astrology belongs. It's part of the kingdom of anti-progress, the exact equivalent of the Christian notion of the kingdom of Antichrist.

The white-hot passion with which so many scientists condemn as-trology and other systems of rejected knowledge thus has its roots in the identity that scientists are taught to assume by their education and their professional culture. From the time of Francis Bacon right down to the present, scientists have been encouraged to think of themselves as laborers in the great cause of progress, leading humanity forward out of the superstitious past toward a brighter and better future of ever-increasing reason, knowledge and power. From the nineteenth century onward, in turn, this is the image of themselves that scientists have by and large tried to project into the wider society, with varying degrees of success.

Acting out an ideal in that manner can be a dangerous thing to do, and civil religions rarely have much sense of the risks involved. Theist faiths with at least a few centuries of experience under their belts tend to be a good deal more cautious. Buddhist monks who visualize themselves as bodhisattvas and Christians practicing the *imitatio Christi* have traditional protections to keep the identification of the self with an ideal figure from spinning out of control into psychological imbalance.

Civil religions rarely have such safeguards. Those of my readers who, as I did, had the chance to spend some time around old-fashioned Communists will have seen some of what happens when those protections are neglected. The leader of the proletariat who goes to great lengths to avoid noticing that the proletariat is not following him and melts down completely when this latter detail becomes too evident to ignore was once a tolerably common type.

That type became much more common in the second half of the twentieth century, when it started to take effort not to notice the fact that the American proletariat wasn't going to follow a Marxist lead. In the same way, I don't think it's accidental that the current rationalist crusade against religion, astrology and everything else it likes to label irrational, medieval, wrong, etc. shifted into overdrive in the final decades of the twentieth century, right about the time that it first became really difficult to justify the blanket claim that progress was always as inevitable as it was beneficent.

≈≋✥≋≈

Like their theist cousins, civil religions fairly often respond to challenges to their core beliefs by moving toward the extremes and looking for somebody to blame. The cultural politics that assigned the label of "anti-progress" to certain traditional philosophies and practices such as astrology gave the civil religion of progress an assortment of easy targets once the onward march of progress began to lose its appeal. The difficulty with such exercises in scapegoat-hunting is that they do nothing to solve the problem that drives them and may actually get in the way of addressing serious challenges.

The status of science in contemporary industrial society is a case in point. Not long ago, when a qualified scientist got up in front of the public and spoke about some matter of scientific fact, most Americans took him at his word. Nowadays? One of the core reasons for the failure of climate activism is that a great many people know that an expert opinion from a distinguished researcher can be bought for the price of a modest research grant and have seen scare tactics used to push political agendas so many times that another round of dire warnings from experts doesn't impress them anymore. When climate activists chose to rely on the prestige of science to back up a standard-issue scare campaign, in other words, they were making a serious strategic mistake, on which their opponents were not slow to capitalize.

To some extent the collapse in the prestige of science has unfolded from the way that scientific opinion has whirled around like a weathervane on certain very public issues in recent decades. Plenty of people alive today still recall when continental drift was crackpot pseudoscience, polyunsaturated fats were good for you and ionizing radiation was measured in "sunshine units." It's important to the workings of science that scientists should be permitted to change their minds on the arrival of new evidence, but that necessary openness clashes with the efforts of the scientific community to claim a privileged place in the wider conversations of our time — for example, by insisting that claims by scientific authorities should not be challenged from outside the discipline no matter how many times these same authorities have changed their minds.

Add to that clash the increasingly visible corruption of science by financial interests — the articles in medical journals that are bought and paid for by pharmaceutical firms eager to promote their products, the studies whose conclusions reliably parrot the propaganda of their funding sources and so on — and you've got the makings of a really serious public relations disaster. That disaster is not going to be prevented or even delayed by denouncing astrologers and their ilk. Mind you, it may succeed in making astrology more popular than it otherwise would be, for the same reason that the Republican Party's bizarre habit of defining anything it doesn't like as "socialism" may yet convince a good many Americans to give Marx a second chance.

Given the very real pressures being brought to bear on scientists and scientific institutions in the current environment of economic contraction and violent political partisanship, it's unlikely that anything more constructive will be on anyone's agenda until well after the damage is done — and it's the bad luck of astronomy, along with a great many other sciences not currently participating in the worst of the abuses, that it's likely to be tarred with the same brush as those who richly deserve it. Factor in the twilight of the civil religion of progress, though, and the ethical and political crisis of contemporary science becomes something considerably larger.

In the most likely future ahead of us, in which sustained economic growth is a subject for history books, a growing fraction of the developed world's population lives in intractable poverty, and access to the latest technological trinkets is out of the question for most people, faith in the inevitability and beneficence of progress will make roughly as much sense to most of them as faith in the worker's paradise of true Communism did to most citizens of the Soviet Union in 1980 or so. In such a future, funding for scientific research will be at the mercy of the first demagogue who realizes that gutting government grant programs for the sciences is a ticket to a landslide victory in the next election.

So long as scientists keep on thinking of themselves as heroic workers in the grand cause of progress, furthermore, any attempt on their part to counter such efforts will labor under the same brutal limits that afflict the clergymen of liberal denominations discussed earlier. The vision of the future central to their identity is already becoming the subject of bitter jokes of the "I believe I was promised a jetpack" variety. As the shift in the collective imagination implied by those jokes continues to spread, scientists — like the old-fashioned Communists mentioned earlier — won't be able to respond to their critics without jettisoning their traditional rhetoric, and they won't be able to jettison the rhetoric without abandoning a set of beliefs that align them with the supposedly invincible onward march of progress. That's a trap from which very few organizations and social movements ever manage to escape.

Thus it's uncomfortably easy to imagine a meeting of the American Association for the Advancement of Science in 2070 or so, say, that resembles nothing so much as the national convention of one of the old-line American Communist parties 80 or 90 years earlier — a small group of old men going through the motions of an earlier time, repeating decades-old slogans, voting on resolutions that matter to no one else on the planet and grimly trying to pretend that history hasn't left them sitting in the dust. In such a future, those astronomical observatories that haven't been stripped of metal by looters and left to the wind and rain might find a second life as homes for the very rich — it's easy to imagine the attendees at the convention I've just described muttering bitterly about the Chinese trillionaire who's just had the former Palomar Observatory remodeled into a mansion and is boasting to reporters from 2070's mass media about the spectacular view from his new home.

The point that needs to be grasped here is that the institutional structure of science — the archipelago of university departments, institutes and specialized facilities for research that provide the economic and practical framework for science as it's practiced today — faces massive challenges as we move forward into a world on the far side of progress. On the one hand, the raw fiscal burden of supporting that structure in an age of economic contraction and environmental payback will become increasingly difficult for any nation to meet. On the other, the emotional commitment of scientists to the civil religion of progress, and to an understanding of the purpose and goals of science that only makes sense in the context of that religion, places harsh burdens on any attempt to preserve that structure once popular faith in progress dissolves.

It might still be possible to maintain scientific research as a living tradition in the centuries immediately ahead of us. Still, it's crucial to realize that nothing guarantees the success of such a project. It's only because scientific research fills an essential role in the civil religion of progress that so few people can imagine a future in which funding for expensive research projects isn't available at all.

≈⚭≈

To make sense of the role of science in today's collective imagination, and thus of the likely impact of the collapse of the myth of progress on the future of science, it's going to be necessary to take what will look like a drastic detour and talk about the role of ritual theater in the world's religions. I don't know of a religious tradition on the planet that doesn't have examples of this very common practice. Modern societies are no exception to the rule. Those of my readers who grew up Christian, for example, and recall Nativity plays and Easter pageants from their childhoods already know as much about ritual theater as they'll need to know to grasp what follows.

Ritual theater doesn't follow the same rules as the secular drama that's found in today's playhouses, cineplexes and DVD racks. There are no surprises in ritual theater, no unexpected plot twists, no unfamiliar characters and for good reason. The point of ritual theater in a religious context is to enact whatever's seen as eternally true in the religious tradition that sponsors it. Depending on your religion, what's eternally true may be revealed in some specific historical event — say, the Buddha beneath the Bo tree or Christ on the cross — or in some recurring natural event — say, the cycle of the seasons — or it may be permanently outside of time, symbolized by myths which "never happened but always are." One way or another, some blend of folk imagination and the creative genius of individuals makes these accepted truths visible in ritual theater, which represents (literally, re-presents) the eternal in a form that everyone can experience.

There's a lot of variation between one religion's ritual theater and another's, but within any given tradition, the plot outline and the emotional reactions that are the point of the performance tend to be as stereotyped as a politician's campaign speech. Pick any of the early Greek tragedies — these were originally enacted at religious festivals in Athens and so are classic examples of ritual theater in more senses than one — and you can pretty much count on watching a proud and gifted individual have his life destroyed by the incomprehensible decrees of the gods. That was the structure of ancient Greek ritual drama, and the response, as Aristotle describes it, was an emotional catharsis of pity and terror in which the members of an ancient Greek audience reconciled themselves to their place in the cosmos as mortals subject to the awesome and inscrutable immortals.

It would have been unthinkable to Aeschylus or Sophocles to have a god pop up in the middle of the stage at the climax of the play and fix everything. What was utterly inappropriate in the early Greek ritual theater, though, became common in the later secular drama of the classical world, where *deus ex machina* — literally, the god out of the stage machinery — was so common as to become a catchphrase. Christian ritual theater, which emerged out of late classical drama, proceeded to take that experience as its central theme. What J.R.R. Tolkien in a brilliant essay called "eucatastrophe"[1] — the sudden, shattering reversal that transforms tragedy into triumph — thus became the core experience of Christian ritual theater, passed on via the mystery plays of the Middle Ages straight through to the passion plays and parochial school pageants of the present time.

Leap to the other end of the Old World and you'll find a completely different mode of ritual theater in the Noh drama of Japan. The most common story line among Noh plays has a wandering priest making his way through unfamiliar country. He happens on someone he takes for an ordinary village girl or some other perfectly natural person. As she sings and dances her story, though, it gradually becomes apparent that she is a supernatural being of some kind — a ghost, a demon, a spirit or a deity — whose destiny the priest may change through his own power and piety, or may simply witness. The whole drama serves to communicate the distinctive religious vision of Japanese folk culture in which the supernatural shimmers through the apparent solidity of the ordinary world like colors in shot silk.

Civil religions have their own traditions of ritual theater. Here in America, school pageants on George Washington's birthday and civic celebrations on the Fourth of July once routinely copied all the standard forms of religious ritual theater, complete with the utterly stereotyped plots and the predictable emotional reactions common throughout the genre. Tolerably often, though, the ritual theater of civil religions takes a less self-consciously dramatic form and gets acted out in some facsimile of real life: think of the show trials of Stalin's Russia, in which thousands of people were coerced into acting out the role of wicked dupes of the capitalists and were then applauded for their performances with a bullet to the brain.

The civil religion of progress by and large has kept its own ritual theater out of the realm of formal performance, but makes up for this by trying to enact its stereotyped dramas in every possible informal venue. Those of my readers who haven't been hiding under a rock since the days of Galileo already know the plot of those dramas, as they follow the mythology sketched out in Chapter Five right down to the finest details. They begin with a lone genius who shakes himself free of the prejudices and superstitions of the ages and thus manages to see some part of the world clearly for the first time. The dramatic action emerges out of the conflict between the lone genius and his (or, very rarely, her) less gifted contemporaries who defend those prejudices and superstitions against the efforts of the genius to upset the applecart of conventional thought.

The plot thus defined includes a few variations, mostly involving the end of the story. The genius may be condemned and killed by the outraged authorities of his time, only to be vindicated and glorified by future generations. He may struggle on gamely to the end of his life, ignored or denounced by all right-thinking people, and then be vindicated and glorified by future generations. Alternatively, he may triumph over the opposition by proving his case conclusively, and having vindicated himself, is then glorified by future generations. In each case, the emotional reaction expected from the audience is the same: identifying themselves with the future generations just mentioned, they are called on to glorify the great heroes of progress, to rejoice in the salvation from the prejudiced and superstitious past that these heroes have conferred on them and to wait expectantly for the even more wonderful things that future heroes of progress will inevitably bring the world in times to come.

A detail worth special attention here, though, is the debate between the lone genius and his prejudiced and superstitious adversaries that always, explicitly or implicitly, fills the middle act of the drama. There's no more thoroughly stereotyped scene in the whole field of ritual theater. The adversaries of progress have a set of standard lines assigned to them by the standard plot. They are supposed to point out that whatever idea or technology the lone genius is championing violates the immemorial order of the cosmos or the authoritative teachings of the past, to insist that whatever it is can't be true or won't work and to warn that if the idea is accepted or the technology put into general use, some kind of horrible fate will follow in short order.

The lone genius, in turn, is assigned a set of standard counterarguments to overcome these ceremonial talking points. He is supposed to say that the onward march of human knowledge has rendered the immemorial order of the cosmos and the authoritative teachings of the past obsolete, that whatever innovation he's championed is true or will work and that it will bring immense benefits to the human race in the years to come. Both sides recite their parts in the second act, fulfilling the requirements of the script, and in the third act the lone genius triumphs, posthumously or otherwise.

I've pointed out already that this stereotyped script has been incessantly pushed onto the history of thought by the popular culture of our age, even when it's been necessary to twist history and falsify facts to make it fit the storyline. It's important to recognize how great a distortion the ritual theater of progress has imposed on our sense of our own past, but it's at least as important to notice the ways in which the same ritual theater structures debates over science and technology here and now. The debates over evolution and the environment discussed in Chapter Five are as stereotyped and ineffectual as they are precisely because they follow, point for point, the plot I've just sketched out, and the speeches assigned to the adversaries of progress can be heard endlessly repeated by the proponents of creationism and environmentalism today.

It's probably worth noting here that the point of discussing science, technology and other holy symbols of the civil religion of progress is not limited to providing venues for the ritual theater of that faith. If fusion power and the Internet were purely spiritual realities — say, two of the blessings that the faithful could expect to receive after death in some kind of techno-heaven buzzing with starships, jetpacks and domed cities — that would be a different matter, but fusion reactors and the like are also expected to solve practical difficulties here on earth. That means that a discussion of their prospects arguably ought to extend beyond the limits of ritual theater and include points that aren't part of the ceremonial dialogue.

Whether a technology makes economic sense in a world of rapidly depleting resources and spiraling economic dysfunction is thus a valid concern, whether or not that concern conforms to the ritual theater of our time. If some future iteration of ITER finally gets a sustained fusion reaction going, that's an intriguing bit of experimental physics, but unless that event leads to the discovery of some commercially viable way to ignite and maintain such a reaction that costs a great deal less than $17 billion per reactor, that's all it is — and since every cheaper option has been tried in half a century of very well-funded experimentation, it's a safe bet that in fact, that's all it is.

It's not at all hard to imagine a future in which, let's say, excited physicists announce to the world that sustained nuclear fusion has finally been accomplished using some elaborate new reactor design an order of magnitude or so more complicated than ITER. Running the numbers, governments and utility companies calculate that, factoring in all possible economies of scale, each new fusion reactor would cost 100 times as much per kilowatt hour as a comparable fission reactor with consumer bills to match. Has the energy crisis been solved? Not in any sense meaningful in the real world.

In the real world, a technology has to be economically feasible to build and use, or it doesn't matter. It really is as simple as that. The galloping economic expansion of the age of cheap abundant energy now visible in history's rearview mirror made it possible to ignore that unwelcome reality for a time, or at least to pretend to ignore it — you'll notice that the grandiose plans to cover Manhattan with a dome and give it a year-round climate of 72 degrees and no rain, along with a great many other economically preposterous projects of the recent past, never even got to the detailed-blueprint stage.

The age of scarcity that's now upon us, though, draws a hard line under such fantasies. From now on into the foreseeable future, the first question that has to be asked about any technological project is "Can we afford to use it?" The second, which needs to be asked immediately after the first, is "Are there ways to do the same thing that cost less?" These questions may not be part of the ritual theater of the civil religion of progress, but I'd like to suggest that consoling true believers in that faith with assurances of the invincibility of their surrogate deity may be less important just now than dealing with the imminent impact of the end of abundance and the twilight of the Industrial Age.

There are any number of issues in the headlines these days that provide a solid object lesson in how questions not found in our current genre of ritual theater might be applied to the real world. Consider the attempts to keep the world's petroleum supply from tipping into decline by mining tar sands, hydrofracturing oil shales and pursuing other difficult and expensive unconventional oil projects. One of the major difficulties here, of course, is a great deal of money is being made off of these various projects by assorted Wall Street office fauna, and their efforts to keep the gravy train rolling for their benefit doubtless have quite a bit to do with the remarkable disregard for mere geological reality to be found in so much energy-industry propaganda these days.[2]

That sort of strained relationship with fact is a sufficiently standard feature of speculative bubbles that it ought to be high up there on the checklist of any connoisseur of financial lunacy. Those of my readers who recall the details of the late housing bubble will doubtless think of the enthusiasm shown then for what were called NINJA loans — that is, loans given to borrowers who had no income and no jobs or assets, but who would one and all, so bankers insisted with straight faces, pay back those loans religiously out of the money they were sure to make flipping properties. The same logic doubtless governs the equally earnest insistence that the ferocious depletion rates that afflict fracked wells simply don't matter, that kerogen shales like the Green River formation that have resisted every previous attempt to get oil out of them have suddenly transformed themselves into nice extractable oil shales for our benefit, and that the results of wells drilled in the best possible "sweet spots" in each formation must inevitably be repeated by every available well site in the region.

Here, as with the countless other examples that might be put on display by some Dickensian Spirit of Speculative Bubbles Past, the understandable desire to make a fast buck off other people's cluelessness might seem to offer an adequate explanation for the bumper crop of fatuous twaddle that's being pushed by the pundits and splashed around so freely by the media these days. Still, I've come to think that there's more going on here than the passion for emptying the pockets of chumps that sets the cold sick heart of Wall Street throbbing, and indeed that there's even more at work than our culture's habit of reenacting the traditional morality plays of the civil religion of progress in order to console the faithful in difficult times.

Plunge into the heart of the current quest to scrape the bottom of the planet's oil barrel, rather, and you'll find yourself face to face with a foredoomed attempt to maintain one of the core beliefs of the civil religion of progress in the teeth of all the evidence. The stakes here go far beyond making a bunch of financiers their umpteenth million, or providing believers in the myth of progress with a familiar ritual drama to bolster their faith; they cut straight to the heart of that faith and thus to some of the most fundamental presuppositions that are guiding today's industrial societies along their road to history's scrapheap.

⁂

Since the days of Sir Francis Bacon, whose writings served as the first draft of the modern mythology of progress, one of the central themes of that mythology has been the conquest of Nature by humanity — or rather, in the more revealing language of an earlier day, by Man. You aren't Man, in case you were wondering, and neither am I. Neither is Sir Francis Bacon, for that matter, nor anyone else who's ever lived or will ever live. This person called Man, rather, is a mythical hero who gives the civil religion of progress its central figure. Just as devout Christians participate vicariously in the life of Christ through the celebration of the sacraments and the seasons of the liturgical year, believers in progress are supposed to participate vicariously in Man's heroic journey from the caves to the stars by purchasing hot new products, and oohing and aahing appreciatively whenever the latest shiny technological trinket is unveiled by Man's lab-coated priesthood.

Man's destiny is to conquer Nature. That's his one and only job, according to the myth, and when Man's not doing that, he's not doing anything worthwhile at all. Read any of the standard histories of Man written by true believers in the civil religion of progress, and you'll see that societies and eras that devoted their energies to art, music, religion, literature, or anything else you care to name other than extending Man's dominion over Nature are dismissed as irrelevant to Man's history, when they're not critiqued outright for falling down on the job.[3]

You may be thinking by this point, dear reader, that a belief system that likes to portray humanity as a tyrant and conqueror rightfully entitled to view the entire cosmos as lebensraum may not be particularly sensible, or for that matter particularly sane. You may well be right, too, but I'd like to focus on a somewhat more restricted point: according to this way of looking at things, Nature is not supposed to put up more than a pro forma struggle or a passive resistance. Above all, once any part of Nature is conquered, it's supposed to stay conquered and do what it's told thereafter — and of course that's where the trouble creeps in, because a great many of the things we habitually lump together as Nature are refusing to go along with the script.

Examples come to mind by the dozens, but one of the most significant and frightening just now is the collapse of the most important health revolution of modern times, the conquest (that word again) of bacterial disease by antibiotics. I'm not sure how many of my readers realize what an immense change in human life followed Alexander Fleming's 1928 discovery that a substance excreted by bread mold killed most bacteria without harming human cells.

A century ago, dysentery and bacterial pneumonia were leading causes of death in most industrial countries, killing far more people than heart disease or cancer, and the odds of living from birth to age five had an uncomfortable resemblance to a throw of the dice even in wealthy countries. Penicillin and the antibiotics that followed it changed that decisively, enabling doctors to stop bacterial diseases in their tracks. It's because of antibiotics that I'm here to write this book; the scarlet fever that had me flat on my back for weeks when I was seven years old would almost certainly have killed me if antibiotics hadn't been available.

Outside the public health and infectious disease fields, most people remain serenely convinced that the relative freedom from bacterial disease that's characterized the recent past in the industrial world is destined to remain fixed in place for the rest of time. Within those fields, by contrast, that comfortable conviction finds few takers.[4] Penicillin, the antibiotic that saved my life in 1969, won't even slow down most microbes now. Diseases that used to yield readily to an injection or two now have to be treated with complex cocktails of increasingly toxic antibiotics, and every year more pathogens turn up that are resistant to some, most, or all available antibiotics.

There's plenty of blame to go around, at least for those who want to play the blame game. It's been common since the 1950s for physicians to prescribe antibiotics for conditions antibiotic therapy can't treat — for example, the common cold. It's been equally common since the 1950s for livestock farms to give their animals daily doses of antibiotics, since (for complex biochemical reasons) this causes the animals to gain weight more quickly, and thus be worth more money at slaughtering time. Both these bad habits helped give bacteria the widest possible range of opportunities to develop resistance. Still, these and other contributing factors simply help feed the main issue, which is that bacterial evolution didn't come to a sudden stop when Fleming started paying attention to bread mold.

Evolution through natural selection, as noted above, is the process by which living things adapt themselves to environmental changes. It works through individual organisms, but its effects are not limited to the individual scale. In the case of the spread of antibiotic resistance among microbes, there are at least three patterns at work. First, microbes are being selected for their resistance to individual antibiotics. Second, as new antibiotics are brought out to replace old ones, microbes are being selected for their ability to develop resistance to one antibiotic after another as quickly as possible. Finally, the pressure exerted on the entire microbial biosphere by the pervasive presence of antibiotics in the modern environment is giving a huge selective advantage to species that have the ability to exchange genes for resistance with other species.

The results are being documented in increasingly worried articles in public health journals. A large and growing number of pathogenic microbes these days are already resistant to the antibiotics that used to treat them; new antibiotics brought onto the market start running into problems with resistant bacteria in a fraction of the time that was once necessary for resistance to emerge; and the transfer of antibiotic resistance from one species to another is becoming an increasingly troubling problem. The possibility of a return to pre-1928 conditions, when a simple bacterial infection could readily turn into a death sentence and most families buried at least one child before the age of five, is seeing serious discussion in the professional literature.

Such worries, though, are falling on deaf ears outside the public health and infectious-disease fields. There's a mordant irony in the reason why, though I suspect it's not often relished. Faced with the prospect of the end of the antibiotic era and the return of bacterial illnesses as major threats to public health, most politicians, like the people they're supposed to serve, respond with an overfamiliar sentence: "Oh, I'm sure they'll think of something." The increasingly frantic efforts of researchers to find new antibiotics and stay ahead of the remorselessly rising tide of microbial resistance get no more attention than the equally frantic efforts, say, of drilling companies to find petroleum deposits to make up for the increasingly rapid depletion of existing oil fields.

In both cases, and in any number of others, the myth of progress is the most important barrier in the way of a meaningful response to our predicament. According to the myth, we can't go backwards to any condition encountered in the past. What Man conquers is supposed to stay conquered, so he can continue his ever-victorious journey from the caves to the stars. It's unthinkable, in terms of the myth, that the supposed conquest of some part of nature — say, bacterial disease — might represent nothing more than a temporary advantage that the pressures of natural selection will soon erase.

Thus when this latter turns out to be the case, those believers in the religion of progress who aren't forced to confront such awkward realities in their work or their daily lives simply repeat the sacred words "Oh, I'm sure they'll think of something," to invoke the blessing of the great god Progress on His only begotten son, Man, and then proceed to act as though nothing could possibly go wrong. The difficulty, of course, is that an embarrassingly large portion of the territory supposedly conquered by Man over the last three centuries is showing an awkward propensity to ignore Man's supposed overlordship and do what it wants instead.

The much-ballyhooed Green Revolution of the mid-twentieth century is another case in point. The barrage of fertilizers and poisons the proponents of that movement turned on agriculture won a temporary advantage over the hard subsistence limits of earlier eras, but it was only temporary. The reckless use of artificial fertilizers turned out to have drastic downsides, while the poisons drove insects and weeds into exactly the same frenzy of intensive natural selection that antibiotics brought to the microbial world. Insects and weeds don't reproduce as quickly or swap genetic material with the same orgiastic abandon as microbes, but the equivalent changes are happening at a slightly slower pace; one of the dirty secrets of conventional agriculture is that herbicide resistance among weeds and pesticide resistance among insects and other agricultural pests are spreading rapidly, erasing the short-term gains of the Green Revolution while leaving the long-term costs in lost topsoil and poisoned water tables to be paid by generations to come.[5]

Farmers faced with resistant weeds and pests, like physicians faced with resistant microbes, are turning to increasingly desperate measures to get the same results that their equivalents decades ago got with much less trouble. That's exactly the situation that's driving the current quest for unconventional oil reserves, too. Back in the glory days of petroleum exploration and discovery, drillers could punch a well a few hundred feet into the ground and hit oil; now it takes hugely expensive deep-water drilling, tar sands extraction, or hydrofracturing of shale and other "tight oil" deposits to keep the liquid fuel flowing, and the costs keep rising year after year.

The implication that has to be faced is that the age of petroleum, and everything that unfolded from it, was exactly the same sort of temporary condition as the age of antibiotics and the Green Revolution. Believers in the religion of progress like to think that Man conquered distance and made the world smaller by inventing internal combustion engines, aircraft and an assortment of other ways to burn plenty of petroleum products. What actually happened, though, was that drilling rigs and a few other technologies gave our species a temporary boost of cheap liquid fuel to play with, and we proceeded to waste most of it on the assumption that Nature's energy resources had been conquered and could be expected to fork over another cheap abundant energy source as soon as we wanted one.

That follows logically from the myth, but it doesn't follow in reality. Instead, the temporary advantage our species gained by exploiting all that cheap, easily accessible petroleum is being brought to an end by factors even more implacable than the constant pressure of natural selection on niche boundaries: the simple facts that a finite planet by definition only contains a finite amount of any given resource and that deposits of every resource are distributed according to the power law — the rule, consistently true across an impressive range of fields, that larger deposits are much less common than smaller ones. Those factors are not going away; the fact that Wall Street office fauna are shoveling smoke about, ahem, "limitless amounts of oil and natural gas" may make them their umpteenth million and keep the clueless neatly sedated for a few more years, but it's not going to do a thing to change the hard facts of the predicament that's closing around us all.

Seen in this light, the mythology of Man's conquest of Nature bears an uncomfortable resemblance to a certain other campaign of conquest launched to the sound of blaring brass bands and overconfident proclamations in the not too distant past. Like German civilians tuning in to news broadcasts from Berlin in the heady summer of 1941, people in the world's industrial nations have taken in any number of proclamations about Man's latest glorious victories in the war against Nature. The conquest of disease, the conquest of hunger, the conquest of air and space and distance itself — is there *any* scientific or technological success, however temporary, that hasn't been praised in those fatuous terms? — each had its 15 minutes of fame as Man's heroic legions of science and progress pursued their allegedly invincible *Drang nach Sternen.*

Some time ago, though, the content of the propaganda broadcasts began to change, though their tone did not. Commercial fusion power seems to have played much the same role in Man's conquest of Nature that Moscow played in that other campaign, the goal that seemed almost in reach time and again, but never quite fell into the hands so greedily outstretched for it. Other campaigns meant to push the frontiers of Man's dominion further out into Nature's unconquered territory have had equally mixed luck, and even the immense effort that put an American flag on the Moon turned out to have no more influence on the course of events than the rather less challenging campaign by an SS mountain battalion that put a different flag on the summit of the highest mountain in the Caucasus range.

It's what followed that relative stalemate, though, that's of importance here. Beginning in 1943, the German civilians tuning in to those radio broadcasts from Berlin had to deal with an increasing burden of cognitive dissonance, as the heroic battles and triumphant victories breathlessly announced by Goebbels' acolytes stopped moving eastwards on the map and started shifting back toward the west. The forces that had been sweeping everything before them in the suburbs of Moscow were now doing the same thing in the vicinity of Smolensk, with no explanation of the change. Nor was there any clearer explanation to be had as Germany's glorious victories shifted steadily westwards, past Minsk and Warsaw and Breslau, until nervous listeners in the Berlin suburbs, just before the broadcasts stopped for good, could hear the sound of artillery rattling their own windows.

The question that all would-be conquerors need to ask themselves, in other words, is what will happen if their planned campaign of conquest fails. None of the seventeenth-century thinkers who played a role in launching humanity on its assault on Nature seems to have posed that question, even in private, much less tried to think through the answers. I'd encourage my readers to have this in mind when the latest reports of glorious victories place these latter more and more often in territory that was supposedly conquered in earlier campaigns. I'd also encourage them, to push the metaphor a step further, to think about what terms of surrender might be demanded of us when Man's grand attempt to conquer Nature ends in defeat.

Seven

Life Preservers for Mermaids

T HE FANTASY OF MAN'S SUPPOSED CONQUEST OF NATURE, though it's played so central a role in the thinking of our age, is not quite the only way that people in the contemporary industrial world try to make sense of the relationship between humanity and the biosphere. Over the last few centuries, and especially in recent decades, a radically different vision has been spreading through the crawlspaces of our culture: a vision that responds to Nature not as an enemy to be defeated and enslaved, but as an unfailing source of comfort, delight and awe. These conflicting visions have become the two sides of a fault line along which the tectonic pressures of the collective imagination are pressing toward crisis.

This fault line is one I've been observing for quite some time now. It so happens that my unpaid day job as the head of a contemporary Druid order brings me into contact with a tolerably large number of people who fall more generally on the latter side of the division I've just traced: whose sense of wonder and instinct for reverence are far more readily roused by the order of Nature, and their own necessary participation in that order, than it is by the overturning of natural order that plays so crucial a role in the theist and civil religions of mainstream Western culture. It also happens that I find myself consistently on that side of the division I've just traced. Reflecting on my own sense of alienation from the conventional religiosity of our time and on what I've learned from the many other people who experience a similar alienation for similar reasons, I've come to believe that what's going on is the emergence, for the first time in more than two thousand years, of a genuinely new religious sensibility in the Western world.

A religious sensibility isn't a religion. It's the substructure of perceptions, emotions and intuitions from which religions draw their appeal to the human heart, and to which religions owe both the deep similarities that link them to other faiths of the same general age and historical origin and the equally deep divides that separate them from faiths of different ages and origins. Between the tendency of modern religions to insist loudly on their uniqueness, on the one hand, and the opposing tendency of modern irreligion to run all religions together into a formless blur on the other, the concept of distinct religious sensibilities is a difficult one for many people nowadays to grasp. The best way to make sense of it is to glance back over the emergence of the religious sensibility that currently dominates the Western world.

If a modern visitor had the chance to survey the religious landscape of the western half of Eurasia and North Africa two or three millennia ago — unless she happened to go looking in some very obscure corners — she would find very few similarities to the religious institutions, practices and ideas of today. People in those days didn't belong to congregations that met regularly inside buildings to pray together; questions concerning life after death weren't considered particularly important to religion, and nobody wasted time waiting for the end of the world. Sacred scriptures in the modern sense were distinctly rare, next to nobody claimed that a god had created the universe, and even the most devout believers in one deity freely conceded that other deities existed and deserved the reverence of their own worshippers.

The core religious institution of that era was the temple, a house for the deity rather than a meeting place for worshippers — rituals in the old temple cults took place out in front in the open air, not inside — and the core ceremony was sacrifice, in which worshippers invited the presence of a deity for a feast and quite literally "killed the fatted calf" to supply the main course for divine and human participants alike. (Food storage technology being what it was at that time, that was the way you provided meat for any honored guest.) The status of priests varied from one place to another, but in most places they were elected or hereditary officials set apart from the laity only in the most pro forma sense, and you didn't have to be a priest to perform a sacrifice.

Behind all the richness and diversity of the religious life of the time was a distinctive sensibility, one that saw the cosmos as a community to which gods and men both belonged. The modern notion of equality had no more place in the cosmos thus conceived than it did in any other ancient community, but the sharp differences in rights and responsibilities didn't prevent every member of the community from having a share in its collective life and benefits.

That sensibility once had the force of revelation. The Jews, for example, were late adopters of the temple cult, and the awe and wonder palpable in Solomon's prayer at the consecration of the temple of Jerusalem[1] convey something of the power of a religious vision in which gods could "in very deed dwell with men on the earth." It was by way of that emotional power that the sensibility of the temple cults superseded a still older sensibility whose traces can just be made out in the oldest written strata of Western religious traditions.

Still, by 600 BCE or so, the initial power of that vision had long since settled into a comfortable routine of thought and practice, and by 600 BCE or so, in turn, the first stirrings of a new and very different religious sensibility were starting to appear. Orphism in the Greek-speaking communities of the Mediterranean basin and the earliest forms of Buddhism in India rejected the celebration of life's good things in the community of gods and men and offered in its place a

radically different vision — a vision of salvation from the natural world
and the human condition, available to an elite few willing to embrace a
life of radical austerity and spiritual practice.

Then and long thereafter, this was a fringe phenomenon that appealed only to a tiny minority of intellectuals. Most people either
believed and practiced as their great-grandparents had, or settled into
fashionably up-to-date materialist philosophies that discarded belief in
gods without stirring the smallest fraction of a cubit from the religious
sensibility that underlay the traditional faiths. Still, the new sensibility
spread into popular culture as the years passed.

You can track its spread by the way that robust traditional celebrations of human sexuality gave way to shamefaced discomfort with the
facts of reproduction. Many Greek religious processions, for example,
carried large wooden penises as emblems of the gods' gifts of fertil-
ity and delight. By the time Greek philosophy was a going concern,
intellectuals were muttering excuses about symbols of the abstract
progenitive power of the divine principles to justify to themselves a
tradition with which they were obviously uncomfortable. Attitudes
toward sexuality of the sort that we now call "puritanical" found an
increasingly public voice as the new sensibility spread, though here
again most people simply rolled their eyes and did what they and their
great-great-grandparents had always done.

The great breakthrough of the new religious sensibility took place
when three popular religious movements — Christianity, Islam and
Mahayana Buddhism — democratized the older vision of salvation for
an elite by proclaiming faith in a uniquely holy person and his doctrine
as a valid substitute for the lifelong austerities and spiritual disciplines
of the older tradition. The shift was never total; ordinary members of
all three movements were expected to take up certain practices and
austerities of the sort that could be pursued alongside an ordinary lifestyle, and all three also evolved roles for those who aspired to the total
immersion of the older tradition (monks and nuns in Christianity and
Buddhism, Sufis in Islam). By the time these traditions found their

voice, the new sensibility had become sufficiently widespread and ·
popular that throwing open the doors of salvation to all and sundry
got an enthusiastic response.

⚜

It's indicative of how deeply the new sensibility had percolated
through the society of the age that by the time Christianity began its
final rise to power in the Roman world, its Pagan rivals were just as
deeply committed to the idea of salvation from the human condition.
As I sit here at my desk, for instance, I'm looking at a copy of *On the
Nature of the Universe* by Ocellus Lucanus, a philosophical treatise
probably written in the second or third century before the Common
Era. Ocellus, like many of the cutting-edge thinkers of his age, wanted
to challenge the popular notion that the cosmos had a beginning and
might therefore have an end. That was part of a broader agenda — one
that's left significant traces in many contemporary currents of thought
— that dismissed everything that came into being and passed away
again as illusion and tried to find a reality outside of the realm of time
and change.

That commitment led to strange convictions. The fourth chapter of
Ocellus' treatise, for example, is devoted to proving that human beings
ought to have sex.[2] If, as Ocellus argues, the cosmos is eternal, it needs
to remain perpetually stocked with its full complement of living things,
and therefore human beings ought to keep on reproducing themselves
— as long as they don't enjoy the process, that is. Back of this distinctly
odd argument lies the emergence, then under way, of one of the more
distinctive doctrines of the new sensibility: the conviction that biological pleasures are always suspect and can be permitted only when
the actions that bring them also have some morally justifiable purpose.

In the generations following Ocellus' time, that same pervasive
distrust of sexuality became standard in intellectual circles across the
Mediterranean world, in modes ranging from the relatively reasonable
to the arguably psychotic.[3] Since Christianity inevitably drew most

of its early converts from people who were unsatisfied by the robust life-affirming traditional faiths the people of that time had inherited from their far from puritanical ancestors, it's hardly a surprise that Christian teachings and institutions ended up absorbing a substantial helping of the attitudes that arose out of the rising religious sensibility of the time.

Every human cultural phenomenon is complex, contested and polyvalent, and the religious landscape of the post-Classical Western world is no exception to this rule. Religious attitudes toward sex in that setting ranged all the way from the Free Spirit movement in late medieval Europe, which indulged in orgies as a sign that its members had returned to Eden, all the way to the Skoptsii of early modern Russia, who castrated themselves as a shortcut to perfect purity. Still, the average fell further toward the puritanical side of the scale than anything that could be found in the older sensibility of temple-cult and fertility-worship.

That shift was as clearly evident outside of Christianity as within it; the writings of late Pagan intellectuals such as Iamblichus and the Emperor Julian show as much discomfort with sexuality and physical embodiment as do those of their Christian contemporaries. What differentiated the two was simply that the Pagan writers defended the older, elitist conception of salvation for those who earned it by austerity and spiritual practice, against the new vision of salvation by faith for all, and made common cause with what was left of the old temple cults because those had long been a focus of Christian animosity. This rearguard action failed, though its literary remains became a lasting resource for those who never did fit in with the new sensibility — or, more to the point, who disagreed with the specific institutional forms that the new sensibility took in its cultural and historical contexts.

A religious sensibility, after all, is not a monolithic thing, and its expressions are even less so. In Europe and the European diaspora, the division between more elitist and more democratic visions of salvation became an enduring fault line, to be joined by the divide between centralized and collective concepts of spiritual authority, on the one hand, and between more this-worldly and more other-worldly concepts of salvation on the other. Fault lines of comparable importance, though radically different, ran through the older religious sensibility as well and can be traced in the very different religious sensibilities of regions outside western Eurasia and the Mediterranean basin.

For that matter, it's entirely possible for older religious sensibilities and their institutional forms to find ways to survive in the interstices of the new. Consider the way that Shinto, a temple-centered polytheism of the classic kind, has been able to hold its own for more than fifteen centuries in Japan side by side with Mahayana Buddhism. The repeated revivals of Pagan worship in the Western world from the late Middle Ages to the present suggests that the same thing could as well have happened in Europe and the European diaspora, if violent intolerance along religious lines had been less of an issue there. Even when a great majority of people take the presuppositions of a given sensibility for granted as unchallengeable truths, there are always those who don't fit in, whose personal sense of the sacred pulls them in directions outside the accepted religious sensibility of their age: some toward sensibilities that have been dominant in the past, others toward sensibilities that may potentially play the same role in the future.

It's important, too, not to impose the traditional folk mythology of progress onto these shifts from one religious sensibility to another. Of course it's been a rhetorical strategy common to many modern religions to do exactly this and to portray the replacement of the old temple cults by the new religions of salvation as a great step forward in the onward march of human progress. Aside from its reliance on a failing mythology, that strategy runs serious risks for the traditions that attempt to make use of it. There's always the danger that some more recently minted theist religion will play the same card and argue that just as Classical Paganism was replaced by Christianity, say, Christianity ought to be replaced by the latest, hottest, newest, most up-to-date revelation, whatever that happens to be this week.

There's also the considerably greater danger that atheists will make exactly the same argument. This latter has been a valuable weapon in the atheist arsenal for centuries now, and it gets much of its power by drawing on the same arguments monotheist religions used against their polytheist predecessors. An edged joke common in Neopagan circles these days phrases the issue concisely: when you've already disbelieved in all the other gods, what's one more?

Still, the contemporary quarrels between atheists and theists, like the equally fierce quarrels between the different theist religions of salvation, take place within a shared sensibility. It's indicative, for example, that theists and atheists agree on the vast importance of what individuals believe about basic religious questions such as the existence of God. It's just that to the theists, having the right beliefs brings salvation from eternal hellfire, while to the atheists, having the right beliefs brings salvation from the ignorant and superstitious past that fills the place of perdition in their mythos.

That obsession with individual belief is one of the distinctive features of the current Western religious sensibility. Different sensibilities define different issues as central or peripheral; in the heyday of the old temple cults, for instance, while acts of impiety toward sacred objects or rites would earn a messy death in short order, nobody cared about what opinions individuals might have about details of religious doctrine. Thinkers could redefine the gods any way they wished so long as they continued to show proper respect for holy things and holy seasons.

The hostilities between Christianity and contemporary atheism, like those between Christianity and Islam, are thus expressions of something like sibling rivalry. Salvation from the natural world and the human condition remains the core premise (and thus also the most important promise) of all these faiths, whether that salvation takes the supernatural form of resurrection followed by eternal life in heaven, on the one hand, or the allegedly more natural form of limitless progress, the conquest of poverty, illness and death, and the great leap outwards to an endless future among the stars.

To a growing number of people nowadays, however, promises
of salvation from the natural world and the human condition fail to
evoke the emotional responses they get from participants in the older
religious sensibility. It's not merely that these promises no longer ring
true, though in many cases that's also an issue; it's that they no longer
have any appeal. What stirs awe and wonder in these people, rather, is
a sense of belonging and of participation in the great cycles of Nature,
an awareness of oneness with life that does not shrink in terror from
life's natural completion in death. What inspires them is not the hope
of a final separation from the realities of nature, life, history and time,
but a conscious and delighted participation in these realities — not the
promise of salvation, but the reality of homecoming.

⚜

The emergence of this new religious sensibility has been, as such
things always are, a gradual process. Historian of religions Catherine
Albanese, in her useful 1990 study *Nature Religion in America*, has
traced it back in American religious life to colonial times, and its roots
in older European cultures go back considerably further still. That said,
it seems to me that the last few decades have seen the new religious
sensibility approach something like a critical mass. It's become much
more common than it once was for me to encounter other people who,
as I do, find more cause for reverence in the curve of a grass blade in
the wind or the dance of energies through an ecosystem than in the un-
substantiated claims of past miracles offered by most of today's theist
religions or the equally dubious promises of future miracles made so
freely by the civil religion of progress.

   If I'm right, and the new religious sensibility I've outlined will play
a significant role in the religious imagination of the Western world in
the decades and centuries to come, a case could be made that its emergence is timely. More than any other single factor, the civil religion of
progress helped to drive the weird astigmatism of the collective imagination that convinces so many people that the right response to the

converging crises of our age is to do even more of what got us in trouble in the first place — as though the only way to get out of a blind alley
is to keep stomping on the accelerator in the hope that the brick wall
ahead must eventually give way.

Ecologist Lynn White pointed out years ago, in a famous essay we'll
be discussing shortly,[4] that the origins of our environmental crisis are
deeply entangled with the religious sensibility of salvation and the beliefs and institutional forms that emerged from that sensibility. Getting
a clear sense of how that entanglement happened and how a different religious sensibility might help to unravel it can offer some useful
insights. Religious sensibilities have an interesting property, though:
they're hard to define with any degree of precision, but remarkably
easy to recognize in practice. It's a little like the old joke about how you
know that an elephant's gotten into your refrigerator. Like the telltale
footprints in the butter dish, the traces left by a given religious sensibility are hard to miss.

The sensibility that seized the imagination of the Western world
after 600 BCE, and that has begun to lose its grip only in our time, is no
exception to this rule. I've already talked about its distinctive central
theme, the passionate insistence that human beings deserve more than
nature, history and the human condition are prepared to give them, and
that there must be some way to escape from the trammels of humanity's
ordinary existence and break free into infinity and eternity. There are
plenty of other tracks in the butter dish of Western culture, for that matter, but the one I want to discuss here is as simple as it is revealing: the
spatial direction in which, according to the sensibility we're discussing,
the way out of the human condition is most likely to be found.

To the cultures of the modern West, it seems self-evident that the
only possible location for heaven is up, and plenty of people assume that
that's universal among human beings. It isn't, not by a long shot. To the
ancient Greeks, for example, the gods and goddesses lived in various
corners of the world — some of them lived on Mount Olympus, a mid-
sized mountain in Thessaly, but Poseidon was normally to be found in

the ocean, Pan in the woodlands of Arcadia, Hades in the underworld and so on; when Zeus wanted to hold a council, he had to send a god or goddess around to summon them all to Olympus. In Shinto, the polytheist religion of Japan, some of the kami live in *Takama no Hara*, the Plain of High Heaven, but others dwell on earth, and every year in the month corresponding to October, they all travel to the Izumo shrine in western Japan and are not to be found elsewhere. The old Irish paradise, Tir na nOg, was on the sea floor of the Atlantic somewhere off west of Ireland — well, I could go on for quite some time with comparable examples.

Within the sensibility that's now fading out across the Western world, by contrast, the route to heaven was by definition a line pointing straight up from the Earth's surface. I want to stress here that this is part of the religious sensibility of an age — that is, a pattern of emotions and images in the collective imagination — rather than a necessary part of the theist and civil religions that existed in that setting and thus were shaped by that sensibility. It's not too hard, in fact, to find ways in which the teachings of these religions were manhandled, sometimes very roughly, to make room in them for the images and emotions that the sensibility of the age demanded.

Here's an example. In the New Testament, the two gospels that describe what later came to be called the Ascension of Jesus describe the event in very simple terms. Mark says "he was received up into heaven," while Luke says "he was parted from them, and carried up into heaven," and "he was taken up; and a cloud received him out of their sight."[5] Christian friends who know their way around theology assure me that heaven is a wholly spiritual state or condition of being, which is no more above the earth than it is, say, northeast of Las Vegas. The pressure exerted by the religious sensibility of the last two millennia, though, is such that the Ascension has nearly always been portrayed as an exercise in levitation.

This has not uncommonly been taken in a very literal manner. It so happens, for example, that Christian symbolism plays a central role in some degrees of Freemasonry, and members of the Knight Templar branch of the York Rite of Masonry celebrate an Ascension Day service annually. In the Appalachian town where I live, the century-old Masonic lodge has an extraordinary early twentieth-century trompe l'oeil painting that plays a part in that service. It's a landscape view of Jerusalem from the Mount of Olives; the Temple is below, with the rest of the city around it, and the Judean landscape reaching away into the distance. The foreground scene on the Mount of Olives is painted on a piece of metal, a little in front of the canvas background, and there are clouds handled the same way at the top of the painting.

There in front, on the Mount of Olives, Jesus stands among his disciples. At the right moment of the ceremony, one of the brethren pulls on a hidden string, and the figure of Jesus rises up from the circle of disciples and soars slowly into the air, rising straight up until he's lost to sight behind the clouds. It's a remarkably powerful image. You can readily imagine the disciples staring openmouthed at the miracle, and people down below in the streets of Jerusalem catching a glimpse of the sight and thinking, good heavens, that looks like a man rising up into the sky!

I don't know of a better example of the way the collective imagination of the modern world shifted gears than when Sputnik I broke free of the atmosphere and opened the Space Age. Until then, the top of the atmosphere might as well have been a sheet of iron, as the Egyptians thought it was. (Their logic was impeccable: polished iron is blue, and so is the sky; iron is strong and heatproof, and the sky would need to be both to deal in order to support the boat named Millions of Years on which Ra the sun god does his daily commute; besides, the only iron they knew came from meteorites, which they sensibly interpreted as stray chunks of sky that had fallen to earth. Many of our theories about nature will likely seem much less reasonable from the perspective of the far future.)

It's an extraordinary experience to go back and read what sensible people in the first half of the twentieth century thought of the claims then being retailed by the small minority who dreamed of going to the Moon and the other planets. Outer space — take a moment to think about the implications of that conventional phrase! — was to most people an abstraction, not a place, and when the Moon and Mars weren't just lights in the sky, they served as convenient new labels for fairyland. Equally, the idea that human machines or human beings, might someday pop through the atmosphere into that "space outside" was raw material for fairy tales.

Nor were the fairy tales slow to appear. Science fiction provided them and ended up playing a remarkably important role in shaping the collective imagination of our age, even when it was considered the last word in lowbrow reading. The civil religion of progress needed a mythic image of salvation from nature, history and the human condition before it could break loose from the competition and become the established religion of our time. Science fiction provided that, and in the process underwent a massive transformation of its own. Until the early 1940s, science fiction was still what it had been in the time of H.G. Wells and Jules Verne, a literature that explored the whole gamut of imaginable technological advances. Thereafter, it fixated more and more precisely on one specific suite of imagined technologies — rocket ships capable of traveling into outer space — and the central image of lift-off, man rising to heaven on a pillar of flame, became a core religious icon of the church of progress.

※〇◎〇※

The close similarity between this image and the ascension of Jesus is no accident. As already noted, civil religions derive their core imagery and emotional tone from the theist religions they replace, and the image of man's ascension into space took on the same role in the religion of progress that Jesus' ascension into heaven has in Christianity. What SF writer Arthur C. Clarke called, in the title of a hugely popular nonfiction book of his, *The Promise of Space* was the precise equivalent — or as precise an equivalent as a materialist and anthropolatrous civil religion could manage — to the promise of salvation at the heart of Christian faith.

Listen to those of today's cornucopian true believers who don't simply put their faith in the endless prolongation of business as usual, and it's rarely difficult to hear the ringing voice of the Christian evangelist coming through the verbiage about limitless energy sources, new worlds for mankind and the rest of it. How many times, dear reader, have you heard the great leap upward into space described as humanity's mission, its destiny, even its sole excuse for existing in the first place? How many times have you read enthusiastic claims about space-based manufacturing, orbital colonies and the like that assume as a matter of course that benefits will outweigh costs and difficulties will inevitably be overcome, because, well, going into space is humanity's mission, its destiny, etc.?

Now it so happens that there's a very good reason to doubt these claims and, in particular, to challenge the notion that orbital colonies, settlements on Mars and the rest of it will inevitably prosper if we just find the quadrillions of dollars necessary to pay for them and the infrastructure necessary to build them in the first place. In an article published in *Nature* in 1997, a team of economists headed by Richard Costanza set out to calculate how much value is contributed to the global economy by the Earth's natural systems; their midrange estimates works out to an annual contribution roughly three times the size of the world's gross domestic product.[6] Put another way, of every dollar's worth of goods and services consumed by human beings each year, around 75 cents are provided free of charge by nature, and only 25 cents have to be paid for by human economic activity.

That immense contribution to human well-being — call it the "biosphere dividend" — isn't available anywhere else in the solar system. Even if Titan, say, has a biosphere of its own, its version of that dividend will apply only to life forms who enjoy sipping liquid methane and gazing at the bright orange sky on a balmy -290-degree afternoon, not to human beings. Here on Earth, human beings get air to breathe, water to drink, shelter from radiation, topsoil in which to grow crops and a dizzying array of other goods and services at no charge from the planetary system. Anywhere else, all these things have to be provided by human labor and require constant inputs of resources that human beings must also provide. That burden somehow gets left out of the sort of glowing rhetoric so often circulated among true believers in progress.

Such arguments have little impact on those who believe. Still, civil religions are considerably more vulnerable to disproof than the theist religions they supplant, in that they belong wholly to the world of ordinary experience and are far more difficult to uphold in the face of ordinary experience than their theist cousins. When advances in rocket science made it impossible to ignore the fact that what was up there above the clouds had nothing in common with heaven, Christians all over the industrial world recalled that most schools of Christian theology define heaven, as already noted, as a spiritual state or condition rather than a physical place at high altitude. Long-established habits of thought had to be changed, to be sure, but those habits didn't touch the core commitments of the faith.

The civil religion of progress didn't have the same advantage, since its core commitments were supposed to manifest in the world of ordinary experience, not in a spiritual condition inaccessible to any eyes but those of faith. Once the religion of progress embraced the fairy-tale logic of science fiction and set out, like Jack climbing the beanstalk, to find the giant's palace of its dreams somewhere up there in the sky, it was vulnerable to catastrophic disproof — and catastrophic disproof is what it got, too, though I'm not at all sure the believers have yet noticed just what it was that hit them.

The vulnerability here was precisely its dependence on borrowed imagery from the theist faiths it supplanted. Decades of science fiction primed the collective imagination of the Western world to see the ascent from earth to space as an ascension from earth to heaven, a passage out of ordinary reality into something wholly other — even if that "wholly other" too often consisted of nothing better than the sort of tacky adventure fantasy that so many SF authors splashed across a galaxy of wholly forgettable imaginary worlds. The torrent of propaganda and pageantry the United States invested in the Space Race against Russia helped feed the sense of expectancy and brought it to a climax that summer day in 1969 when Neil Armstrong stepped down a spidery ladder onto the surface of the Moon.

After the speeches and the TV specials and the ticker-tape parades were done with, though, something very different began to whisper through the crawlspaces of the industrial world's collective imagination — something that could be summed up fairly neatly as "Was that all?" We went to the Moon, not once but repeatedly, and every trip made it harder to ignore the fact that the Moon wasn't wholly other at all. It wasn't fairyland. It was monotonous gray desert without air, water or life, and the only thing you could see there that was of interest to anybody but a handful of scientists was the extraordinary blue-and-white sphere of Earth hanging motionless in the black and starless sky.

To make matters worse, that's more or less what orbiters and landers found everywhere else in the solar system, too. Mars, the scene of countless fantasies since the dawn of science fiction, turned out to have a remarkable resemblance to the less interesting corners of Nevada, without even rattlesnakes or poisonous scorpions to lend it a bit of human interest. Every world in the solar system that human spacecraft reached offered the same less than overwhelming spectacle: sand, scattered rocks and basically nothing else.

Even if Mars had turned out to have some analogue of blue-green algae huddled on the underside of the occasional damp rock, even if the Huygens lander on Titan had spotted unmistakably biological growths basking in the dim glow from the distant sun, a few space missions and a few more National Geographic specials later, the same reaction would inevitably have followed in due time, because the emotions and fantasies that gathered around the promise of space had nothing to do with what was actually out there in the solar system. They had everything to do, rather, with images and ideas of salvation and transcendence that had been surreptitiously borrowed from older theist religions and applied to the physical universe where they turned out to be woefully out of place.

The difficulty here is as simple as it is insuperable: you can't actually transcend nature, history and the human condition by riding a rocket to the Moon, to Mars, or even to some hypothetical exoplanet circling Proxima Centauri, any more than you can do it by riding a cross-country bus to Nevada. You can pretend that this is an option so long as no one actually makes the attempt. Once the goal actually comes within sight, though, the gap between the misplaced hopes and the mundane realities becomes a chasm that even the most enthusiastic true believers have trouble leaping across.

Ironically, a close reading of science fiction could have given warning of that chasm well in advance of its actual appearance. The sense of wonder and exaltation that came to early readers of the genre as they read of voyages to the Moon soon palled, and had to be rekindled with ever more elaborate journeys to ever more distant worlds, until finally characters in SF novels were voyaging across multiple universes in an effort to give readers the same rush they got in Verne's time from a simple trip in a balloon. That's what happens when you try to make a quantitative difference fill in for a qualitative one, and use mere distance or size as a surrogate for a change in the essential character of existence.

It's rather as though some misguidedly materialist believer in the Ascension had convinced himself that heaven really was somewhere up there in the upper atmosphere, and worked out some way to copy those artistic depictions and levitate straight up into the air from the Mount of Olives. His disciples would no doubt have stared with equal awe as he rose into the clouds, and people down below on the streets of Jerusalem might well have caught a glimpse of the sight and thought, good heavens, there goes another one!

It's what follows, though, that makes the difference. According to the Bible, the Ascension ended with Jesus being received into heaven and being seated on the right hand of God the Father. For our imaginary imitator, of course, no such welcome would await. Somewhere above 8,000 feet, altitude sickness would cut in; somewhere above that, depending on the weather, frostbite; above 26,000 feet, the oxygen content of the air is too low to support human life, and death from anoxia would follow if hypothermia hadn't done the job first. If nothing interrupted the ascent, the planet's collection of orbiting space junk would shortly thereafter be enriched by the addition of a neatly freeze-dried corpse.

⚜

All metaphors aside, it's rarely if ever a good idea to take a vision of transcendence and try to enact it in the world of matter. That effort is the stock in trade of civil religions, which tend to emerge in ages that have lost the capacity to believe in transcendence but still have the emotional needs once met by the theist religions of their cultures, and it accounts for the way civil religions have of failing catastrophically when their efforts to act out simulacra of transcendence collide with the awkward realities of the world as it is.

The implosion of the civil religion of Communism thus promptly followed the collision between fantasies of the Worker's Paradise and the bleak bureaucratic reality of the Eastern Bloc nations. The implosion of the civil religion of Americanism is taking place right now as a consequence of the collision between what America thinks it stands for and what it's all too plainly become. The implosion of the civil religion of progress, in turn, is arguably not too far off, as the gaudy dream of infinite knowledge and power through technology slams face first into the hard limits of a finite planet and a solar system uninterested in fueling human fantasies.

The distinction made earlier between religions and religious sensibilities is crucial to making sense of the implications of that collision. Most discussions of the interfaces between religion, ecology and the future have missed this distinction and focused either on specific religious traditions or on the vague abstraction of religion as a whole. The resulting debates were not especially useful to anybody. A classic example is the furor kickstarted by the 1967 publication of the Lynn White essay already cited, "The Historical Roots of Our Ecological Crisis."

White argued that the rise of Christianity to its dominant position in the religious life of the Western world was an essential precondition for the environmental crisis of our time. The old polytheist religions of the West, in his analysis, saw nature as sacred, the abode of a galaxy of numinous powers that could not be ignored with impunity. Christianity, by contrast, brought with it an image of the world as a lifeless mass of matter, an artifact put there by God for the sole benefit of human beings during the relatively brief period between the creation of the world and the Second Coming, after which it would be replaced by a new and improved model. By stripping nature of any inherent claim to human reverence, he suggested, Christianity made it easier for post-Christian Western humanity to treat the earth as a lump of rock with no value beyond its use as a source of raw materials or a dumping ground for waste.

The debate that followed the appearance of White's paper followed a familiar trajectory.[7] Partisans of White's view defended it by digging up examples from history in which Christianity had been used to justify the abuse of nature and had no trouble finding a bumper crop of instances. Opponents of White's view attacked it by showing that the abuse of nature was not actually justified within a Christian worldview, and by and large they had no trouble finding a bumper crop of good theological grounds for their case.

What's more, both were right. On the one hand, there's nothing in Christian theology that requires the abuse of nature, and a very strong case can be made, drawing on the traditions of Christian faith and morals, for the preservation of the environment as an imperative duty. On the other hand, over the course of the last 2,000 years, very few Christians anywhere have recognized that duty, and a great many have used (and continue to use) excuses drawn from their faith to justify their abuse of the environment.

Factor in the influence of religious sensibilities and the paradox evaporates. A religious sensibility, again, is not a religion; it's the cultural substructure of perceptions, emotions and intuitions that shape the way religious traditions are understood and practiced within a given culture or a set of related cultures. The religious sensibility that shaped Christian attitudes toward nature, and of course a great many other things besides, wasn't unique to Christianity in any sense. As we've seen, it emerged in the Mediterranean world before Jesus of Nazareth was born, and only the fact that Christianity happened to come out on top in the bitter religious struggles of the late classical world and suppressed nearly all its rivals gave White's condemnation as much plausibility as it had.

When White pointed to the sacred groves, outdoor worship and ecological taboos of classical Mediterranean pagan religion and contrasted this with the relative lack of veneration for natural ecosystems in Christianity, he was confusing a religion with a religious sensibility. It's certainly possible to point to counterexamples within the Christian tradition, from St. Francis of Assisi through the Anglican natural theology of the Bridgewater Treatises to the impressive efforts currently being made by Patriarch Bartholomew of Constantinople to establish ecological consciousness throughout the Eastern Orthodox Church. So far these have been the exception rather than the rule, but given the sensibility in which the Christian church came to maturity, it's hard to see how things could have gone any other way.

As the theist religions of the west gave way to civil religions, in turn, the same patterns held. Once again, that wasn't true in a monolithic sense, and the first great wave of civil religion to hit the Western world — the nationalism of the eighteenth and nineteenth centuries — went the other way, embracing reverence for nature and the irrational dimensions of life as a counterpoise to the cosmopolitan rationalism of the age. That's why the first verse of "America the Beautiful" — consider the title, to start with — is about the American land, not its human history or political pretensions.

Still, the ease with which such thinking was dropped by the self-proclaimed patriots of today's American pseudoconservatism shows how shallow its roots were in the collective consciousness of our civilization. Other ages have seen the same process at work: it's when the balancing act among traditional narratives, mystical experience and religious sensibility finally fails, and the theist religions of a civilization's childhood and youth give way to the civil religions of its maturity and decay, that the underlying logic of its religious sensibility gets pushed to the logical extreme and appears in its starkest form. In our case, that's biophobia: the pervasive terror and hatred of biological existence that forms the usually unmentioned foundation for so much of contemporary culture.

Does that seem too strong a claim to you, dear reader? If so, I encourage you to consider your attitudes toward your own biological life, that normal and healthy process of ripening toward death in which you're busily engaged right now. Life in that sense is not a nice clean abstract essence. It's a wet and sloppy reality of blood, mucus, urine, feces and other sticky substances, proceeding all the way from the mess in which each of us is born to the mess in which most of us will die. It's about change, growth and decay, and death — especially about death.

Death isn't the opposite of life any more than birth is. It's the natural completion and fulfillment of the process of being alive, not its antithesis, and it's something that people in a great many other cultures have been able to meet calmly, even joyfully, as a matter of course. Our terror of death is a good measure of our terror of life.

It's an equally good measure of the complexity of religious sensibilities that some of the most cogent critiques of modern biophobia come from Christian writers. I'm thinking here especially of C.S. Lewis, who devoted the best of his novels — the interplanetary trilogy that includes *Out of the Silent Planet, Perelandra,* and *That Hideous*

Strength — to tracing out the implications of the religion of progress that was replacing Christianity in the Britain of his time.

Into the mouths of the staff of the National Institute for Coordinated Experiments, the villains of the third book, Lewis put much of the twaddle about limitless progress being retailed by the scientists of his time. Why should we put up with having the earth infested with other living things? Why not make it a nice, clean, sterile planetary machine devoted entirely to the benefit of human beings — or, rather, that minority of human beings who are capable of rational cooperation in the grand cause of Man? Once we outgrow sentimental attachments to lower life forms, outdated quibbles about the moral treatment of other human beings and suchlike pointless barriers to progress, nothing can stop our great leap outward to the stars![8]

You don't hear the gospel of biophobia preached in quite so unrelenting a form very often these days, but the implications are still there. The religion of progress and its apocalyptic antireligion both promise that the future will be without life in the richly and messily biological sense described above. To believers in progress, biological existence and nature itself will have been replaced by something new, shiny and wholly subservient to the human ego; to believers in apocalypse, both will have dissolved in the orgiastic unity of mass death. Different as though those alternatives might seem, both ultimately promise an escape from life — a future in which we all become bubbles of abstract intellect in robot bodies zooming through deep space, after all, is just as lifeless as a future in which we all become cold ash on the smoldering corpse of a once-living planet.

Now of course these paired myths offer something else in common: both serve as excuses for inaction. Claim that progress is certain to save us all and so there's nothing we have to do, or claim that some catastrophe or other is certain to doom us all and so there's nothing we can do, and either way you have a great justification for staying on the sofa and doing nothing. Both thus represent a refusal of what Joseph Campbell called the "call to adventure," the still small voice summoning each of us to rise up in an age of crisis and decay to become the seedbearers of an age not yet born. In this way, as well as the more abstract sense defined by their shared biophobia, both stand in opposition to a living future.

᷎᷎᷎

The search for less futile options starts from a recognition that these dubious choices are both offshoots of a common religious sensibility and that there's at least one alternative in play at this point in history. I've already discussed the way that civil religions like the modern faith in progress are derivative from, even parasitic on, the older theist religions that they replace. Partly that's because theist religions inevitably get there first and make extensive use of whatever superlatives their culture happens to prefer, so the civil religions that come afterwards end up borrowing images and ideas already shaped by centuries of theology.

Still, there's more to it than that. Many of the people who abandoned Christianity for a belief in the future triumph of science, progress and human reason in a godless cosmos, for example, still had the emotional needs that were once met by Christianity, and inevitably sought fulfillment of those needs from their new belief system. Those needs, in turn, aren't universal to all human beings everywhere; they're functions of a particular religious sensibility that began to emerge in the western half of Eurasia around 600 BCE. That sensibility shaped a variety of older and newly minted religious traditions in at least as diverse a range of ways, but the core theme with which all of them contended was a profound distaste for nature, history and the human condition, and the conviction that there had to be an escape hatch through which the chosen few could leap straight out of the "black iron prison" of the world into the infinity and eternity that was supposed to be humankind's true home.

Exactly where to find the escape hatch and how to get through it was a matter of fierce and constant disagreement. From one perspective, the hatch would only fit one person at a time and could be passed through by rigorous spiritual discipline. From another, the unique qualities of a prophet or savior had opened the escape hatch wide, so that everyone who embraced the true faith wholeheartedly and kept some set of moral or behavioral precepts could expect to leap through at some point after physical death. From still another, the hatch would someday soon be opened so wide that the whole world and everyone on it would slip through, in an apocalyptic transformation that would abolish nature, history, time and change all at once.

Much of the complexity of the last 2,000 years or so of Eurasian religious history comes from the fact that devout believers in any faith you care to name embraced each of these options and blended them together in a dizzying assortment of ways. As our civilization moved through the same historical transformations as its predecessors, and the rise of rationalism drove the replacement of traditional theist religions with civil religions, the same quest for an escape hatch from nature, history and the human condition expressed itself in different ways.

The civil religion of progress was arguably the most successful of all in coopting the forms of older religions. It had an abundance of saints, martyrs and heroes, and as we've seen, it was entirely willing to twist history out of shape to manufacture others as needed. The development of technology, buoyed by a flood of cheap abundant energy from fossil fuels, allowed it to supplant the miracle stories of the older faiths with secular miracles of its own, however temporary and ambivalent those replacements turned out to be in practice. The rise of scientific and engineering professions with their own passionate subcultures of commitment to the myth of progress gave it the equivalent of a priest-hood, complete with ceremonial vestments in the form of the iconic white lab coat. The spread of materialist atheism as the default belief system among most scientists and engineers gave it a dogmatic creed that could be used, and in many circles is being used, as a litmus test for loyalty to the faith and a justification for warfare — so far, at least, mostly verbal — against an assortment of unbelievers and heretics.

What the civil religion of progress didn't have, in its early stages, was the escape hatch from nature, history and the human condition that the religious sensibility of the age demanded. This may well be why belief in progress remained a minority faith for so long. The nationalist religions of the eighteenth century, of which Americanism is a survivor, and the social religions of the nineteenth, of which Communism was the last man standing, both managed the trick far earlier — nationalism by calling the faithful to ecstatic identification with the supposedly immortal spirit of the national community and the eternal ideals for which it was believed to stand, such as liberty and justice for all; social religions such as Communism by offering believers the promise of a Utopian world "come the revolution" hovering somewhere in the tantalizingly near future.

It was science fiction that finally provided the civil religion of progress with the necessary promise of salvation from the human condition. One consequence of that choice of escape hatch has been a dependence on overtly theistic imagery far more open and direct than anything in the other civil religions we've discussed. From H.G. Wells' *Men Like Gods* straight through to the latest geek-pope pontifications about the Singularity, the idea that humanity will attain some approximation to godhood, or at least give metaphorical birth to artificial intelligences that will accomplish that feat, pervades the more imaginative end of the literature of progress — just as the less blatantly theological ambition to banish poverty, want, illness and death from the realm of human experience has played a central role in the rhetoric of progress all along.

There are, as it happens, at least two serious problems with the project of perching humanity on some technological approximation of a divine throne in heaven. The first is that the project isn't exactly performing well at the moment. Three hundred years of accelerating drawdown of the Earth's irreplaceable natural resources, and the 300 years of accelerating damage to the Earth's biosphere made inevitable by that process, have exempted a rather small fraction of our species from the more serious kinds of poverty and the more readily curable diseases and handed out an assortment of technological toys that allow them to play at being demigods now and then, when circumstances permit. As nonrenewable resources run short and the impacts of ecological blowback mount, it's becoming increasingly clear that only drastic efforts are likely to preserve any of these advantages into the future — and those drastic efforts are not happening.

Talk, as Zen masters are fond of saying, does not cook the rice, and enthusiastic chatter about artificial intelligence and space manufacturing does nothing to keep contemporary industrial society from stumbling down the same ragged trajectory toward history's compost heap as all those dead civilizations that came before it. If anything, the easy assumption that the onward march of progress is unstoppable, and that the artificial intelligences and orbital factories are therefore guaranteed to pop into being in due time, has become one of the major obstacles to collective action at a time when collective action is desperately needed. The equally easy assumption that some world-wrecking catastrophe will shortly show up on cue to remove our responsibility for the future is another such obstacle. The use of these emotionally appealing fantasies as a source of soothing mental pabulum for those who, for good reason, are worried about the future is wildly popular these days, to be sure, but it's hardly helpful.

Yet it's at this point that the new religious sensibility discussed earlier throws a wild card into the game. It's been my repeated experience that for those who already feel the new sensibility, the old promises haven't just lost their plausibility; they've lost their emotional appeal. It's one thing to proclaim salvation from nature, history and the human condition to those who want that salvation but no longer believe that the ideology you're offering can provide it. It's quite another to do the same thing to people who no longer want the salvation you're offering — people for whom nature, history and the human condition aren't a trap to escape, as they have been for most people in the Western world for the last two millennia, but a reality to embrace in delight and wonder.

That's the unexpected void that's opening up beneath the feet of the most popular civil and theist religions alike at this turn of history's wheel. In order to appeal to societies in which most people embraced the older religious sensibility, with its desperate craving for escape from the world of ordinary experience, religious traditions of both kinds have come to picture their role as that of lifeguards throwing life preservers to clumsy swimmers who are at risk of drowning in the waters of existence. What are they to do when a growing number of the swimmers in question ignore the flotation devices and, diving back into the depths of the water, show mermaid's tails?

Eight

Religion Resurgent

O NE OF THE STANDARD TROPES OF THE CONTEMPORARY FAITH in progress insists that religion is an outworn relic sure to be tipped into history's compost heap sometime very soon. By "religion," of course, those who make this claim inevitably mean "theist religion," or more precisely "any religion other than mine" — the civil religion of progress is of course supposed to be exempt from that fate, since its believers insist that it's not a religion at all.

This sort of insistence is actually quite common in religious life. To ordinary, sincere, unreflective believers, "religion" means the odd things that other people believe; in their eyes, their own beliefs are simply the truth, obvious to anyone with plain common sense. It's for this reason that many languages have no word for religion as such, even though they're fully stocked with terms for deities, prayers, rituals, temples and the other paraphernalia of what we in the West call religion. It's by and large only those societies that have had to confront religious pluralism repeatedly in its most challenging forms that have, or need, a label for the overall category to which these things belong.

The imminent disappearance of all (other) religion that has featured so heavily in rationalist rhetoric for the last century and a half or so thus fills a role in the religion of progress roughly the same as that of the Second Coming in Christianity: the point at which the Church Militant morphs into the Church Triumphant. So far, at least to the best of my knowledge, nobody in the atheist scene has yet proclaimed the date by which Reason will triumph over Superstition — the initial capitals tell you when an abstraction has turned into a mythic figure — but it's probably just a matter of time before some rationalist prophet gladdens the heart of the faithful by giving them a date on which to pin their hopes.

If the evidence of history is anything to go by, though, those hopes will inevitably be misplaced. As noted earlier, the rationalist revolt against religion that's been so large a factor in Western culture over the last few centuries is far less unique than its current publicists like to think. Some such movement rises in every literate civilization in which the art of writing escapes from the control of the priesthood and a significant literate class emerges in secular society. In ancient Egypt, that started around 1500 BCE; in China, around 750 BCE; in India and Greece alike, around 600 BCE; in what Spengler called the Magian culture, the cauldron of competing Middle Eastern monotheisms that finally came under the rule of Islam, about 900 CE. The equivalent point in the history of the West was reached around 1650.[1]

If you know your way around the history of Western rationalism from 1650 to the present, furthermore, you can track the same patterns straight through these other eras. Each movement began with attempts at constructive criticism of religious traditions no one dreamed of rejecting entirely and moved step by step toward an absolute rejection of the traditional faith in one way or another: by replacing it with a rationalized creed stripped of traditional symbolism and theology, as Akhenaten and the Buddha did; by dismissing religion as a habit appropriate to the uneducated, as Confucius and Aristotle did; and by denouncing it as evil, as Lucretius did and today's "angry atheists" do — there aren't that many changes available, and the rationalist movements of the past have wrung them all at one time or another.

Each rationalist movement found an audience early on by offering conclusive answers to questions that had perplexed earlier thinkers, and blossomed in its middle years by combining practical successes in whatever fields mattered most to their society, with a coherent and reasonable worldview that many people found more appealing than the traditional faith. It's the aftermath, though, that's relevant here.

Down through the centuries, only a minority of people have ever found rationalism satisfactory as a working philosophy of life. The majority can sometimes be bullied or shamed into accepting it for a time, but such tactics don't have a long shelf life and commonly backfire on those who use them. Thus the rationalist war against traditional religion in ancient Greek and Roman society succeeded in crippling the old faith in the gods of Olympus, only to leave the field wide open to religions that were less vulnerable to the favorite arguments of classical rationalism: first the mystery cults, then a flurry of imported religions from the East, among which Christianity and Islam eventually triumphed.

That's one of the two most common ways for an era of rationalism to terminate itself with extreme prejudice. The other is the straightforward transformation of a rationalist movement into a religion — consider the way that Buddhism, which started off as a rational protest against the riotous complexity of traditional Hindu religion, ended up replacing Hinduism's crores of gods with an equally numerous collection of bodhisattvas, to whom offerings, mantras, prayers and so on were thereafter directed.

The Age of Reason currently moving into its twilight years, in other words, is not quite as unique as its contemporary publicists like to think. Rather, it's one example of a recurring feature in the history of human civilization. Ages of Reason usually begin as literate civilizations finish the drawn-out process of emerging from their feudal stage, last varying lengths of time and then wind down. Again, the examples

cited earlier are worth recalling: the rationalist movement of the
Egyptian New Kingdom ended in 1340 BCE with the restoration of
the traditional faith under Horemheb; that of China ended with the
coming of the Qin dynasty in 221 BCE; that of India faded out amid a
renewal of religious philosophy well before 500 CE; that of Greece and
Rome ceased to be a living force around the beginning of the Christian
era; and that of the Muslim world ended around 1200 CE.

In each case, what followed was what Oswald Spengler called the
Second Religiosity — a renewal of religion fostered by an alliance
between intellectuals convinced that rationalism had failed and the
masses that never really accepted rationalism in the first place. The
coming of the Second Religiosity doesn't always mean the end of rationalism itself, though this can happen if the backlash is savage enough.
What it means is that rationalism is no longer the dominant cultural
force it normally is during an Age of Reason and settles down to become one intellectual option among many others. Religion is one of
those others, but it normally becomes the most important of them,
and among the reasons that this happens are some that are unexpect-
edly practical — in fact, wholly economic — in nature.

Those economic reasons will require careful exploration because of
certain pervasive blind spots in contemporary thinking. It's axiomatic in
today's economic thought that economic growth is the normal state of
affairs, and any interruption in growth is simply a temporary problem
that will inevitably give way to renewed growth sooner or later. When an
economic crisis happens, then, the first thought of political and financial
leaders alike these days is to figure out how to keep business as usual
running until the economy returns to its normal condition of growth.

The rising spiral of economic troubles around the world in the last
decade or so has caught political and financial officials flatfooted, precisely because that "normal condition of growth" is no longer normal.[2]
After the tech-stock bubble imploded in 2000, central banks in the US
and elsewhere forced down interest rates and flooded the global economy with a torrent of cheap credit. Under more familiar conditions,

this would have driven an investment boom in productive capital of various kinds: new factories would have been built, new technologies brought to the market and so on, resulting in a surge in employment, tax revenues and so on.

While a modest amount of productive capital did come out of the process, the primary result of the central banks' actions was a speculative bubble in real estate even more gargantuan than the tech boom. That was a warning sign too few people heeded. Speculative bubbles are a routine reality in market economies, but under ordinary circumstances they're self-limiting in scale because there are so many other less risky places to earn a decent return on investment.

It's only when an economy has run out of other profitable investment opportunities that speculative bubbles grow to gargantuan size. In the late 1920s, the mismatch between investment in industrial capital and unbalanced distribution of income meant that American citizens could not afford to buy all the products of American industry, and this pushed the country into a classic overproduction crisis. Further investment in productive capital no longer brought in the expected rate of return, and so money flooded into speculative vehicles, driving the 1929 stock market bubble and bust.

The parallel bubble-and-bust economy that we've seen since 2000 followed similar patterns on an even more extreme scale. Once again, income distribution in the United States got skewed drastically in favor of the well-to-do, so that a growing fraction of Americans could no longer support the consumer economy with their purchases. Once again, returns on productive investment sank to embarrassing lows, leaving speculative paper of various kinds as the only option in town. It wasn't just overproduction that made investment in productive capital fail to produce adequate returns, though — there was something considerably more dangerous involved, which was also rather less easy for political and financial elites to recognize.

The dogma that holds that growth is the normal state of economic affairs, after all, did not come about by accident. It was the result of three centuries of experience in the economies of Europe and the more successful nations of the European diaspora. Those three centuries, in turn, saw the most colossal economic boom in all of recorded history, the one that we call the Industrial Age. Two factors drove that boom: first, the global expansion of European empires in the seventeenth, eighteenth and nineteenth centuries and the systematic looting of overseas colonies that resulted; second, the breakneck exploitation of half a billion years of stored sunlight in the form of coal, petroleum and natural gas.[3]

Both those driving forces remained in place through the twentieth century. The European empires gave way to a network of US client states that were plundered just as thoroughly as old-fashioned imperial colonies, while the exploitation of the world's fossil fuel reserves went on at ever-increasing rates. The peaking of US petroleum production in 1972 threw a good-sized monkeywrench into the gears of the system and brought a decade of crisis, but a variety of short-term gimmicks postponed the crisis temporarily and opened the way to the final extravagant blowoff of the age of cheap energy.

The peaking of worldwide conventional petroleum production in 2005 marked the end of that era and the coming of a new economic reality that no one in politics or business seems yet to be prepared to grasp. Claims that the peak would be promptly followed by plunging production, mass panic and apocalyptic social collapse proved to be just as inaccurate as such claims always are. What happened instead was that a growing fraction of the world's total energy supply has had to be diverted, directly or indirectly, to the task of maintaining fossil fuel production.

Not all that long ago, all things considered, a few thousand dollars was enough to drill an oil well that can still be producing hundreds of barrels a day decades later; these days, a fracked well in oil-bearing shale can cost $5 to 10 million to drill and hydrofracture, and three years down the road it'll be yielding less than ten barrels of oil a day. Nor do these increased costs and diminished returns take place in a vacuum. The energy and products of energy that have to be put into the task of maintaining energy production, after all, aren't available for other economic uses.

In monetary terms, oil prices upwards of $100 a barrel, and comparable prices for petroleum products, provide some measure of the tax on all economic activity that's being imposed by the diversion of energy, resources and other goods and services into petroleum production. Meanwhile fewer businesses are hiring, less new productive capital gets built, new technologies languish on the shelves: the traditional drivers of growth aren't coming into play, because the surplus of real wealth needed to make them function isn't there anymore, having had to be diverted to keep petroleum and other fossil fuels flowing at the levels needed to keep today's global economy from pitching forward onto its face.

⚜

The broader pattern behind all these shifts is easy to state, though people raised in a growth economy often find it almost impossible to grasp. Sustained economic growth is made possible by sustained increases in the availability of energy for purposes other than energy production itself. That's the core implication of White's Law, one of the fundamental principles of human ecology, which states that economic development in a society corresponds precisely to the energy per capita available in that society.[4] The only reason economic growth seems normal to us is that we've just passed through 300 years in which, for the fraction of humanity living in western Europe, North America and a few other corners of the world, the supply of energy and other resources soared well past any increases in the cost of production. That era is now over, and so is sustained economic growth.

The end of growth, though, has sweeping implications of its own, and those conflict sharply with expectations nurtured by the long boomtime of the Industrial Age. It's only when economic growth is normal, for example, that investments reliably earn a profit. It's because the economy as a whole can be expected to gain value over time that investments, each of which represent ownership of a minute portion of the whole economy, can normally be expected to do the same thing. On paper, at least, investment in a growing economy is a positive-sum game; everyone can profit to one degree or another, and the goal of competition is to profit more than the other guy.

In an economy that has stopped growing, by contrast, investment is by definition a zero-sum game. Since the economy neither grows nor contracts from year to year, the total value of all investments must remain approximately the same. Under those conditions, the average investment breaks even, and for one investment to make a profit, another must suffer a comparable loss. In a contracting economy, by the same logic, investment is a negative-sum game, the average investment loses money, and an investment that merely succeeds in breaking even can do so only if steeper losses are inflicted on other investments.

It's precisely because the conditions for sustained economic growth are over, and have been over for some time now, that the political and financial establishments in the industrial nations find themselves clinging to the ragged end of a bridge to nowhere, with an assortment of crocodiles gazing up hungrily from the waters below. The stopgap policies that were meant to keep business as usual running until growth resumed have done their job, but economic growth has gone missing in action, and the supply of gimmicks is running short. How long it will remain possible to keep funding the galaxy of giveaways that keep the social machinery of a modern industrial state running smoothly is an interesting question, but "indefinitely" is one of the least likely answers.

Nor is this the only consequence of the end of growth. In a contracting economy, again, the average investment loses money, and that rule doesn't simply apply to financial paper. If a business owner in a contracting economy invests in capital improvements, on average, those improvements will not bring a return sufficient to pay back the investment; if a bank makes a loan, on average, the loan will never be paid back in full and so on. Thus it's not just that the production of every kind of good or service in an industrial economy depends on the expectation that somebody or other can make a profit out of the deal, though of course that's of huge importance. Every other mechanism in a modern industrial society that keeps wealth circulating depends directly or indirectly on the same expectation. Taxes, fees, rent, interest on loans and every other detail of economic activity rests on the assumption that every business, on average, will produce enough profit that its banker, landlord, local and state governments, and so on can all be supported without bankrupting the business.

Nowadays, that's not always a safe assumption to make. If you walk the downtown streets in Cumberland, Maryland, the old red brick Appalachian mill town where I live, you'll see scores of empty storefronts in excellent locations. Many of them haven't had a tenant in 20 or 30 years. Now and then a new business opens in one of these spots, but it's very rare for one of those still to be in business a year after its opening.

Cumberland is a Rust Belt town. The factories that were once its main employers all shut down in the early 1970s, pushing it through the same deindustrial transition that the industrial world as a whole is facing in the years immediately before us. Businesses here have to survive on a very thin profit margin. The difficulty is that bankers, landlords, local and state officials and so on still want their accustomed cut, which is substantially more than that margin will cover. This isn't mere greed — they all have their own bills to pay and an equal or larger number of people and institutions clamoring for a share of their own take.

The result, though, is that storefronts stay empty despite an abundance of unmet economic needs and an equal abundance of people who would be happy to work if they had the chance. The businesses that could meet those needs and employ those people can't make enough of a profit to keep their doors open. The inability of most economic activities to turn a profit in an age of contraction is already an issue at many levels, and one with which contemporary economic thought is almost completely unprepared to deal.

That same challenge occurs reliably in the twilight years of every civilization. The late Roman world is a case in point: by the beginning of the fifth century CE, it was so hard for Roman businessmen to make money that the Roman government had laws requiring sons to go into their fathers' professions, whether they could earn a living that way or not, and there were businessmen who fled across the borders and went to work as scribes, accountants and translators for barbarian warlords, because the alternative was economic ruin in a collapsing Roman economy.

Meanwhile rich landowners converted their available wealth into gold and silver and buried it, rather than cycling it back into the economy, and moneylending became so reliable a source of social ills that lending at interest was a mortal sin in medieval Christianity and remains so in Islam right down to the present. When Dante's *Inferno* consigned people who lend money at interest to the lowest part of the seventh circle of Hell,[5] lower down than mass murderers, heretics and fallen angels, he was reflecting a common opinion of his time and one that had real justification in the not so distant past.

Left to itself, the negative-sum game of economics in a contracting economy has no necessary endpoint short of the complete collapse of all systems of economic exchange. In the real world, it rarely goes quite that far, though it can come uncomfortably close. In the aftermath of the Roman collapse, for example, it wasn't just lending at interest that went away.[6] Money itself dropped out of use in most of post-Roman Europe — as late as the twelfth century, it was normal for most people to go from one year to the next without ever handling a coin — and market-based economic exchange, which thrived in the Roman world, was replaced by feudal economies in which most goods were produced by those who consumed them, customary payments in kind took care of nearly all the rest, and a man could expect to hold land from his overlord on the same terms his great-grandfather had known.

More broadly, there's one reliable way to deal with the collapse of growth-dependent economic institutions and practices in an age of economic contraction, which is to move productive activities into spheres that don't depend on the profit motive to guide economic activity. The household economy is one obvious place, and so is that expansion of the household economy — all but universal in agricultural societies except during the few centuries in which a civilization peaks and falls — in which each family in a community cultivates grains, legumes and other bulk food crops for its own use on village farmland.

Gift economies hardwired into the social hierarchy are also standard in such ages. There's a good reason why generosity is always one of the most praised virtues in feudal and protofeudal societies. From Saxon England to Vedic India to the First Nations of the Pacific Northwest coast, giving lavish gifts to all and sundry has always been the most important economic activity of the aristocrat. As the key player in a feudal or protofeudal gift economy, he makes up for the lack of a viable profit motive in ages of economic contraction or stasis.

During the implosion of the Roman world's complex market economy and the emergence of the post-Roman economics of agrarian feudalism across Europe, though, there was another reliable source of investment in necessary infrastructure and other social goods: the Christian church. It thrived when all other economic and political institutions failed because it did not care in the least about the profit motive and had ways to motivate and direct human energies to constructive ends without having to rely on the lure of profit. In other dark ages, other religions have filled similar roles with similar effects — Buddhism, for example, in the dark ages that followed the collapse of Heian Japan, or the Egyptian priesthoods in the several dark ages experienced by ancient Egyptian society.

It's worth noting that dark ages in those societies that had some such religious tradition in place were considerably less dark and preserved a substantially larger fraction of the cultural and technological heritage of the previous society than those in which no institution of the same kind existed. When other institutions fail, in fact, religion is one of the few options capable of providing a framework for organized collective activity of any kind. The revival of religion in the twilight of an age of rationalism and its rise to a position of cultural predominance in the decline of a civilization thus have a potent practical rationale in addition to any other factors that support it.

That same rationale also has a great deal to say about which social institutions can expect to remain viable during an age of economic contraction, because it's not only whole economies that have to find some motive that will inspire people to invest their time, labor and commitment in the necessary work. Every institution within a society has to face the same challenge. If modern science, or for that matter, modern religious organizations, are to have any hope of weathering the crises ahead, their leaders and ordinary members alike will have to take into account the need to find ways to motivate human action in an age of decline — and this may require changes that a great many people these days will find distinctly unwelcome.

⚜

A morphological comparison will be useful here, for more than the obvious reasons, and the one I have in mind involves two communes that existed in rural eastern Massachusetts in the first half of the nineteenth century. The first of them will be familiar to those who know their way around the history of the Transcendentalist movement, America's first homegrown counterculture. It was called Brook Farm; it was founded with high hopes and much fanfare in 1841 by a bunch of Boston hippies — for all practical purposes, that's what the Transcendentalists were — and it imploded in a series of crises in 1846 and 1847.

Its trajectory will be painfully familiar to anybody who watched the rise and fall of rural communes in the aftermath of the Sixties. As usual, the central conflict pitted middle-class expectations of adequate leisure, comfort and personal independence against the hard economic realities of subsistence farming, and both sides lost. Unable to support

its members' lifestyles solely from the results of their labor, Brook
Farm ran through its savings and as much money as it could borrow,
and when the money ran out, it went under.

One of the commune's founding members, Nathaniel Hawthorne,
set his novel *The Blithedale Romance* at a lightly fictionalized Brook
Farm. Back when American public schools still expected their stu-
dents to read literature, most teenagers who grew up in the United
States could count on getting assigned to read Hawthorne's *The Scarlet
Letter* or *The House of the Seven Gables*, but not *The Blithedale Romance*.
Partly, I suspect, that was because its edgy portrayal of the psychology
of the true believer, via the character of Hollingsworth the social re-
former, cuts far too close to the bone. Partly, though, it's because the
United States has long suffered from a frantic terror of all the most innovative parts of its own past and has assigned the relics thereof to a
variety of memory holes to which schoolchildren are emphatically not
introduced.

Brook Farm, in point of fact, was one of hundreds of communes
in the United States in the nineteenth century. The concept wasn't
new even then, but went back to colonial days. The first American
commune I know of, Johannes Kelpius' "Woman in the Wilderness"
community of Rosicrucian ascetics, was founded in the trackless forests of Pennsylvania in 1694. There are dozens of good books on these
communities from nineteenth- and early twentieth-century historians
— Charles Nordhoff's 1875 survey *The Communistic Societies of the
United States* is a classic — and a flurry of research on them in academ-
ic circles more recently, but you'll rarely hear about any of that in any
public venue these days.

During the years when Brook Farm was stumbling through its short
and troubled life, though, there were several other communes in the
neighborhood — Massachusetts in the early nineteenth century had
roughly the same cultural role in American life that California held in
the middle of the twentieth, with communes to match. One of them,
which deserves special mention here, was only 35 miles away by road.

Long before Brook Farm's rise and long after its fall, it was a prosper-
ous egalitarian community with around 200 members, growing all its
own food and meeting all its financial needs with room to spare. The
Harvard Village, as it was called, was everything Brook Farm's founders claimed they wanted their commune to be, and it was thus almost
by definition everything Brook Farm's founders rejected most heatedly
in practice: that is, it was a Shaker community.

The United Society of Believers in Christ's Second Appearing, better known then and now as the Shakers, had its start in Manchester,
England, where Ann Lee — "Mother Ann" to Shakers ever after — led
a tiny religious group that spun off from the Quakers over the course of
the 1760s. In 1774, Mother Ann and eight followers came to what was
about to become the United States and found no shortage of interest
in their new gospel. From 1787 on, the United Society was run by its
American converts, and these latter proceeded to accomplish one of
the most remarkable feats of convergent evolution in human cultural
history: starting wholly from first principles and with apparently no
knowledge of the historical parallels, they reinvented almost every detail of classic monasticism.

Like monks and nuns everywhere, Shakers were celibate — one
of Mother Ann's revelations was that sexuality is the principal source
of human sinfulness — and lived communally, owning no personal
property. Men and women lived in separate dormitories in a Shaker
village and led essentially separate lives; Shaker meetinghouses, where
Sunday services were held, had two doors, one for Brothers and one
for Sisters, and the two sexes sat on opposite sides. Despite the rule of
celibacy, there were always children in Shaker villages, some of them
orphans, some left by destitute or deadbeat parents, some brought
into the United Society when their parents joined; they had their own
dormitories, one for girls and one for boys. The children could choose
to leave or stay when they reached adulthood. To stay was to give up
sexuality, family, property and a great deal of autonomy, but it was a
choice many made.

There were consolations, to be sure, and not all of them were wholly spiritual. The opportunities open to women among the Shakers were much more substantial than anything available in what Shakers called "the World." Both sexes had equal roles in each village, each regional bishopric and the entire Society — the Central Ministry, the body of four senior Shakers who ran the organization, consisted of two Elders and two Eldresses. Ordinary members could expect a life of hard work, but that was common enough in nineteenth-century America, and the lifelong support of a close-knit community provided by the Shaker system was something most people in that rough-and-tumble era did not have.

The Shakers thus had to be on the watch for freeloaders — "bread-and-butter Shakers" was the usual term — who wanted to join the Society for the sake of free meals and medical care, but had no interest in the religion or, for that matter, in putting in an honest day's work. Still, the United Society found so many sincere converts that new Shaker communities were being founded into the 1830s, and membership declines didn't become an issue until well after the Civil War. Nor is the United Society quite gone even today; there are still a few Shakers left at the last remaining Shaker village at Sabbathday Lake, Maine, supporting themselves by the traditional Shaker trade of drying and selling herbs.

Compare a Shaker community with a Christian or Buddhist monastery and the parallels are impossible to miss. The Christian monastic virtues of poverty, chastity and obedience are all present and accounted for; so is the commitment to labor as a form of religious service. For that matter, the clean, simple, spare esthetic that the Shakers made famous in their furnishings and architecture has a great deal in common with the elegant simplicity that Zen Buddhism introduced to Japanese art and design, or close equivalents in Christian monastic traditions.

The parallels aren't accidental. Set out to live on a monastic plan, and the kind of simplicity prized by Shakers, Cistercians, Zen monks and so many of their fellow monastics, have a great many practical advantages. Whether it takes the form of a Shaker village, a Catholic abbey, a Zen monastery, or what have you, the monastic life is one of the few consistent success stories in the history of communal living. That's exactly the problem, of course, because the vast majority of people who imagine themselves living in a communal setting these days aren't willing to push their enthusiasm to the point of giving up sex, family personal property and personal autonomy.

The result, predictably enough, has been a steady stream of projects, proposals and actual communities launched by people who want to have their cake and eat it too: that is, to live in a self-supporting communal setting while still retaining comfortable middle-class values of ownership, autonomy and unhindered sexual activity. Brook Farm was one of those attempts, and it lasted longer than most. There have been a few that have done better, to be sure, but it's remarkable how often those have ended up adopting at least some of the traditional monastic values, such as community ownership of property.

There's a wholly pragmatic reason for the failure of the others. The kind of lifestyles that most people consider normal in industrial societies is only possible if you're helping to burn through half a billion years of stored sunlight via a modern industrial economy. You can't support such a lifestyle with hand labor on a rural commune. Even the much less resource-intensive lifestyles of the Brook Farm era were too costly to be met by working the land, which is why Brook Farm went broke in five years. Most of the communes of the Sixties crashed and burned sooner than that. Unless there was a sugar daddy available to cover the bills, the amount and kind of work the residents were willing to do failed to meet the costs of the lifestyles they wanted to lead, and collapse followed promptly.

The exceptions have almost all been religious communities. In the Sixties, that usually meant that they clustered around a spiritual leader who was charismatic or convincing enough to get away with telling his followers what to do, and had the common sense to do the math and figure out that it takes a lot of hard work and at least as much willing acceptance of poverty to make communal living viable. Some of the religious communities launched by the Sixties' counterculture thus are still around; others got past the economic problems that wrecked most of their secular counterparts, only to crash headlong into one of the other standard traps that face communal projects.

You can see all these same patterns traced out in the communes launched by earlier American countercultures from the Transcendentalists on. By and large, the only ones that survive their founding generation are those that conform more or less precisely to the model of classic monasticism sketched out above. It's a pattern that has been notably effective in dealing with dark ages in the past and thus has some claim to be considered as a means for dealing with the troubled era that will inevitably follow the decline of the Industrial Age — provided, of course, that the lessons of history are taken into account.

I spoke of convergent evolution earlier, and the borrowing from biology is a deliberate one. Darwin's theory, at its core, is simply a recognition that some things work better than others, and those organisms who stumble across something that works better — in physical structure, in behavior, or what have you — are more likely to survive whatever challenges they and their less gifted counterparts face together. Why one thing works better than another may or may not be obvious, even after close study. When one set of adaptations consistently results in survival, while a different set just as consistently results in collapse, it nonetheless seems quite reasonable to draw the obvious lesson from that experience.

That inference seems reasonable to me, at least. I'm quite aware that many other people in the modern industrial world don't seem to see things that way. Point out that X has failed every single time it's been tried, without a single exception, and people will insist that this doesn't matter unless you can detail the reasons why it has to fail; then, when you do so, they try to argue with the reasons. In the opening lines of his essay *The Eighteenth Brumaire of Louis Napoleon,* Karl Marx commented acidly: "Hegel says somewhere that history always repeats itself. He forgot to mention: the first time as tragedy, the second as farce." One of the most potent forces driving those repetitions, by turns tragic and farcical, is the endlessly repeated insistence that it's different this time, and so the lessons of history don't matter.

Thus it's an interesting question why celibacy, for example, should foster the long-term survival of monastic systems. Perhaps celibacy works because it prevents sexual jealousies from spinning out of control, as they so often do in the hothouse environment of communal living. Perhaps celibacy works because pair bonds between lovers are the most potent source of the private loyalties that so often distract members of communal groups from their loyalty to the project as a whole. Perhaps celibacy works because all that creative energy has to go somewhere — the Shakers birthed an astonishing range of artistic and creative endeavors, from a musical corpus of more than 11,000 original hymns, through graphic arts, architecture and a style of furniture and other crafts that's widely considered one of the great traditions of American folk culture.

Perhaps it's some other reason entirely. The point that needs to be kept in mind, though, is that in a monastic setting, celibacy works, and many other ways of managing human sexuality in that setting pretty reliably don't. The question "does *x* happen?" is logically distinct from the question "why does *x* happen?" It's possible to be utterly correct about the fact that something is the case while being just as utterly clueless about the reasons why it is the case. This is why the fact that medieval philosophers believed that rocks fall because they're in love with the earth didn't prevent them from recognizing that rocks do indeed fall when you pick them up and let go.

The value and the limitations of history as a guide to the present and the future come out of the hard fact that the morphology of history tells us what happens, but not why it happens. More than three centuries of communal experiments in North America, and more than 3,000 years of similar experiments elsewhere, have a lot to teach about what works and what doesn't work when people decide to pursue a communal lifestyle. Those who are willing to learn from those experiences have a much better chance of coming up with something that works than those who insist that the past doesn't matter and thus repeat its most common mistakes all over again.

Reinventing the wheel has its uses, but if your efforts at reinvention consistently turn out square wheels, it may be helpful to look at other examples of the wheelwright's craft and see if you can figure out what they got right and you got wrong. That applies to details such as the role of traditional monastic rules in keeping a commune going for the long term, but it also applies to the much more general question of what works and what doesn't in eras of decline — and if the evidence of history is to be taken into account, religion is one of the few things that works.

⚜

The great difficulty with this otherwise straightforward point is that trying to make religion serve secular purposes reliably runs into intractable problems. To be sure, this has done nothing to stop such attempts from being made. It's far from uncommon these days, for example, for intellectuals to talk wistfully about how good it would be if people could be induced to believe in an ecological religion. That possibility has been aired fairly often, most notably in the circle of ecologically literate intellectuals that formed around Gregory Bateson, Stewart Brand and *The Whole Earth Catalog* in the San Francisco region in the 1970s.

Their motivations were anything but opaque. What made a green religion interesting to Bateson, Brand and their associates was their recognition that something more than material incentives would have to be used motivate people to make the changes that would be necessary to keep industrial civilization from slamming face first into the consequences of its own environmental mistakes. Only an ecological religion, they believed, would call forth from its believers the commitment, and indeed the fanaticism, that a transformation to sustainability

would require. Nor was this just empty talk — there were several earnest attempts to launch such a religion and at least one effort to provide
it with a set of sacred scriptures.[7] All of them fizzled.

Another attempt of much the same sort, though it's aimed at a different set of secular goals, is in the process of going down the same
well-greased slope. This is the Charter for Compassion launched
by pop-spirituality author Karen Armstrong a few years back.[8] The
Charter is being marketed by the TED Foundation under the slogan
"The best idea humanity has ever had." Those of my readers who know
their way around today's yuppie culture may not be surprised by the
self-satisfied smugness of the slogan, but it's the dubious thinking that
underlies the Charter itself that I want to point up here.

The Charter starts by claiming that "The principle of compassion
lies at the heart of all religious, ethical and spiritual traditions." There's
a far from minor difficulty with this claim, which is that it simply isn't
true. All religions? There are many in which compassion falls in the
middling or minor rank of virtues and quite a few that don't value compassion at all. All ethical traditions? Aristotle's *Nichomachean Ethics*,
widely considered the most influential work on ethics in the Western
tradition, doesn't even mention the concept, and many other ancient,
medieval and modern ethical systems give it less than central billing.
All spiritual traditions? That vague and mightily misused word "spirituality" stands for a great many things, many of which have nothing to
do with compassion or any other moral virtue.

I noted in an earlier chapter the monumental confusions that pop
up when values get confused with facts, and this is a good example.
Armstrong clearly wants to insist that in her opinion, everyone *should*
put compassion at the center of their religious, ethical and spiritual
lives. In a society that disparages values, it's easier to push such an argument using claims of fact — even when, as here, those claims are
obviously false. Mind you, Armstrong's charter also finesses the inevitable conflict between the virtue she favors and other virtues that have
at least as good a claim to central status, but that's a different subject.

The deeper falsification I want to address here is contained in the passage already cited, though it pops up elsewhere in the Charter as well: "We therefore call upon all men and women to restore compassion to the centre of morality and religion" is another example. What's being said here, in so many words, is that moral virtue either is or ought to be the central focus of religion: more, that religion is in essence a system of ethics dressed up in ornate mythological drag. That was the view popularized by Immanuel Kant, as mentioned back in Chapter One, and it remains a very popular view these days, especially among the liberal intelligentsia from which Armstrong and the TED Foundation draw most of their audiences. It's essentially the same falsification that guided the efforts to manufacture an eco-religion mentioned earlier; some form of it nearly always becomes a commonplace of popular thought in ages of rationalism, but it's still a falsification.

It so happens that a large minority of human beings — up to a third, depending on the survey — report having at least one experience, at some point in their lives, that appears to involve contact with a disembodied intelligent being.[9] Many of these experiences are spontaneous; others are fostered by religious practices such as prayer, meditation and ritual. Any number of causes have been proposed for these experiences, but I'd like to ask my readers to set aside the issue of causation for the moment and pay attention to the raw data of experience.

As noted above, there's a crucial difference between the question "Does *x* happen?" and the question "Why does *x* happen?" — a difference of basic logical categories — and it's a fruitful source of confusion and error to confound them. Whether these experiences — which we may as well call "religious experiences" — are caused by autohypnosis, undiagnosed schizophrenia, archetypes of the collective unconscious, the real existence of gods and spirits, or something else, these experiences happen to a great many people; they have done so as far back as records go, and *religion is the traditional human response to them*. If nobody had ever had the experience of encountering a god, an angel, a saint, an ancestor, a totem spirit, or what have you, it's probably safe to say that our species would not have religions.

Human beings under ordinary conditions encounter two kinds or, if you will, worlds of experience: one that's composed of things that can be seen, heard, smelled, tasted and touched, which we can call the biosphere, and one composed of things that can be thought, felt, willed and imagined, which we can call the noosphere (from Greek *nous*, "mind"). The core thesis offered by the great majority of religions, around the world and throughout time, is that there is a third world, which we can call the theosphere, and that some part or power or inhabitant of this third world is what breaks through into human consciousness in religious experience.

It's important not to make this very broad concept more precise than the data permit, or to assume more agreement among religious traditions than actually exists. The idea of a theosphere — a kind, mode, or world of human experience that appears to be inhabited by disembodied intelligences — is very nearly the only common ground you'll find among religious traditions, and attempts to hammer the wildly diverse religious experiences of different individuals and cultures into a common tradition inevitably tell you more about the person or people doing the hammering than they do about the raw material being hammered.

In particular, the role played by moral virtue in human relationships with the theosphere and its apparent denizens varies drastically from one tradition to another. There are plenty of religious traditions in which ethics play no role at all and in which moral thought is assigned to some other sphere of life, while even among those religions that do include moral teaching, there's no consensus on which virtues are central. In any case, it's the relationship to the theosphere that matters, and the moral dimension is there to support the relationship, not vice versa.

This is pretty much the explanation you can expect to get, by the way, if you ask ordinary, sincere, unreflective believers in a theist religion what their religious life is about. They'll normally use the standard terminology of their tradition — your ordinary churchgoing American Protestant, for example, will likely tell you that it's about getting right with Jesus, your ordinary Shinto parishioner in Japan will explain that it's about maintaining a proper relationship with the *kami* and so on through the diversity of the world's faiths — but the principle is the same. If morals come into the discussion, the role assigned to them is a subordinate one: the Protestant, for example, will likely explain that following the moral teachings of the Bible is one part of getting right with Jesus, not the other way around.

That's the thing that attempts to construct or manipulate religion for some secular purpose always miss, and it explains why such attempts reliably fail. The atheists who point out that it's not necessary to worship a deity to lead an ethical life, even a life of heroic virtue, are quite correct. The religious person whose object of reverence expects moral behavior may have an additional incentive to ethical living, but no doubt the atheists can come up with an additional incentive or two of their own.

It's religious experience, the personal sense of contact with a realm of being that transcends the ordinary affairs of material and mental life, that's the missing element. You can replace it over the short to middle term with some other source of powerful emotions, such as patriotism or class loyalty, and then you get a civil religion — more or less equivalent to a theist religion in its emotional power, but as discussed earlier, much more brittle in practice. If you don't have any such replacement, you're left with yet another set of moral preachments that appeal only to those who already agree with them.

This is what guarantees that Armstrong's Charter for Compassion will presently slide into oblivion, following a trajectory marked out well in advance by dozens of equally well-meant and equally ineffectual efforts of the past. How many people even remember these days, for example, that nearly all of the world's major powers actually sat down in 1928 and signed a treaty to end war forever? The Kellogg-Briand Pact failed because the nations that needed to be restrained by it weren't willing to accept its strictures, while the nations that were enthusiastic about it weren't planning to invade anybody in the first place. In the same way, the people who sign the Charter for Compassion, if they really intend to guide their behavior by its precepts, are exactly the ones who don't need it in the first place, while people who see no value in compassion either won't sign or won't let a signature on a document restrain them from doing exactly what they want, however uncompassionate that happens to be.

That's exactly what happened to the efforts of green thinkers in the 1970s either to manufacture a green religion, or to manipulate existing religions into following a green agenda. The people who proposed such a project didn't actually believe in the religion they were trying to promote — they believed that other people ought to believe in it, which is far from the same thing. Thus the only people they were able to interest in the project were those who didn't need it, because they were already motivated to follow ecologically sound lifestyles by some other factor. The theosphere wasn't brought into the project, or even consulted about it, and so the only source of passionate commitment that could have made the project more than a daydream of Sausalito intellectuals went by the boards. So, in due time, did the project.

What makes the involvement of the theosphere essential to any such program is precisely that the emotional and intellectual energies set in motion by religious experience trump all other human motivations in intensity and durability. Every rationalist movement throughout history has embraced the theory that all this can, should and must be dispensed with, in order to make society make rational sense. Every rationalist movement has then found it necessary to make a covert compromise with the religious needs of its members by erecting a civil religion to fill the place of the despised theist faith.

Every rationalist movement, in turn, has collapsed in frustration and disarray when the civil religion proved unable to fulfill its promises in the material world, and any transcendent factor that might have made up the difference had been excluded from the beginning. That's the stone over which civil religions keep stumbling: lacking contact with the theosphere — the experiential dimension of theist religion, which civil religions always try to replace with some substitute that never quite does the job — religion simply won't work for long.

The collapse of the rationalist agenda, and the civil religion or religions in which that agenda is typically embodied, is thus one of the forces that launches what Oswald Spengler called the Second Religiosity. Another is the economic factor discussed earlier in this chapter. Another is the simple fact that most people never do accept the rationalist agenda, and as polemics against traditional religion from rationalist sources become more extreme, the backlash mentioned earlier becomes a potent and ultimately unstoppable force. Still, there seems to be a great deal more to it than that.

Without getting into the various arguments, religious and antireligious, about just exactly what reality might lie behind what I've called the theosphere, it's probably fair to say that this reality isn't a passive screen onto which individuals or societies can project whatever fantasies they happen to prefer. What comes out of the theosphere, in the modest religious experiences of ordinary believers as well as the world-shaking visions of great prophets, changes from one era to another according to a logic (or illogic) all its own. Such changes correspond closely to shifts in religious sensibility, but they also relate to a further dimension of the crisis of our age — a dimension that will be central to this book's final chapter.

Nine

At the Closing of an Age

IT'S CRUCIAL TO REMEMBER THAT THE CRISIS OF OUR AGE is not just a function of depleted resources and the buildup of pollutants in the biosphere. It's also a matter of depleted imaginations and the build-up of dysfunctional ideas in the collective consciousness of our time. Toxic ideas such as the biophobia discussed in Chapter Seven, just like more material kinds of toxic waste, have lasting effects on the systems that surround us, and those effects need to be taken into account in trying to find meaningful responses to the end of the Industrial Age.

Most of the rising spiral of problems we face, after all, could have been prevented with a little foresight and forbearance, and even now — when most of the opportunities to avoid a really messy future have long since gone whistling down the wind — there's still much that could be done to mitigate the worst consequences of the end of the Industrial Age and pass on the best achievements of the last few centuries to our descendants. Of the things that could be done to fur-ther these worthwhile ends, though, very few are actually being done, and those have received what effort they have only because scattered individuals and small groups out on the fringes of contemporary industrial society are putting their own time and resources into the task.

Meanwhile the billions of dollars, the vast public relations campaigns and the lavishly supplied and funded institutional networks that could have helped make these same things happen on a much larger scale are by and large devoted to projects that are simply going to make things worse. That's the bitter irony of our age and, more broadly, of every civilization in its failing years. No society has to be dragged kicking and screaming down the slope of decline and fall; one and all, they take that slope at a run, yelling in triumph, utterly convinced that the road to imminent ruin will lead them to paradise on Earth.

That's one of the ways that the universe likes to blindside believers in a purely materialist interpretation of history. Modern industrial society differs in a galaxy of ways from the societies that preceded it into history's compost heap, and it's easy enough — especially in a society obsessed with the conviction that it's superior to every other civilization in history — to jump from the fact of those differences to the conviction that modern industrial society must have a unique fate: uniquely glorious, uniquely horrible, or some combination of the two: nobody seems to care much as long as it's unique. Then the most modern industrial social and economic machinery gets put to work in the service of stupidities that were old before the pyramids were built, because human beings rather than machinery make the decisions, and the motives that drive human behavior don't actually change that much from one millennium to the next.

What does change from millennium to millennium, and across much shorter eras as well, are the sensibilities, ideas and beliefs built atop the foundation provided by the motivations just mentioned. Oswald Spengler, whose work has been discussed repeatedly in earlier chapters, had much to say about the way that different cultures come to understand the world in ways so different that even the most basic conceptions about reality vary from one culture to another.

Still, there's another dimension to the way thoughts and beliefs change over time, and it takes place within the historical trajectory of a single culture. This is the dimension that we recall, however dimly, when we speak of the Age of Faith and the Age of Reason. Since these same ages recur in the life of every literate urban society, we might more usefully speak of ages of faith and ages of reason in the plural; we will also need to discuss a third set of ages, the ages of memory, that succeed ages of reason in much the same way that the latter supplant ages of faith.

Now of course the transition between ages of faith and ages of reason carries a heavy load of self-serving cant these days. The rhetoric of the civil religion of progress presupposes, for all practical purposes, that every human being who lived before the scientific revolution was basically just plain stupid, since otherwise they would have gotten around to noticing centuries ago that modern atheism and scientific materialism are the only reasonable explanations of the cosmos. Thus a great deal of effort has been expended over the years on creative attempts to explain why nobody before 1650 or so ever realized that everything they believed about the cosmos was so obviously wrong.

A more useful perspective comes out of the work of Giambattista Vico, the modern world's first great theorist of historical cycles. Vico's *The New Science* focuses on what he called "the course the nations run," the trajectory that leads a new civilization up out of one dark age and eventually back down into the next. Vico wrote in an intellectual tradition that's long been extinct, the tradition of Renaissance humanism, saturated in ancient Greek and Roman literature and wholly at ease in the nearly forgotten worlds of mythological and allegorical thinking. Even at the time, his book was considered difficult by most readers, and it's far more opaque today than it was then, but the core ideas Vico was trying to communicate are worth teasing out of his convoluted prose.

One useful way into those ideas is to start where Vico did, with the history of law.[1] It's a curious regularity in legal history that law codes start out in dark-age settings as lists of specific punishments for specific crimes — "if a man steal a loaf of bread, let him be given twelve blows with a birch stick" — without a trace of legal theory or even of generalization. Later, all the different kinds of stealing get lumped together as the crime of theft, and the punishment assigned to it usually comes to depend at least in part on the abstract value of what's stolen. Eventually laws are ordered and systematized, a theory of law emerges, and great legal codes are issued providing broad general principles from which jurists extract rulings for specific cases.

By the time this level of abstraction is reached, the civilization that created the legal code is usually stumbling toward its end, and its fall is the end of the road for its legal system; when the rubble stops bouncing, the law codes of the first generation of successor states go right back to lists of specific punishments for specific crimes. As Vico pointed out, the Twelve Tables — the oldest code of Roman law — and the barbarian law codes that emerged after Rome's fall were equally concrete and unsystematic, even though the legal system that rose and fell between them was one of history's great examples of legal systematization and abstraction.

What caught Vico's attention is that the same process appears in a galaxy of other human institutions and activities. Languages emerge in dark-age conditions with vocabularies rich in concrete, sensuous words and very poor in abstractions, and transform those concrete words into broader, more general terms over time — how many people remember that "understand" used to mean to stand under, in the sense of getting in underneath to see how something works? Political systems start with the intensely personal and concrete feudal bonds between liege lord and vassal, and then shift gradually toward ever more abstract and systematic notions of citizenship. Vico barely mentioned economics in his book, but it's a prime example: look at the way that wealth in a dark-age society means land, grain and lumps of gold, which get replaced first by coinage, then by paper money, then by various kinds of paper that can be exchanged for paper money and eventually by the electronic hallucinations that count as wealth today.

What's behind these changes is a shift in the way that thinking is done, and it's helpful in this regard to go a little deeper than Vico himself did and remember that the word "thinking" can refer to at least three different kinds of mental activity. The first is the process of figuration discussed in Chapter Two — the activity that turns the jumbled input of your senses into a world of recognizable objects. As noted earlier in this book, your mind is busy doing this all the time, though you don't usually notice how the world you experience around you is being assembled by your mind moment by moment.

Figuration is a more complex process than most people realize. If you look at a good optical illusion, you can watch that process at work, as your mind flops back and forth between the available options. If you look at an inkblot from the Rorschach test and see two bats having a romantic interlude, that's figuration too, and it reveals one of the things that happens when figuration gets beyond the basics: it starts to tell stories. Listen to children who aren't yet old enough to tackle logical reasoning, especially when they don't know you're listening, and you'll hear figuration in full roar: everything becomes part of a story, which may not make any sense at all from a logical perspective but connects everything together in a single narrative that makes its own kind of sense of the world of experience.

It's when children, or for that matter adults, start to compare figurations to each other in something other than a narrative sense that a second kind of thinking comes into play, which we can call *abstraction*. You have this figuration over here, which combines the sensations of brown, furry, movement, barking and much more into a single object; you have that one over there, which includes most of the same sensations in a different place into a different object; from these figurations, you abstract the common features and give the sum of those features a name, "dog." That's abstraction.

The child who calls every four-legged animal "goggie" has just started to grasp abstraction and does it in the usual way, starting from the largest and broadest abstract categories and narrowing down from there. As she becomes more experienced at it, she'll learn to relabel that abstraction "animal," or even "quadruped," while a cascade of nested abstractions allows her to grasp that Milo and Maru, originally both "goggie," are both animals, but one is a dog and the other a cat. As the categories grow richer, the further potentials of abstraction start to come into play; just as figuration allowed to run free starts to tell stories, abstraction given the same liberty starts to construct theories.

A child who's old enough to abstract but hasn't yet passed to the third kind of thinking can usually provide you with any number of examples of theorizing in its most basic form. Ask her to speculate about why something happens, and you'll get a theory instead of a story. The difference between the two is that, where a story simply flows from event to event, a theory tries to make sense of the things that happen by fitting them into abstract categories and making deductions on that basis. The categories may be inappropriately broad, narrow, or straight out of left field, and the deductions may be whimsical or just plain weird, but it's from such tentative beginnings that logic and science gradually emerge in individuals and societies alike.

Figuration, then, assembles a world out of fragments of present and remembered sensation, using ideas held unconsciously or half-consciously in the mind as a framework. Abstraction takes these figurations and sorts them into categories, then tries to relate the categories to one another in a fully conscious framework. It's when the life of abstraction becomes richly developed enough that there emerges a third kind of thinking, which we can call *reflection*.

Reflection is thinking about thinking: stepping outside the world constructed by figuration to think about how figurations are created from raw sensation, stepping outside the cascading categories created by abstraction to think about where those categories came from and how well or poorly they fit the sensations and figurations they're meant to categorize. Where figuration tells stories and abstraction creates theories, reflection can lead in several directions. Done capably, it yields that elusive but crucial quality we call wisdom; done clumsily, it loses its way in self-referential tailchasing; pushed too far, it can all too easily end in madness.

⁂

Map these three modes of thinking onto the historical trajectory of any civilization and the connections are hard to miss. Complex literate societies aren't born complex and literate, after all, even if history has given them the raw materials to reach that status in time. They normally take shape in the smoking ruins of some dead civilization, and their first centuries are devoted to the hard work of clearing away the intellectual and material wreckage left behind by their predecessors. Figuration, the process of creating meaningful forms out of the chaos of perception, dominates the centuries of a society's emergence and early growth; language, law and the other phenomena mentioned above focus on specific examples or, as we might as well say, specific figurations.

The most common form of intellectual endeavor in such times is storytelling — it's not an accident that the great epics of our species and the vast majority of its mythologies come out of the early stages of high cultures. Over time, as barbarian warlords and warbands settle down and become the seeds of a nascent feudalism and religious institutions take shape, the myths and epics of the newborn culture are told and retold. All these are tasks of the figurative stage of thinking, in which telling stories that organize the world of human experience into a single meaningful pattern is the most important task, and no one worries too much about whether the stories are consistent with each other or make any kind of logical sense.

If the logical method of a previous civilization has been preserved into the figurative age of the next, which has been true often enough in recent millennia, abstraction exists in a social bubble, cultivated by a handful of intellectuals but basically irrelevant to the conduct of affairs. Instead, religion dominates intellectual and cultural life, and feudalism or some very close equivalent dominates the political sphere. It's usually around the time that feudalism is replaced by some other system of government that the age of faith gives way to the first stirrings of an age of reason or, in the terms used here, abstraction takes center stage.

The hard work of the figurative stage is an essential preliminary to this shift. Once that has been accomplished and the cosmos has been given an order that makes sense within the religious sensibility and cultural habits of the age, people have the leisure to take a second look at the political institutions, the religious practices and the stories that explain their world to them, and start to wonder whether they actually make sense. At first, the new abstraction sets itself the problem of figuring out what religious myths really mean, but since those narratives don't "mean" anything in an abstract sense — they're ways of assembling experience into emotionally compelling stories the mind can readily grasp and recall, not theories based on internally consistent categorization and logic — the myths eventually get denounced as a pack of lies, and the focus shifts to creating rational theories about the universe. Epic poetry and mythology give way to literature, religion loses ground to some secular pursuit such as classical philosophy or modern science, and written constitutions and law codes replace feudal custom.

That isn't a fast process, and it usually takes some centuries either to create a set of logical tools or to adapt one from some older civilization so that the work can be done. The inevitable result, as already mentioned, is that the figurations of traditional culture are weighed in the new balances of rational abstraction and found wanting. Thus the thinkers of the newborn age of reason examine the Bible, the poems of Homer, or whatever other collection of mythic narratives has been handed down to them from the figurative stage, and discover that it doesn't make a good textbook of geology, morality, or whatever other subject comes first in the rationalist agenda of the time. Now of course nobody in the figurative period thought that their sacred text was anything of the kind, but the collective shift from figuration to abstraction involves a shift in the way that even such basic notions as truth are conceived.

Partisans of abstraction always like to portray these shifts as the triumph of reason over superstition, but there's another side to the story. Every abstraction is a simplification of reality, and the further you go up the ladder of abstractions, the more certain it becomes that the resulting concepts will fail to match up to the complexities of actual existence. Nor is abstraction as immune as its practitioners like to think to the influences of half-remembered religious narratives or the subterranean pressures of ordinary self-interest — it's standard, for example, for the professional thinkers of every age of reason to prove with exquisite logic, just as ours currently do, that whatever pays their salaries is highly reasonable and whatever threatens their status is superstitious nonsense. The result is that what starts out proclaiming itself as an age of reason normally turns into an age of unreason, dominated by a set of closely argued, utterly consistent, universally accepted rational beliefs whose only flaw is that they fail to explain the most critical aspects of what's happening out there in the real world.

In case you haven't noticed, that's more or less where we are today. It's not merely that the government of every major industrial nation is trying to achieve economic growth by following policies that are supposed to bring growth in theory but have never once done so in practice; it's not merely that the populace of every major industrial society eagerly forgets all the lessons of each speculative bubble and bust as soon as the next one comes along and makes all the same mistakes with the same dismal results as the previous time; it's not even that allegedly sane and sensible people have somehow managed to convince themselves that limitless supplies of fossil fuels and other nonrenewable resources can somehow be extracted at ever-increasing rates from the insides of a finite planet: it's that only a handful of people out on the furthest fringes of contemporary culture ever notice that there's anything at all odd about these stunningly self-defeating patterns of behavior.

It's at this stage of history that reflection becomes necessary. It's only by thinking about thinking, by learning to pay attention to the way we transform the raw data of the senses into figurations and abstractions, that it becomes possible to notice what's being excluded from awareness in the course of turning sensation into figurations and sorting out figurations into cascading levels of abstraction. It's at this same stage of history, though, that reflection also becomes a lethal liability, because as noted above, wisdom is far from the only possible outcome of sustained reflection.

Vico points out that there's a barbarism of reflection that comes at the end of a civilization's life, exactly parallel to the barbarism of sensation that comes at the beginning — and also ancestral to it.[2] Reflection is a solvent; skillfully handled, it dissolves abstractions and figurations that obscure more than they reveal so that less counterproductive ways of assembling raw sensation into meaningful patterns can be pursued. Run riot, it makes every abstraction and every figuration as arbitrary and meaningless as any other, until the collective conversation about what's real and what matters dissolves in a cacophony of voices speaking past one another — and it's in this context that religions play the most critical of their historic roles.

※✿❀✿※

Human intelligence, it bears remembering, was not evolved for the purpose of understanding the entire cosmos, and attempts to use it for that purpose run into predictable problems. It's useful, in fact, to think of intelligence as a remarkable but fragile capacity, recently acquired in the evolutionary history of our species and still full of bugs that the remorseless beta testing of natural selection hasn't yet had time to find and fix. The three kinds of thinking just discussed — figuration, abstraction and reflection — are at different stages in that Darwinian process, and a good many of the challenges of being human unfold from the complex interactions of older and more reliable kinds of thinking with newer and less reliable ones.

Figuration is the oldest kind of thinking as well as the most basic. There's every reason to think that animals assemble the fragmentary data received by their senses into a coherent world in much the same way that human beings do, and assemble their figurations into sequences that allow them to make predictions and plan their actions. Abstraction seems to have come into the picture with spoken language; the process by which a set of similar figurations (this poodle, that beagle, the spaniel over there) get assigned to a common category with a verbal label, "dog," is a core example of abstract thinking as well as the foundation for all further abstraction. To a figurative thinker, a narrative is true because it fits with other narratives seen as true and thus makes the world make intuitive sense and fosters human values in hard times; to an abstractive thinker, a theory is true because it's passed whatever tests the rationalism of the age accepts as grounds for accepting a claim of truth.

That's not necessarily as obvious an improvement as it seems at first glance. To begin with, of course, it's by no means certain that knowing the truth about the universe is a good thing in terms of any other human value; for all we know, H.P. Lovecraft may have been quite correct to suggest that if we actually understood the nature of the cosmos in which we live we would all, like the hapless Arthur Jermyn, douse ourselves with oil and reach for the matches.[3] Still, there's another difficulty with rationalism, which is that it leads people to think that abstract concepts are more real than the figurations and raw sensations on which they're based — and that belief doesn't happen to be true.

Abstract concepts are simply mental models that more or less sum up certain characteristics of certain figurations in the universe of our experience. They aren't, and should never be confused with, the figurations or the sensory data that they seek to explain. The laws of nature so eagerly pursued by scientists, for example, are generalizations that explain how certain quantifiable measurements are likely to change when something happens in a certain context, and that's all they are.

It seems to be an inevitable habit of rationalists, though, to lose track of this crucial point and convince themselves that their abstractions are more real than the figurations or the raw sensory data on which the latter are based — that the abstractions are the truth, in fact, behind the world of appearances we experience around us. It's wholly reasonable to suppose that there is a reality behind the world of appearances, to be sure, but the problem comes in with the assumption that a favored set of abstract concepts *is* that reality, rather than merely a second- or third-hand reflection of it in the less than flawless mirror of the human mind.

The laws of nature make a good example of this mistake in practice. To begin with, of course, the entire concept of "laws of nature" is a medieval Christian religious metaphor with the serial numbers filed off, ultimately derived from archaic notions of God as a feudal monarch promulgating laws for his subjects to follow. We don't actually know that nature has laws, in any meaningful sense of the word — she could simply have habits or tendencies — and we have less than no reason to think that our figurations, or the abstractions built atop them, are identical to whatever laws, habits or tendencies nature might happen to have. Nonetheless the concept of natural law is so firmly hardwired into the structure of contemporary science that it has become a presupposition that few ever think to question.

Treated purely as a heuristic, a mental tool that fosters exploration, the concept of natural law has proven to be very valuable. The difficulty creeps in when natural laws are treated, not as useful summaries of regularities in the world of experience, but as the invisible realities behind the world of experience. It's this latter sort of thinking that drives the insistence, very common in some branches of science, that a repeatedly observed phenomenon can't actually have taken place because the existing body of theory provides no known mechanism capable of causing it.

That's the kind of difficulty that lands rationalists in a trap of their own making and turns ages of reason into ages of unreason: eras in which all collective action is based on some set of universally accepted, mutually supporting, logically arranged beliefs about the cosmos that somehow fail to make room for the most crucial issues of the time. It's among history's richer ironies that those beliefs consistently end up clustering around a civil religion — that is, a figurative narrative no more subject to logical analysis than the theist religions it replaced, which is treated as self-evidently rational and true precisely because it can't stand up to any sort of rational test, but provides a foundation for collective thought and action that can't be supplied in any other way — and that it's usually the core beliefs of the civil religion that turn out to be the Achilles' heel of the entire system.

All of the abstractions of classical Roman culture thus ended up orbiting around the central conceptions of the civil religion of the Empire, a narrative that defined the cosmos in terms of a benevolent despot's transformation of primal chaos into a well-ordered community of hierarchically ranked powers. Jupiter's role in the cosmos, the Emperor's role in the community, the father's role in the family, reason's role in the individual — all these mirrored one another and provided the core narrative around which all the cultural achievements of classical society assembled themselves. The difficulty, of course, was that the cosmos refused to behave according to the model, and the failure of the model cast everything else into confusion. In the same way, the abstract conceptions of contemporary industrial culture have come to rely on the civil religion of progress and are at least as vulnerable to the spreading failure of that secular faith to deal with a world in which progress is rapidly becoming a thing of the past.

It's here that reflection, the third mode of thinking discussed here, takes over the historical process. Reflection, thinking about thinking, is the most recent of the modes and the least thoroughly debugged by evolution's slow but relentless process of testing to destruction. During most phases of the historical cycle, it plays only a modest part, because its vagaries are held in check either by traditional religious figurations or by popular rational abstractions, either of which may be considered unquestionably true in their day. Many religious traditions, in fact, teach their followers to practice reflection using formal meditation exercises; most rationalist traditions do the same thing in a somewhat less formalized way; both are wise to do so, since reflection framed by some set of accepted beliefs is an extraordinarily powerful way of educating and maturing the mind and personality.

The trouble with reflection is that thinking about thinking eventually shows up just how limited the human mind actually is as a means for knowing truth. Once the formerly unquestioned truths come under question, it takes only a modest amount of sustained reflection to demonstrate that it's not actually possible to be sure of anything, and that way lies nihilism, the conviction that nothing means anything at all. Abstractions subjected to sustained reflection dissolve into an assortment of unrelated figurations; figurations subjected to the same process dissolve just as promptly into an assortment of unrelated sense data, given what unity they apparently possess by nothing more solid than the habits of the human nervous system and the individual mind.

Jean-Paul Sartre's fiction expressed the resulting dilemma memorably:[4] given that it's impossible to be certain of anything, how can you find a reason to do anything at all? It's not a minor point, nor one restricted to twentieth-century French intellectuals. Shatter the shared figurations and abstractions that provide a society with its basis for collective thought and action, and you're left with a society in fragments, where biological drives and idiosyncratic personal agendas are the only motives left, and communication between divergent subcultures becomes impossible because there aren't enough common meanings left to bridge the widening gap.

This plunge into nihilism becomes almost impossible to avoid once abstraction runs into trouble on a collective scale, furthermore, because reflection is the automatic response to the failure of a society's abstract representations of the cosmos. As it becomes painfully clear that the beliefs of the civil religion central to a society's age of reason no longer fit the world of everyday experience, the obvious next step is to reflect on what went wrong and why, and away you go.

It's probably necessary here to note that the fact that human thinking has certain predictable bugs in the programming and tends to go haywire in certain standard ways does not make human thinking useless or evil. We aren't gods, disembodied bubbles of pure intellect, or anything else other than what we are: organic, biological, animal beings with a remarkable but not unlimited capacity for representing the universe around us in symbolic form and doing interesting things with the resulting symbols. Being what we are, we tend to run up against certain repetitive problems when we try to use our mental apparatus to do things for which evolution did little to prepare it — or us. It's only the bizarre collective egotism of contemporary industrial culture that convinces so many people that we ought to be exempt from limits to our intelligence. That mistaken notion is just as unproductive as claiming that we're exempt from limits in any other way.

Fortunately, there are also reliable patches for some of the more familiar bugs. It so happens, for example, that there's one consistently effective way to short-circuit the plunge into nihilism and the psychological and social chaos that results from it. In theory, there may be others, but so far as I know, there's only one that has a track record behind it, and it's the same one that provides the core around which societies come together in the first place: the raw figurative narratives of religion. What Spengler called the Second Religiosity — the renewal of religion in the aftermath of an age of reason — is driven not only by the economic and pragmatic factors discussed in Chapter Eight, but also by the failure of rationalism either to deal with the multiplying crises of a society in decline or to provide some alternative to the infinite regress of reflection run amok.

Religion can accomplish this because it has a workable answer to the nihilist's insistence that it's impossible to prove the truth of any statement whatsoever. That answer, as already noted, is faith: the recognition that some choices have to be made on the basis of values rather than facts, because the facts can't be known for certain but a choice must be made anyway — and choosing not to choose is still a choice. Put another way, nihilism becomes self-canceling once reflection goes far enough to show that a belief in nihilism is just as arbitrary and unprovable as any other belief. That being the case, the figurations of a religious tradition are no more absurd than anything else and provide a more reliable and proven basis for commitment and action than any other option.

The Second Religiosity of any given society may or may not involve a return to the beliefs central to the older age of faith. In recent millennia, far more often than not, it has not. As the Roman world came apart and the civil religion and abstract philosophies of the Roman world failed to provide any effective resistance to the corrosive skepticism and nihilism of the age, it wasn't the old cults of the Roman gods who became the nucleus of a new religious vision but new faiths imported from the Middle East, of which Christianity and Islam turned out to be the most enduring.

Similarly, the implosion of Han dynasty China led not to a renewal of the traditional Chinese religion but to the explosive spread of Buddhism and of the religious Taoism of Zhang Daoling and his successors. On the other side of the balance is the role played by Shinto, the oldest surviving stratum of Japanese religion, which survived alongside Buddhism and became a potent source of cultural stability all through Japan's chaotic medieval era. Which of the many significant forces at work is most important in leading a society one way or another is an extraordinarily difficult question to answer, and the wild card discussed in Chapter Eight — the influence of that transcendent dimension I've termed the theosphere — can hardly be ruled out.

The traditions of older societies had a distinctive way of talking about shifts of the kind we've just discussed — a way that shocks most modern ears, though readers of this book have encountered it in a different context already. They spoke, not of the rise and fall of religious sensibilities or religions, but as Nietzsche did, of the birth and death of gods. Plutarch's famous dialogue on the silence of the Greek oracles[5] introduces a narrative of this kind as a way to talk about some of the religious transformations then under way in the Classical world, and it's a narrative with no small relevance to our time.

During the reign of the Roman Emperor Tiberius, a character in Plutarch's dialogue recounts, passengers aboard a ship sailing from Greece to Italy heard a mysterious voice calling out from the island of Paxi, telling the ship's steersman to pass on word to the coastlands further on that Great Pan was dead. The steersman, an Egyptian named Thamus, relayed the message as directed, and a great cry of lamentation went up from the uninhabited shore. Word of this got to the emperor, who was himself a serious student of mythology; he referred the matter to a committee of experts, who determined that the Pan who had just died was the third of that name, the son of Penelope by Hermes (or, in a scandalous variant, by all of her suitors during Odysseus' absence — thus the name given the horned and horny god).

There's a fine irony, and probably a deliberate one, in Plutarch's choice of an Egyptian as the message bearer in his story. The Egyptians of Plutarch's time were no strangers to dead gods; Osiris, one of the greatest of the Egyptian deities, was believed to have died twice and only rose from the dead the first time, a detail that apparently did nothing to keep him from his divine duties. That's commonplace for divinities; pilgrims to Tsubaki Grand Shrine in Japan, for example, can visit the grave of Sarutahiko no Okami, whom believers in Shinto consider to be the chief of all the earthly *kami* and still very much a living spiritual presence. Two millennia ago, in much the same spirit, pilgrims on Crete paid their respects at the grave of Zeus and then offered prayers and sacrifices to him as an immortal god, and of course my Christian readers will doubtless be thinking of the Church of the Holy Sepulcher in Jerusalem in this context. Dying simply isn't that much of a hindrance for gods.

Early in this book I discussed the way that civil religions inevitably copy the habits of theist religions, to the extent that their narratives and underlying religious sensibility permit, and the same principle applies here in an interesting way. Every human society has its own collective image of what human beings are like in the abstract, which serves more or less the same role in that society as the ego or self-image in the psychology of the individual. When a given society makes the momentous shift from theist to civil religions, as its Age of Reason approaches its zenith and collapse, its collective human image very often becomes a substitute deity — and that deity, like Great Pan, may not have an indefinite lifespan.

Whether or not it has yet become the center of a civil religion, the collective image of humanity in any given society is always a polymorphous thing, subject to constant redefinition in the competing interests of subgroups within the society, and it's also subject to changes driven by historical cycles as well as something not too far removed from genetic drift. Still, variants of the collective human image in any human society always have a close family resemblance with one another and very often a set of common features that aren't subject to change, no matter how much debate piles up around other aspects of the image.

The imaginary figure of Man, conqueror of Nature, is exactly such a collective image — and for the last few centuries, it's been the dominant image of humanity in Western industrial societies. As mentioned in Chapter Six, Man isn't you, or me, or anyone else who ever lived or ever will live. He's a fictional character who plays the central role in the grand mythic narrative at the core of the civil religion of progress, the square-jawed hero whose destiny it is to conquer Nature and march gloriously onward and upward to the stars.

To refer to the abstraction Man as the protagonist of a hero myth is not merely a figure of speech. In a brilliant book, *Narratives of Human Evolution*, paleoanthropologist Misia Landau showed that the stories that have been spun around "the ascent of Man" — think about that phrase for a bit — are in fact classic hero tales embracing all the conventions of that very distinctive genre, complete with all the standard motifs that are traced out in studies of the subject by Joseph Campbell and other scholars of mythology. She examined the classic nineteenth- and twentieth-century accounts of human evolution in detail and showed how in every case, the facts unearthed by scientific research were hammered into shape to fit a far from scientific narrative.

It probably needs repeating that the narrative in question is not evolution. The evolution of species is one of the facts unearthed by scientific research; in the case of the hominids, in particular, the rambling family tree that led from East African forest apes to the author and readers of this book has been worked out in precise detail, backed up by an assortment of fossils and artifacts impressive enough that the term "missing link" dropped out of use among scientists a long time ago. No, what's happened is that the normal process by which a successful species adapted to challenging conditions and spread beyond its original ecosystem has been turned into the central myth of a civil religion and used to redefine the entire two million years or so of hominid existence in the image of the last three centuries of Western history.

In that myth, the conquest of Nature — more precisely *our* conquest of Nature, the specific way of conquering Nature that modern industrial society thinks it's engaged in — is treated as the normal, natural, and inevitable goal of all human aspiration. That myth is by no means limited to the cheerleaders of progress; there's a rich irony in the fact that nowadays, many of those who hate Man, conqueror of Nature, and everything he stands for are as convinced as any scientific rationalist that this cultural construct, this abstract and arbitrary fictional character who represents nothing more solid than one civilization's most popular notion of human nature and destiny, is the simple and literal truth about our species.

It bears recalling here that Man the conqueror of Nature is a mythological character, not an adequate reflection of the complexity of human relationships with Nature over the whole sweep of human history. The vast majority of humans, across the vast majority of the time our species has been around, have lived in relative balance and harmony with the ecosystems around them. The vast majority of the exceptions have taken place either when humans reached a part of the planet they hadn't settled before, when humans were in the early stages of adopting some new means of subsistence and hadn't worked the bugs out yet, or when environmental changes driven by planetary forces have destabilized existing human ecologies and left the survivors scrambling to find some new means of subsistence. Other species in similar situations undergo the same kinds of crisis, and then find their way back to balance — and so do we.

It so happens that all of us were born and raised, and are descended from a dozen generations of people who were born and raised, during a period of drastic instability caused by the second factor just listed. Some members of our species stumbled onto a new means of subsistence, which we haven't yet figured out how to use in a sustainable manner and at this point almost certainly never will. This sort of thing has happened many times before to our species and to countless other species as well; our behavior has been shaped by it, as the behavior of other humans and other species has been shaped by similar conditions. All this is normal for living things on a changing planet.

Human beings, that is, are noticeably less sapient than the moniker of our species would suggest. Since the conditions of the recent past are all that any of us has ever known, most of us have taken the temporary state of instability that has dominated the last few centuries and projected it onto the far from blank screen of the human past and future. Meanwhile the temporary state of instability is rapidly drawing to an end. One core dimension of the crisis of our age, in other words, is that our collective personification of humanity, our sense of the meaning and destiny of our species, is well past its pull date.

≈☙◉❧≈

The image of Man the conqueror of Nature was adaptive, in the strict Darwinian sense, during the brief age of extravagance that followed our discovery of ways to break into the planet's geological cookie jar of fossil sunlight. Those who embraced that image of humanity prospered and reproduced their kind, both in the straightforward biological sense and in the subtler, cultural sense by which success attracts imitators. Now that the rate at which fossil fuels can be extracted from the planet is running up against hard geological limits, and the net energy yield from such exercises is stuck in a remorseless decline, the image of Man the conqueror of Nature has stopped being adaptive.

That fact, however, has not yet led to any general recognition of the need to change. That's a common challenge in individual psychotherapy, or so I'm told by therapists of my acquaintance, and it's certainly a challenge in the training of the personality that's a crucial part of Druid spirituality. People who have not yet grasped the failure of their existing self-images will cling like grim death to the most disastrously dysfunctional senses of identity and defend them fiercely against the suggestion that they could see themselves in a different way. Our need for a sense of stable identity is so powerful that many of us would rather be wretchedly miserable than risk the leap into the unknown that surrendering a self-image always involves.

One of the great challenges faced by the teacher in any spiritual tradition — and I suspect that psychotherapists see things the same way — is thus to find ways to encourage students to get to the point at which they're willing to risk treating their self-concepts as concepts, abstractions created by the mind, rather than simply the way things are. One of the core difficulties we face in the modern industrial world, in turn, is the same need expressed the collective level.

There's a voice calling out to all of us from the island of Paxi, announcing that Great Man is dead. The only difference between our situation and that of Plutarch's time is that few people are willing to listen to that cry, as Thamus the steersman did, and fewer still show any willingness to carry the message to those who are waiting to hear it. Thus we've circled back around to the place where this book began, Friedrich Nietzsche's proclamation of the death of God, for it was that death — the collapse of Christianity as the accepted public foundation of Western cultures — that made the transformation of Man the conqueror of Nature into a substitute deity both possible and (in a certain sense) necessary.

The problem with Nietzsche's proposed solution, in turn, was that it simply postponed for a little while the problem it was intended to address. The Overman, the free human being who flings himself into the abyss of a meaningless universe to give it meaning through a sacrificial act of endless self-overcoming, was never much more than a pale reflection of Christ, who descended into the universe of matter and human incarnation on something like the same mission. It was a brave attempt but not a particularly smart one, and the results, both for Nietzsche and for the European society he proposed to put on new foundations, were far from good.

Dying, as it turns out, isn't the only thing that gods do easily and human beings find considerably more awkward. Nietzsche may have been right when he wrote that "one must have chaos within one to give birth to a dancing star;"[6] he certainly had the chaos and arguably gave birth to the star in the form of some of the most brilliant of German prose and some of the most challenging philosophical writings in any language. Still, it's probably fair to extend the metaphor a bit further and suggest that the radiation emitted by his newborn star proceeded to fry his brain and reduce one of the keenest minds of Europe to the status of catatonic vegetable. As any astrophysicist could have told him, human beings are not equipped to give birth to stars.

In less metaphorical language, as already noted, the ramshackle structures of the human mind tend to break down in certain highly predictable ways when pushed beyond the tasks for which evolution has equipped them. The plunge into nihilism discussed earlier is one of these predictable malfunctions. In Nietzsche's case, that ended up taking the form of a mental illness that, though it's been blamed on syphilis, had all the symptoms and progressive course of acute schizophrenia, paranoid and megalomaniac at the time of his psychotic break in Turin and phasing gradually into catatonia before his death in

1900. In the case of European society as a whole, a strong case could be made that much the same thing happened in the half century or so after Nietzsche's time: the collapse of Europe into a maelstrom of war, delusion, and mass murder that followed the continent-wide psychotic break of 1914 was only brought to an end more than three decades later and at the cost of equally continental destruction.

Western cultures in the nineteenth century thus replaced their traditional monotheism with a newly minted monanthropism — a belief system that flattened out the rich diversity of humanity into a single abstract figure, Man, and loaded that figure with most of the titles and attributes of the divinity he was expected to replace. Nineteenth- and twentieth-century writings that referenced our species almost always made use of that capitalized abstraction and proclaimed him the lord of creation, the goal of evolution, the inheritor of the cosmos and so on through the whole litany of self-important hogwash that surrounded the human project in those days.

At that time, as I've suggested, it was adaptive in a purely pragmatic sense. It helped to encourage the rapid growth of industrial systems during the brief historical epoch when abundant fossil fuels and other nonrenewable resources made such systems possible. The downside of the experiment was that it left very few barriers in place to the barbarism of reflection, and those barriers fell down promptly once kicked by jackboots.

Still, the era when that expedient seemed to work is over, terminated with extreme prejudice by the paired and relentless realities of dwindling resource stocks and an increasingly destabilized biosphere. Whatever form the Second Religiosity of our age takes, whatever ways we and our descendants cobble together to counter the barbarism of reflection and keep the unsteady structures of human thought from the same plunge into chaos that left Nietzsche babbling incoherently with his arms around the neck of a beaten horse, the basic requirements of the time before us include giving Man the conqueror of Nature a decent burial and finding a way to imagine ourselves that has some relation to the realities of the human condition in a world after progress.

In meeting those requirements, the perspectives and practices of theist religion have a central role. I'm aware that that's a controversial claim — not least because, as already noted, so many devout believers in the contemporary cult of progress insist so loudly on seeing all religions but theirs as so many outworn relics of the superstitious past. This is a common sentiment among rationalists, especially in the twilight years of ages of reason, and it tends to remain popular right up until the Second Religiosity goes mainstream and leaves the rationalists sitting in the dust wondering what happened.

⚜

The question that comes first to many minds when a renewal of religion is discussed, though, is what religion or religions are most likely to provide the frame around which a contemporary Second Religiosity will take shape. It's a reasonable question, but for several reasons it's remarkably hard to answer.

The first and broadest reason for the difficulty is that the overall shape of a civilization's history may be determined by laws of historical change, but the details are not. It was as certain as anything can be, for example, that some nation or other was going to replace Britain as global superpower when the British Empire ran itself into the ground in the early twentieth century. That it turned out to be the United States, though, was the result of chains of happenstance and choices of individual people going back to the eighteenth century if not further. If Britain had conciliated the American colonists before 1776, for example, as it later did in Australia and elsewhere, what is now the United States would have remained an agrarian colony dependent on British industry; there would have been no American industrial and military colossus to come to Britain's rescue in 1917 and 1942, and we would all quite likely be speaking German today as we prepared to celebrate the birthday of the Weltkaiser Wilhelm VII.

In the same way, that some religion will become the focus of the Second Religiosity in any particular culture is a given; which religion it will be is a matter of happenstance and the choices of individuals. It's possible that an astute Roman with a sufficiently keen historical sense could have looked over the failing rationalisms of his world in the second century CE and guessed that one or another religion from what we call the Middle East would be most likely to replace the traditional cults of the Roman gods, but which one? Guessing that would, I think, have been beyond anyone's powers; had the Emperor Julian lived long enough to complete his religious counterrevolution, for that matter, a resurgent Paganism might have become the vehicle for the Roman Second Religiosity, and Constantine might have had no more influence on later religious history than his predecessor Heliogabalus.

The sheer contingency of historical change forms one obstacle in the way of prediction, then. Another factor of more local relevance comes from a distinctive rhythm that shapes the history of popular religion in the United States and has varying equivalents elsewhere. From colonial times on, American popular spiritualities have had a predictable lifecycle. After a formative period of varying length, they grab the limelight, hold it for between 30 and 40 years, and then either crash and burn in some colorful manner or fade quietly away.

What makes this particularly interesting is that there's quite a bit of synchronization involved; in any given decade, that is, the pop spiritualities then in the public eye in the United States will all be going through roughly the same stage in their life cycles. The late 1970s, for example, saw the near-simultaneous emergence of four popular movements of this kind: evangelical Protestant fundamentalism, Neopaganism, the New Age and the evangelical atheist materialism of the so-called Sceptic movement.

In 1970, none of those movements had any public presence worth noticing. Fundamentalism was widely dismissed as a has-been phenomenon that had last shown any vitality in the 1920s, the term "Neopagan" was mostly used by literary critics talking about an assortment of dead British poets, the fusion of surviving fragments of 1920s New Thought and Theosophy with the UFO scene that would give rise to the New Age was still out on the furthest edge of fringe culture, and the most popular and visible figures in the scientific community were more interested in studying parapsychology and Asian mysticism than in denouncing them. The popular spiritualities that were on their way out in 1970, in turn, had emerged together in the Great Depression and replaced another set that came of age around 1900.

That quasi-generational rhythm has to be kept in mind when making predictions about American pop religious movements, because very often, whatever's biggest, strongest and most enthusiastically claiming respectability at any given time will soon be heading back out to the fringes or plunging into oblivion. It may return after another three or four decades — Protestant fundamentalism had its first run from just before 1900 to the immediate aftermath of the 1929 stock market crash, for example, and then returned for a second pass in the late 1970s — and a movement that survives a few such cycles may well be able to establish itself over the long term as a successful denomination. Even if it does accomplish this, though, it's likely to find itself gaining and losing membership and influence over the same cycle thereafter.

The stage of the cycle we're in right now, as the four movements just mentioned near the end of their normal span, is the one in which established pop spiritualities head for the fringes or the compost heap, and new movements vie for the opportunity to take their places. Which movements are likely to replace fundamentalism, Neopaganism, the New Age and today's "angry atheists" at the center of the public spotlight as those movements move toward the fringes? Once again, that depends on happenstance and individual choices, and neither of those are easy to predict in advance.

There are certain regularities in the cycle, to be sure, and those allow a few educated guesses to be made. For example, liberal and conservative Christian denominations seem to take turns in the limelight, so it's fairly likely that the next major wave of American Christianity will be aligned with liberal causes rather than conservative ones. It's anyone's guess, though, which liberal and moderate denominations will take the lead here, and which will remain mired in the fashionable agnosticism and the entirely social and secular understanding of religion that's made so many liberal churches irrelevant to the religious needs of their potential congregations.

In much the same way, American scientific institutions alternate over the same 30 to 40 year span between openness to spirituality and violent rejection of it. The era of the American Society for Psychical Research was followed by that of the war against the Spiritualists, that gave way to a postwar era in which physicists read Jung and the Tao Te Ching and physicians interested themselves in alternative medicine, and that was followed in turn by the era of the Committee for Scientific Investigation of Claims of the Paranormal and today's strident evangelical atheism. A turn back toward an openness to spirituality on the part of science is thus reasonably likely in the decades ahead.

Still, those are probabilities, not certainties, and many other aspects of American religious culture are a good deal less subject to repeating patterns of this kind. Other parts of the world, furthermore, have their own distinctive rhythms of popular religion, and how those will influence the American experience is another question entirely. All this puts up serious barriers to guessing the shape of the Second Religiosity as that takes shape in deindustrializing America, and I'm not even going to try to sort out the broader religious future of the rest of today's industrial world — that would take a level of familiarity with local religious traditions, cultural cycles and collective thinking that I simply don't have.

Here in the United States, it's hard enough to see past the large but faltering popular spiritual movements of the current cycle, guess at what might replace them and try to anticipate which of them might rise to the immense challenges facing any religious movement in the wake of the failed rationalism of the recent past. It's still an open question, for that matter, whether the religious forms that will be central to the Second Religiosity of industrial civilization's twilight years will be drawn from the existing religious mainstream of today's Western societies, or whether they're more likely to come either from the bumper crop of religious imports currently in circulation or from an even larger range of new religious movements contending for places in today's spiritual marketplace.

⚜

History strongly suggests, though, that whatever tradition or traditions break free from the pack to become the common currency of thought in the post-rationalist West will have two significant factors in common with the core religious movements of equivalent stages in previous historical cycles. The first is the capacity to make the transition from the religious sensibility of the previous age of faith to the emerging religious sensibility of the approaching age of memory. The second is a willingness to abandon the institutional support of the existing order of society and stand apart from the economic benefits as well as the values of a dying civilization. Both of those are real challenges to existing and newly minted faiths alike.

The religious sensibility fading out around us has for its cornerstone the insistence that humanity stands apart from nature, and that we — or at least the elect among us — deserve some better world than the one in which we happen to find ourselves. The pervasive biophobia of that sensibility, its obsession with imagery of rising up from the earth's surface and most of its other features, unfolds from a basic conviction that, to borrow a phrase from one currently popular denomination of progress-worshippers, humanity is only temporarily "stuck on this rock" — the "rock" in question, of course, being the living Earth in all her beauty and grandeur — and will be heading for something bigger, better and a good deal less biological just as soon as God or technology or some other supposedly benevolent power gets around to rescuing us.

This is exactly what the rising religious sensibility of our age rejects. More and more often these days, I encounter people for whom "this rock" is not a prison, a place of exile, a cradle, or even a home, but the whole of which human beings are an inextricable part. These people aren't looking for salvation, at least in the sense that word has been given in the religious sensibility of the Western world over the last two millennia or so and which was adopted from that sensibility by so many theist and civil religions during that time. They are not pounding on the doors of the human condition trying to get out, or consoling themselves with the belief that sooner or later someone or something is going to rescue them from the allegedly horrible burden of having bodies that pass through the extraordinary journey of ripening toward death that we call life.

They are seeking, many of these people. They are not satisfied with who they are or how they relate to the cosmos, and so they have needs that religions can meet. What they are seeking, though, is not escape from the world but wholeness within the world's greater whole, a sense of connection and community that embraces not only other people but the entire universe around them, and reaches out also to the creative powers that move through that universe and sustain its being and theirs. Many of them are comfortable with their own mortality and at ease with what Christian theologians call humanity's "creaturely status," the finite and dependent nature of human existence. What troubles them is not the inevitability of death or the reality of limits, but a lack of felt connection with the cosmos and with the whole systems that sustain their lives.

Can the traditions of the current religious mainstream or its established rivals speak to such people? Yes, though it's going to take some significant rethinking of habitual language and practice to shake off the legacies of the old religious sensibility and find ways to address the needs and possibilities of the new one. This is by no means impossible, and indeed it's happening now; I've spoken and corresponded at length with devout Christians, for example, whose religious sensibility belongs wholly to the rising current — who, for example, see the first chapter of the Gospel of John as a ringing proclamation of the living incarnation of Christ throughout nature, which is rendered holy by his indwelling presence — and talked theology with Buddhists whose affirmation of the Buddha-nature in all things has similar implications.

It's thus entirely possible that one or another denomination of Christianity or Buddhism, or of some other already well-established religious tradition, might succeed in shaking off the legacies of the old religious sensibility and providing a framework for the Second Religiosity in the decades and centuries ahead. That said, the jury's still out, and it's entirely possible that the religious tradition that defines the Second Religiosity in a world after progress will be something entirely different — possibly something that has not yet been born.

The second requirement for a successful response to the challenge of the Second Religiosity bears down with particular force against established religious institutions. Most American denominations of Christianity and Buddhism, for example, have a great deal of expensive infrastructure to support — churches and related institutions in the case of Christianity; monasteries, temples and retreat centers in the case of Buddhism. Most of the successful denominations of both faiths, in order to pay for these things, have by and large taken to the same strategy to meet those costs, which amounts to pandering to the privileged classes of American society. That's a highly successful approach in the short term, but the emergence of a Second Religiosity is not a short-term phenomenon.

It has to be remembered that the economic implications of decline bear just as forcefully against religious institutions as they do against any other organized body with infrastructure to maintain and expenses to pay. In a world in which the average investment loses money, religious organizations that rely too heavily on trust funds and invested money are facing likely ruin as both they and their donors run short of cash. Those religious movements that tie themselves too tightly to middle- or upper-middle-class audiences are thus likely to find, as the floodwaters of change rise, that they've lashed themselves to a stone and will sink along with it.

It's those traditions that can handle poverty without blinking that are best able to maintain themselves in hard times, just as it's usually traditions with that same feature that an increasingly impoverished society finds least difficult and most congenial to support. Christianity in the Roman world was primarily a religion of the urban poor, with a sprinkling of downwardly mobile middle-class intellectuals adding spice to the mix; Christianity in the post-Roman dark ages was typified by monastic establishments whose members were even poorer than the impoverished peasants around them. Buddhism was founded by a prince, but very quickly learned that absolute nonattachment to material wealth was not only a spiritual virtue but a very effective practical strategy.

In both cases, though, that was a long time ago, and most American forms of both religions — and most other popular faiths, for that matter — are heavily dependent on access to middle- and upper-middle-class donors and their funds. If that dependence continues, those denominations will not survive the era of economic contraction ahead. Their fall may well leave the field wide open to the religions of the poor, to new religious movements that grasp the necessity of shoestring budgets and very modest lifestyles, or to further imports from abroad that retain Third World attitudes toward wealth.

I'm often asked in this context about the possibility that Druidry, the faith that I follow, might end up filling a core role in the Second Religiosity of industrial civilization. It's true that we embraced the new religious sensibility long before it was popular elsewhere, and equally true that shoestring budgets and unpaid clergy are pretty much universal in Druid practice. For that matter, though we're sometimes confused with the currently popular Neopagan movement, we've been around for quite a bit longer — many of today's Druid orders can trace their ancestry straight back to the Druid Revival of the eighteenth century — and we've cycled in and out of popularity often enough to know how to weather the inevitable shifts in public opinion.

Still, the only way I can see Druidry becoming a major factor in the religious history of the deindustrial age is if every other faith that makes the attempt were to trip and fall flat on its nose. A small, quirky and highly intellectual tradition with a passion for diversity and independence of thought, an ingrained dislike of proselytizing, a shortage of simple formulations of the kind that make good slogans and a tendency to focus on personal spiritual practice rather than the sort of activities that can draw a congregation, simply isn't that well suited to become a mass movement of the kind that can provide a framework for meaning to an entire civilization. Stranger things have happened in the history of religions, but not very often, and it would display a wry sense of humor on the part of the theosphere to choose so eccentric a faith for so immense a task.

⚜

One way or another, we are in the interval between a death and a difficult birth. The religion of progress, the established faith of the industrial world, is facing the fate of every civil religion that fails to make good on its promises. As the dream of a Utopian future somewhere out there among the stars joins the imaginary paradises of other civil religions on the compost heap of history, older sources of value, meaning and purpose will have to be updated, or new ones invented, to respond to the immense transformations that will accompany the end of the Industrial Age.

It's almost impossible to overstate the impact these tectonic shifts will have on contemporary culture. Ideas, institutions and ways of life forged in an era of cumulative economic expansion and rapidly expanding human mastery over the natural world are unlikely to hold up well in an era of prolonged economic contraction and environmental blowback. As they collapse, other ideas, institutions and ways of life will have to be found and deployed, and that work of rebuilding will have to be done amid the stresses and unpredictable impacts of a troubled time. It's a harrowing task, and the one source of reassurance I know is that other human societies, in other ages, have managed the same thing within the hard limits of the resources, opportunities and wisdom available to them at the time.

Seen from another perspective, however — the perspective of the emerging religious sensibility I've discussed in this book — the time ahead of us takes on a different meaning. At the heart of the older sensibility that's now guttering out around us was a daring if not necessarily wise attempt to break free of the natural world entirely so that humanity could launch itself beyond all limitations and break through into eternity and infinity. The religions, the intellectual movements and ultimately the superlative technological achievements of Western civilization were all pressed into service in making that attempt.

In a certain very limited sense, that effort succeeded. A modest number of human beings were tossed briefly outside the atmosphere and circled around our planet for a while before returning home, while a handful went further still, to stand on the surface of the Moon or orbit through the void surrounding it. Their voyages may well provide our descendants with a powerful symbol of the subtler but equally real journey of billions of people in the world's industrial societies, who managed to talk themselves for a while into believing that they were outside nature, superior to it, waiting only for some final dramatic change — spiritual, social, technological, or some blending of the three — to bring ordinary existence to a close forever.

In a deeper sense, though, the grand attempt to transcend the human condition forever has been a resounding flop, and its failure has brought harsh consequences to the biosphere that supports us and to our own humanity. The task before us at this point in the turning of time's wheel, though, is prefigured by those short journeys outside the atmosphere that simultaneously fulfilled and betrayed the dream of the space age, that strange cultural phenomenon that briefly loaded hopes of transcendence onto a collection of rocketry. Once the astronauts had finished gathering rocks, taking photos and pursuing their other chores on the Moon, the remainder of their journey beckoned: not a

leap further outward through some bleaker void to some yet more des-
olate destination, but the simple task of returning to the living planet
they had so briefly left behind.

That same task awaits the people of the world's industrial nations
today. We have taken the old quest to break free of nature and the
human condition very nearly as far as our considerable technological
powers would permit, and in the process created landscapes — spiritual, cultural and in some places physical as well — very nearly as bleak
as the Moon's silent and airless wastes. Whether that was a good idea
or a bad one, a choice or a necessity, a triumph or a terrible failure, is
ultimately less relevant than the fact that the effort has run its course.

A different quest calls us now, murmuring through the emerging
religious sensibility of our age, rising stark before us in the cold gray
dawn of a world after progress: to return to the living Earth and come
to know it again as the whole of which each of us is a part. After all our
wanderings, it is time to come home.

Notes

Chapter One:

1. Nietzsche 1974, p. 181.
2. Nietzsche 1990, pp. 79-80.
3. See Brown 2010 for an entertaining account of the controversy.
4. Bellah 1967.
5. www.valleyforge.org, accessed 7 April 2013.
6. Nietzsche 1961, p. 41.
7. Nietzsche 1961, p. 78.

Chapter Two

1. For a useful analysis, see Heinberg 2013.
2. Goethe 1993.
3. Bacon 1952.
4. Kurzweil 2005.
5. See especially Daly 1991.
6. Barfield 1965, p. 24.
7. Brown 1983, p. 37.

8. Hesiod 1973.
9. Chew 2001, pp. 41-62.
10. Hesiod 1973, p. 62.
11. See the appendices to Wilhelm 1967, especially pp. 325-336.
12. Da 1981.
13. Hanson 1995 is an accessible study.

Chapter Three:

1. Greer 2010.
2. From the poem "Archaischer Torso Apollos," 1908.
3. Godwin 1994, pp. 340-1.
4. See especially Nietzsche 1990, pp. 50-1.
5. Nietzsche 1992, p. 99.
6. Hadot 1998 is perhaps the best introduction to Stoicism as a praxis and way of life.
7. Spengler 1926, pp. 291-5.
8. Spengler 1928, pp. 505-507.
9. Bateson 1972, pp. 194-278.

Chapter Four:

1. Gould 1989 is a good introduction.
2. *On the Gods and the World*, ch. 4. Taylor's translation (Sallust 1976, p. 20) gives the same phrase as "these things indeed never took place at any particular time, because they have a perpetuity of subsistence."

Chapter Five:

1. Toynbee 1939.
2. Grant 1990 is among the best surveys.
3. Seife 2008 is an excellent summary.
4. Webb 2002, p. 217.
5. Williams ab Ithel 1862, p. 227.
6. From the poem "Cad Goddeu" ("The Battle of the Trees").

7. Greer 2005.
8. I am indebted to Austen Ringwode for e-mail conversations that clarified this point for me.
9. See Russell 1991.
10. See, for example, de Moll and Coe 1978 and Todd 1977.

Chapter Six:
1. Tolkien 1966, pp. 33-99.
2. Again, Heinberg 2014 is a good starting place for the issues involved in the current unconventional-oil situation.
3. See, for a classic example, the discussions of history in Sagan 1985.
4. See Garrett 2000, especially chapter 4.
5. See, for example, Shiva 1991 and Ponting 1992.

Chapter Seven:
1. 2 Chronicles 6.
2. Ocellus 1976, pp. 21-28.
3. Osborne 1993.
4. White 1967.
5. Mark 16:19, Luke 24:51, and Acts 1:9, respectively.
6. Costanza 1997.
7. See Jenkins 2009 for a useful summary.
8. Lewis 1996; see also Lewis 1947.

Chapter Eight:
1. Spengler 1926, Table 1 (following p. 428).
2. See Greer 2011 for a more detailed discussion.
3. See Catton 1980 for the dependence of industrial society on these two factors.
4. White 1959.
5. Dante 1954, pp. 106-8.
6. Ward-Perkins 2005.
7. For example, Goldsmith 1992 and Sender and Bay Laurel 1973.

8. charterforcompassion.org/the-charter (accessed 12 April 2014).
9. For a survey of the evidence, see Greer 2005, ch. 5.

Chapter Nine:

1. Vico 1948, pp. 93-96 and 386-93.
2. Vico 1948, pp. 397-418.
3. Lovecraft 1921.
4. See Sartre 1949 among many others.
5. Plutarch 1898.
6. Nietzsche 1961, p. 46.

Bibliography

Albanese, Catherine, *Nature Religion in America* (Chicago: University of Chicago Press, 1990).

Bacon, Sir Francis, *The Advancement of Learning*, in Sir Francis Bacon, *Advancement of Learning, Novum Organum, New Atlantis* (Chicago: William Benton, 1952).

Barfield, Owen, *Saving the Appearances* (New York: Harcourt Brace Jovanovich, 1965).

Bateson, Gregory, *Steps to an Ecology of Mind* (New York: Ballantine, 1972).

Bellah, Robert, "Civil Religion in America," *Daedalus* Vol. 96 no.1 (Winter 1967), pp. 1-21.

Berton, Pierre, *The Comfortable Pew* (Philadelphia, PA: J.B. Lippincott, 1965).

Brown, Mike, *How I Killed Pluto and Why It Had It Coming* (New York: Spiegel and Grau, 2010).

Brown, Tom, Jr., *Tom Brown's Field Guide to Nature Observation and Tracking* (New York: Berkley Books, 1983).

Catton, William R., Jr., *Overshoot: The Ecological Basis of Revolutionary Change* (Urbana, IL: University of Illinois Books, 1980).

Chew, Sing C., *World Ecological Degradation* (Walnut Creek, CA: Altamira Press, 2001).

Clarke, Arthur C., *The Promise of Space* (New York: Harper & Row, 1968).

Costanza, R., R. d'Arge, R. de Groot, S. Farber, M. Grasso, B. Hannon, K. Limburg, S. Naeem, R. O'Neill, J. Paruelo, R. Raskin, P. Sutton, and M. van den Belt, "The value of the world's ecosystem services and natural capital," *Nature* 387 (1997), pp. 253-260.

Da Liu, *T'ai Chi Ch'uan and I Ching* (London: Routledge and Kegan Paul, 1981).

Daly, Herman, *Toward a Steady-State Economy* (Washington, DC: Island Press, 1991).

Dante Alighieri, *The Inferno*, trans. John Ciardi (New York: New American Library, 1954).

de Moll, Lane, and Gigi Coe, ed., *Stepping Stones: Appropriate Technology and Beyond* (New York: Schocken Books, 1978).

Galbraith, John Kenneth, *The Great Crash 1929* (Boston, MA: Houghton Mifflin, 1954).

Garrett, Laurie, *Betrayal of Trust: The Collapse of Global Public Health* (New York: Hyperion, 2000).

Glassman, James K., and Kevin A Hassett, *Dow 36,000* (New York: Times Business, 1999).

Godwin, Joscelyn, *The Theosophical Enlightenment* (Albany, NY: State University of New York Press, 1994).

Goethe, Johann Wolfgang von, *The Metamorphosis of Plants* (Junction City, OR: Biodynamic Farming and Gardening Association, 1993).

Goldsmith, Edward, *The Way: An Ecological Worldview* (London: Rider, 1992).

Gould, Stephen Jay, *Time's Arrow, Time's Cycle* (New York: Penguin, 1990).

_____, *Wonderful Life* (New York: Norton, 1989).

Grant, Michael, *The Fall of the Roman Empire: A Reappraisal* (New York: Colliers, 1990).

Greer, John Michael, *Apocalypse Not* (San Francisco, CA: Cleis Press, 2010).

_____, *A World Full of Gods* (Santa Fe, NM: ADF Press, 2005).

_____, *The Wealth of Nature: Economics as if Survival Mattered* (Gabriola Island, BC: New Society Publishers, 2011).

Hadot, Pierre, *The Inner Citadel*, trans. Michael Chase (Cambridge, MA: Harvard University Press, 1998).

Hanson, Victor Davis, *The Other Greeks* (Los Angeles, CA: University of California Press, 1995).

Hawthorne, Nathaniel, *The Blithedale Romance* (New York: W.W. Norton & Co., 1978).

Heinberg, Richard, *Snake Oil* (Santa Rosa, CA: Post Carbon Institute, 2013).

Hesiod, *Theogony* and *Works and Days*, in Dorothea Wender, trans., *Hesiod and Theognis* (London: Penguin, 1973).

James, William, *The Principles of Psychology* (Boston, MA: Henry Holt, 1890).

Jenkins, Willis, "After Lynn White; Religious Ethics and Environmental Problems," *Journal of Religious Ethics* Vol. 37 no. 2, 2009.

Kurzweil, Ray, *The Singularity is Near* (New York: Viking, 2005).

Landau, Misia, *Narratives of Human Evolution* (New Haven, CT: Yale University Press, 1991).

Lereah, David, *Why the Real Estate Boom Will Not Bust* (New York: Currency/Doubleday, 2005).

Lewis, C.S., *That Hideous Strength* (New York: Simon & Schuster, 1996).

_____, *The Abolition of Man* (New York: Macmillan, 1947).

_____, *The Discarded Image* (Cambridge: Cambridge University Press, 1964).

Lovecraft, H.P., "The White Ape" (aka "Facts Concerning The Late Arthur Jermyn And His Family"), *The Wolverine* no. 9, March 1921.

Lucanus, Ocellus, *On the Nature of the Universe*, trans. Thomas Taylor (Los Angeles, CA: Philosophical Research Society, 1976).

Marx, Karl, *The Eighteenth Brumaire of Louis Napoleon* (New York: International Publishers, 1963).

Nietzsche, Friedrich, *Ecce Homo* trans. R.J. Hollingdale (London: Penguin Books, 1992).

____, *The Gay Science*, trans. Walter Kaufmann (New York: Vintage, 1974).

____, *Thus Spoke Zarathustra*, trans. R.J. Hollingdale (Baltimore, MD: Penguin Books, 1961).

____, *Twilight of the Idols* and *The Anti-Christ*, trans. R.J. Hollingdale (London: Penguin Books, 1990).

Nordhoff, Charles, *The Communistic Societies of the United States* (New York: Schocken Books, 1965).

Ocellus Lucanus, *On the Nature of the Universe*, trans. Thomas Taylor (Los Angeles, CA: Philosophical Research Society, 1976).

Osborne, Laurence, *The Poisoned Embrace: A Brief History of Sexual Pessimism* (London: Bloomsbury, 1993).

Plutarch, "On the Failure of Oracles," in *Plutarch's Morals: Theosophical Essays*, trans. Charles William King (London: G. Bell, 1898).

Ponting, Clive, *A Green History of the World* (New York: St. Martin's Press, 1992).

Robinson, John A.T., *Honest To God* (London: SCM Press, 1963).

Russell, Jeffrey Burton, *Inventing the Flat Earth* (New York: Praeger, 1991).

Sagan, Carl, *Cosmos* (New York: Random House, 1985).

Sallust, *On the Gods and the World*, trans. Thomas Taylor (Los Angeles, CA: Philosophical Research Society, 1976).

Sartre, Jean-Paul, *Nausea*, trans. Lloyd Alexander (New York: New Directions, 1949).

Seife, Charles, *Sun In A Bottle: The Strange History of Fusion and the Science of Wishful Thinking* (New York: Penguin, 2008).

Sender, Ramón, and Alicia Bay Laurel, *Being of the Sun* (New York:

Harper & Row, 1973).

Shiva, Vandana, "The Green Revolution in the Punjab," *The Ecologist* vol. 21 no. 2, March/April 1991.

Spengler, Oswald, *The Decline of the West, Vol. I: Form and Actuality*, trans. Charles Francis Atkinson (New York: Alfred A. Knopf, 1926).

____, *The Decline of the West, Vol. II: Perspectives of World-History*, trans. Charles Francis Atkinson (New York: Alfred A. Knopf, 1928).

Todd, Nancy Jack, *The Book of the New Alchemists* (New York: E.P. Dutton, 1977).

Tolkien, J.R.R., "On Fairy-stories," in *The Tolkien Reader* (New York: Ballantine Books, 1966).

Toynbee, Arnold, *A Study of History, Vol 4: The Breakdowns of Civilizations* (London: Oxford University Press, 1939).

Vico, Giambattista, *The New Science of Giambattista Vico*, trans. Thomas Goddard Bergin and Max Harold Fisch (Ithaca, NY: Cornell University Press, 1948).

Ward-Perkins, Bryan, *The Fall of Rome and the End of Civilization* (Oxford: Oxford University Press, 2005).

Webb, Stephen, *Where Is Everybody?* (New York: Springer-Verlag, 2002).

White, Lynn, *The Evolution of Culture* (New York: McGraw-Hill, 1959).

____, "On the Historical Roots of our Ecological Crisis," *Science* Vol. 155 no. 3767, 10 March 1967.

Wilhelm, Richard, *The I Ching or Book of Changes*, trans. Cary Baynes (Princeton, NJ: Princeton University Press, 1967).

Williams ab Ithel, J., ed., *Barddas* (London: Longman & Co., 1862).

Index

S
Satanism, 17, 18
science
  and civil religion of progress,
    143–44
  collapsing prestige of, 141
  and progress, 139
  relationship to religion, 116, 125
science fiction, 171, 173–75, 183
scientific and technical progress,
  39, 42, 83
  and law of diminishing returns,
    40, 105, 107
scientism, 107–11
Second Religiosity, 97, 190, 211,
  227–28, 235–37, 239–40,
  242–43
Shakers, 200–201, 204
shape of time, 44, 46–54, 64
Shintoism, 165, 169, 228
Singularitarian movement,
  39–40, 183
socialism, 19, 23, 26, 142
Society for Creative
  Anachronism, 139
Spengler, Oswald, 35, 64–72, 76,
  81, 97, 188, 190, 211, 214, 227
Stoicism, 60, 62

T
Taoism, 228
theism, classical, 120–23, 166
theist religions, 15–16, 18, 29,

140, 165, 169, 175–76, 241
  believers in, 130, 208
  as declining, 187
  differences among, 22
  history of, 79
  institutional infrastructure of, 24
  as motivating factor, 37
  relation to civil religions, 17,
    19, 27, 54, 171, 173, 178,
    182, 185, 209, 211, 225
Theosophy, 238
time, as cyclical, 51–52
  See also shape of time
Toynbee, Arnold, 35, 71–72, 76,
  101, 103
Transcendentalist movement,
  198, 203

U
United Society of Believers in
  Christ's Second Appearing,
  200–201

V
Vico, Giambattista, 35, 71–72,
  215–17, 222

W
White, Lynn, 168, 177–78, 193
world, after progress, 4, 80, 112,
  133, 236, 242, 246

Z
Zen Buddhism, 201–2
Zhang Daoling, 228

About the Author

JOHN MICHAEL GREER — Archdruid, historian, and one of the most influential figures in the peak oil movement, writes the widely cited weekly blog "The Archdruid Report" and has published more than twenty books on nature, spirituality and the future of industrial society. His involvement in sustainability issues dates back to the early 1980s, when he was active in the Appropriate Technology movement and became certified as a Master Conserver. He is the author of numerous titles, including *The Long Descent*, *The Ecotechnic Future* and *The Wealth of Nature*. He lives in Cumberland, MD, an old mill town in the Appalachians, with his wife Sara.

If you have enjoyed *After Progress* you might also enjoy other

BOOKS TO BUILD A NEW SOCIETY

Our books provide positive solutions for people who want to make a difference. We specialize in:

Sustainable Living • Green Building • Peak Oil
Renewable Energy • Environment & Economy
Natural Building & Appropriate Technology
Progressive Leadership • Resistance and Community
Educational & Parenting Resources

New Society Publishers

ENVIRONMENTAL BENEFITS STATEMENT

New Society Publishers has chosen to produce this book on recycled paper made with **100% post consumer waste,** processed chlorine free, and old growth free.

For every 5,000 books printed, New Society saves the following resources:[1]

27	Trees
2,465	Pounds of Solid Waste
2,713	Gallons of Water
3,538	Kilowatt Hours of Electricity
4,482	Pounds of Greenhouse Gases
19	Pounds of HAPs, VOCs, and AOX Combined
7	Cubic Yards of Landfill Space

---

[1]Environmental benefits are calculated based on research done by the Environmental Defense Fund and other members of the Paper Task Force who study the environmental impacts of the paper industry.

For a full list of NSP's titles, please call 1-800-567-6772 *or check out our website* at:

www.newsociety.com